TRADE UNIONISM IN GERMANY FROM BISMARCK TO HITLER 1869–1933

Volume One 1869–1918

TRADE UNIONISM IN GERMANY FROM BISMARCK TO HITLER 1869–1933

Volume One 1869–1918

by

John A. Moses

GEORGE PRIOR PUBLISHERS

London · England

First published in the United Kingdom by
George Prior Publishers
Lower Ground Floor
High Holborn House
52–54 High Holborn
London WC1V 6RL, England

ISBN 0 86043 483 4

British Library Cataloguing in Publication Data
_____

Moses, John A.
  Trade Unionism in Germany from Bismarck to
  Hitler, 1869–1933
  Vol. 2
  1. Trade-unions—Germany—History
  I. Title
  331.88′0943   HD6596

  ISBN 0 86043 483 4

Printed in Great Britain by
Mansell (Bookbinders) Ltd., Witham, Essex

For Ingrid, Dirk and Rolf

CONTENTS

PREFACE

While doing the research for this book on German trade unionism I was frequently asked by colleagues in Australia and Britain
why I felt it to be an important subject. After all, I was told, trade
unions are much the same the world over. Their chief concern
was with working conditions, shorter hours, larger wages and
better housing—all very mundane and predictable goals. The
image one had of trade unionists was of dour and stolid men who
could not see beyond the immediate parochial issues of their
concern to the great issues of politics and the survival of humanity
as a whole. My 'historical' encounter with the trade union leaders
of Germany in the period covered here did not confirm at all this
image. On the contrary I met men who had set themselves a
mighty and daunting task: how to transform the most feared
militaristic and authoritarian capitalist society into what they
called an economic democracy. And they were going to do it not
by revolution but by peaceful, rational and parliamentary means.
This to me appeared to be an imaginative goal of the highest
order.

As no account of this specific struggle exists either in German
or English I felt the time had come to attempt it. Many of my
German colleagues, trained in their traditional thoroughness,
warned that the time span to be covered was far too large. One
should rather concentrate on a shorter, more manageable period
in great detail. This indeed is the kind of scholarly monograph
which is considered to be necessary before one is regarded as
having become a fully trained professional historian in Germany.
However, as an Australian who teaches German history for a
living, it seemed impractical to proceed along the accepted German way for several compelling reasons. A detailed monograph
on, say, the few years at the beginning of the 1890s or simply the
phase of the Great War would not have communicated the pers-

pective on the overall movement that I believe English-speaking students would need. Secondly, there is the perennial 'tyranny of distance' that oppresses the antipodean academic who tries to write about European subjects. One is condemned to searching archives, as it were, on the run. When one is on study leave, even for a year, there is not enough time to do the burrowing one would like to do and so one has to rely on the more readily available sources which enable one to make a broader intelligible sweep.

Another very serious problem associated with getting at sources is the competition one encounters from German colleagues who have the advantage of living on the spot. They are not always particularly edified to meet a foreigner working in their field for fear that the outsider might find some sensationally revealing documents before they do. If these scholars happen to have close contact with archivists and other custodians of historical records, then it is virtually certain that the archivists in question will give preference to their own countrymen. This is a natural and human enough practice, especially understandable in a period of intense competition for academic honours and posts. However, it puts the outsider at a distinct disadvantage, and it is a practice which in my case, together with the other points considered, has predetermined what kind of book I was to write.

None of the foregoing should be interpreted to mean that I am in any way ungrateful for the help I have received. Indeed, the research for this book was made possible partly by the German Academic Exchange Service when I was a student in Germany (1961–65), by the Humboldt Foundation when I was on study leave in Hamburg for the twelve months 1972–73 and also by the Historische Kommission zu Berlin who kindly invited me to further my researches there during the winter of 1975–76. Throughout these periods I have benefited from the advice of many scholars such as Werner Jochmann, Fritz Fischer, Imanuel Geiss, Rainer Tamchina, Joachim Bieber, Dirk Müller, Günter Krüschet, Dietrich Recke and in particular, Henryk Skrzypczak and Gerhard Beier. All were most generous with their time and practical help. The librarian at the Historische Kommission in Berlin, Frau Sigrid Krüger, merits my particular thanks for her invaluable professional expertise. Again, as all researchers who work in extreme remoteness from their sources know, nothing can be done without the assistance of the inter-library loan service. The University of Queensland possesses an extremely efficient reference service staff. Over the years the chief reference librarian, Mr. Spencer Routh, and his colleagues have procured for me many items unavailable in this country. Without their cheerful aid this book would have taken even longer to write.

Finally, the senior administrative officer of the University of Queensland History Department, Miss Margaret Burke and her able secretarial staff were responsible for the typing of the manuscript. To them I owe a very special debt of gratitude.

John A. Moses   *Brisbane*
(January 1980)

INTRODUCTION

This book is an attempt to analyse the self-perception of the German socialist trade union leadership and to trace how it developed over the decades between Bismarck's period of office and Adolf Hitler's seizure of power. Studies devoted to the growth and policies of the Social Democratic Party and those parties which split off from it during the First World War and its immediate aftermath are available in both English and German. Research has rightly concentrated on these fateful developments because of their very great revelance to the present. The fact that there are now two German states is, to a great extent, the result of the split (described by Carl Schorske) in the SPD which occurred under the strains of the Great War. Scant attention, however, has been paid to what might be called the real muscle of the labour movement, as distinct from the mind (represented by the various parties), namely the socialist or 'free trade unions'. Yet the metaphor 'muscle' is only a comment on the organizational size and numbers of workers organized, for this great body had a head, and it was one which followed its own path towards democratic socialism. It did not by any means blindly follow the ideological lead of the SPD before 1918, and thereafter the unions, confronted with the existence of three working class parties, the SPD, the USPD (until 1922) and the KPD, had all the more reason to act independently of these competing groups, although of course, the free trade unions (ADGB) continued to regard the SPD as their parliamentary spokesman.

The account of the development of the socialist trade union struggle to change the character, first of the Wilhelmine Reich and then of the Weimar Republic, is also one of relevance to the present. It shows that in industrial societies the so-called industrial wing of the labour movement tends to follow laws peculiar to its unique position in the capitalist system. In Germany, the doctrinaire character of the socialist parties conflicted with what might be called the natural behaviour of the trade unions, and as a result of this conflict the political strength of the working class was always weakened. Moreover, the conflict was misunderstood by the bourgeoisie and the forces of the right so that the mass of the working class, particularly the trade union organized workers were regarded as second class citizens. The effects of this were catastrophic not only for Germany but for the world at large.

In order here to state the problem as concisely as possible, let it be understood that we are concerned with the socialist trade union attempt to achieve a more modern, rational relationship to the German state. In the mind of the union leadership the state had functioned chiefly in the interests of the bourgeoisie, the aristocracy, the bureaucracy, the army, the church and the universities. It was beyond the understanding of the union leaders that the working class be excluded from membership in this state and nation, particularly in view of the fact that the greatness of Germany in no small measure resulted from the efficiency of the German industrial workers. Ever since the Reich had been founded, the working-class political movement had been suspect; and particularly since the Paris Commune of 1871, with which Bebel, the socialist leader, proclaimed his sympathy at the time, had the politically organized and militant workers of Germany been regarded as dangerous to the fatherland. This reputation was never really lived down. The relationship, therefore, of labour to the fatherland was a crucial domestic political issue in the period under consideration.

As far as method is concerned, no new trends will be followed here. The question as to which factors are the more decisive ones in history—ideas or structures—is left open, while the so-called *Wechselwirkung* (reciprocal relationship) between ideas and structures is assumed. This book focuses, though, more on ideas and individual champions of these ideas. There was a clearly recognizable movement within German labour in the years 1890 to 1933 which was borne aloft by an elite—a kind of labour aristocracy—but which received the endorsement of an ever-growing number of the work force. For this reason it is essential to analyse the ideas and policies of the leadership because these are a central factor in the overall process, although not of course the whole process. The work therefore is organized as follows.

Chapter One attempts to locate the problem in its historiographical context. It shows that the various competing ways of looking at the history of German trade unionism depend to a large extent on the political-ideological sympathies of the historian, hence the conflicting theses. This subject is one that is being vehemently debated in Germany because of its roots in the ideological controversy over the collapse of the Weimar Republic, the rise of fascism and ultimately, the division of Germany. Perhaps only by analysing these views in perspective, it is possible for an outsider, such as the present writer, to extract what is valuable from all of them. Of course, no historian is or can be ideologically neutral. The present account is essentially that of a liberal point of view. The first chapter also serves to state the problem in more detail than in this introduction and really provides the justification for the book.

Chapter Two seeks to focus on the role of trade unionism in the rival socialist theories of Lassalle and Marx, for their separate ideological legacies were at once a strength and a weakness of German labour in general and of unionism in particular. The respective impacts of Lassalle and Marx with regard to trade unionism were very much live issues throughout the period under consideration, and they therefore need further clarification here.

In the case of both Chapters One and Two, the general historiographical and theoretical frameworks have been erected so as to enable the unfolding of the socialist trade union movement to be investigated. Attention is focused on the socialist-influenced unions rather than on those inspired by liberals (the Hirsch–Duncker unions) or those founded under the influence of the Roman Church in Germany, the so-called Christian trade unions. Although these latter movements were considerable, they never reached anywhere near the size of the free (socialist) unions, nor did they stand in any problematic relationship to the existing state. Neither the Hirsch–Duncker nor the Christian unions affirmed the class struggle or subscribed to any republican or revolutionary ideology. Reliable information on the broad sweep of German trade union history is now provided by Helga Grebing. By taking cognizance of this work and the more detailed studies of both East and West German scholars it has been possible to survey in Chapter Three the beginnings of German socialist trade unionism prior to 1878 when the broad outlines of future developments were already becoming discernible.

Chapter Four, which deals with the critical period of the Anti-Socialist Law, stresses the very central role played by unions in keeping the ideals of socialism alive in the working class when it had been the aim of Bismarck to stamp them out. As such, this chapter provides the indispensable background for what is to come, in particular, the conflict within German social democracy over the usefulness of unions in the class struggle, as well as the goals of the Wilhelmine state to draw the sting from the socialist trade union movement. Indeed, the way in which militant labour was treated under the law of the Reich is the subject of Chapter Five, along with trade union conceptions of how to reform the Wilhelmine state in the interests of labour.

Intimately linked with the subject matter of Chapter Five is the content of Chapters Six and Seven in which the party–union relationship is examined. This forms a central section in the overall work because in the period 1890 to 1914, the 'trade-unionization' of the German social democratic movement occurred. And it is precisely because this process was resisted by the more doctrinaire elements on the left that the subsequent fateful split in German social democracy came about. Clarity concerning the period when the SPD became the largest political party in the Reich and when the union organization developed to become the most powerful in the industrialized world, is an essential prerequisite to understanding those tensions within the German labour movement which came to the surface during the Great War.

Chapter Eight is by way of being an extended footnote on the relationship between the German free trade unions and the Second International. This is so placed because it sheds light on the additional aspect of union–party relations as well as explaining the reasons why German trade unions were reluctant to submit to the principle of internationalism in the vital general strike issue. As such, this chapter forms the logical prelude to Chapters Nine and Ten which analyse the policies of the trade union leadership during the 1914–18 War. These chapters illuminate an area of German labour history which has recently attracted the interest of such scholars as Gerald D. Feldman and Jürgen Kocka. Their seminal studies are here augmented by focusing on the trade union self-perception during the war, with respect both to the state and to the SPD. The dominant theme is the determination of the union leadership to pursue a course which would win for the working class an improved legal and social status within the Wilhelmine state. For this reason, the unions were the chief object of criticism among those more radical Social Democrats who opposed the war effort. In union eyes, this jeopardized hopes for future concessions from the state.

The consistency of the union policy of cooperation with the state comes under discussion in Chapter Eleven, and it is here that the union tight-rope walk between bolshevism and capitalism is fully explained. This is an essential exercise for understanding how the parliamentary form of government emerged in the wake of the confusion of the German Revolution of 1918/19. Chapter Twelve then examines the way in which the union leadership consolidated its position against the critics of its wartime policy and rather conservative role in the revolution. The first post-war congress at Nuremberg in 1919 was a milestone in German labour history, and this is examined to illustrate the self-perception of the unions in the new state which was neither monarchist nor soviet in constitution.

Chapter Thirteen examines the actual constitutional position which the unions won for themselves in the Weimar Republic. This is of central importance in understanding the inner political and social struggles of the pre-Nazi period. Among the chief reasons for the ultimate collapse of the Weimar state and the triumph of nazism was the growing right-wing and capitalist criticism that the constitution had virtually turned Germany into a 'trade union state'. On the other hand, the way in which the unions successfully parried all efforts of the extreme left to turn Germany into a soviet republic is also examined.

That 'Weimar' was to be a modern welfare state was largely due to trade union policies. This conception, however, was opposed by both the left and right. Chapter Fourteen then deals with trade union responses to the first great challenge from the right in the so-called Kapp Putsch of March 1920, and also how the unions coped with the Ruhr invasion and the great inflation of 1923. This highlights the union concern to protect both the social-political provisions of the constitution and at the same time to maintain the viability and competitiveness of the national economy.

Emerging from those crises which signalled the breakdown of union–management cooperation were the more strident union demands for a so-called economic democracy. This concept, though not peculiar to German labour history, was perhaps developed to its highest point in Germany in the years prior to the world economic crisis of 1929. Chapter Fifteen examines the evolution of the union theory of economic democracy in the German context.

Chapter Sixteen traces the collapse of union optimism during the depression and their various attempts to advance social–economic solutions to the vast economic difficulties in order to salvage the constitution from the increasingly vehement right-wing and fascist attacks upon it. It will be shown that, contrary to Marxist–Leninist assertions, the collapse of democracy in Germany was not due to trade union betrayal, but rather to the lack of understanding among capitalist and right-wing circles of trade union conceptions of economic democracy. The Communists, of course, had constantly sabotaged this concept as well and therefore hastened the demise of what was at once an imaginative and modern attempt to realize economic democracy in a highly industrialized society.

Finally, Chapter Seventeen addresses itself to the currently controversial question of whether the trade union leadership, without any thought of resistance, voluntarily submitted to nazism. This debate has taken an interesting turn in recent years and its ventilation in this way is an attempt to achieve some clarity over what is a very controversial and emotion-charged issue.

ABBREVIATIONS

ADAV	Allgemeiner Deutscher Arbeiter Verein (General German Workers Association)
ADB	Allgemeiner Deutscher Beamtenbund (General Federation of German Public Servants)
ADGB	Allgemeiner Deutscher Gewerkschaftsbund (General German Trade Union Federation)
AfA	Allgemeiner freier Angestelltenbund (General Federation of Salaried Employees)
AFS	*Archiv für Sozialgeschichte*
AFSSP	*Archiv für Sozialwissenschaft und Sozialpolitik*
AHR	*American Historical Review*
AJPH	*Australian Journal of Politics and History*
APUZ	*Aus Parlament und Zeitgeschichte.* Beilage zur Wochenzeitung *Das Parlament*
ARG	*Das Argument*
ASSA	*American Social Science Association*
ASEER	*The American Slavic and East European Review*
BGDA	*Beiträge zur Geschichte der deutschen Arbeiterbewegung*
BUSBLS	*Bulletin of the US Bureau of Labor Statistics*
Corr.	*Correspondenzblatt* (Organ of the General Commission of the Free Trade Unions)
CR	*Contemporary Review*
DA	*Die Arbeit* (Theoretical Journal of ADGB)
DAF	Deutsche Arbeitsfront (German Labour Front)
DBB	Deutscher Beamtenbund (German Federation of Public Servants)
DDP	Deutsche Demokratische Partei (German Democratic Party)
DFI	*Documents of the First International*

DG	*Die Gesellschaft*
DVP	Deutsche Volkspartei (German People's Party)
ESR	*European Studies Review*
GA	*Gewerkschafts-Archiv*
GDA	*Geschichte der Deutschen Arbeiterbewegung*
GDR	German Democratic Republic
GMH	*Gewerkschaftliche Monatshefte*
GWU	*Geschichte in Wissenschaft und Unterricht*
GZ	*Gewerkschafts-Zeitung* (Organ of the ADGB)
HIKO	Historische Kommission zu Berlin
HJ	*The Historical Journal*
HT	*History and Theory*
HZ	*Historische Zeitschrift*
IFTU	International Federation of Trade Unions
IISH	*International Institute for Social History*
ILR	*International Labour Review*
IWK	*Internationale Wissenschaftliche Korrepondenz zur Geschichte der deutschen Arbeiterbewegung*
JCH	*Journal of Contemporary History*
JCEH	*Journal of Central European History*
JEH	*Journal of Economic History*
JES	*Journal of European Studies*
JFG	*Jahrbuch für Geschichte*
JIDG	*Jahrbuch des Instituts für deutsche Geschichte*
JMH	*Journal of Modern History*
JSH	*Journal of Social History*
KPD	Kommunistische Partei Deutschlands (Communist Party of Germany)
KUER	*Kyoto University Economic Review*
LH	*Labour History* (Canberra)
MESW	*Marx, Engels. Selected Works in two Volumes*
MEW	*Marx-Engels Werke*
MGM	*Militärgeschichtliche Mitteilungen*
NSDAP	Nationalsozialistische Deutsche Arbeiterpartei (German National Socialist Workers' Party, i.e. Nazi Party)
NSBO	Nationalsozialistische Betriebszellen Organisation (National Socialist Factory Cells Organization)

NZ	*Die Neue Zeit*
PP	*Past and Present*
PVS	*Politische Vierteljahresschrift*
Rapp	*Rapports V Histoire Contemporaine*
RDA	*Revue d'Allemagne*
RDI	Reichsverband Deutscher Industrieller (Reich Association of German Industrialists)
RGBL	Reichsgesetzblatt
RM	Reichsmark
RUO	*Revue de l'Université d'Ottowa*
SA	Sturmabteilung (Storm Troops, i.e. Nazi Brown Shirts)
SDAP	Sozialdemokratische Deutsche Arbeiterpartei (Social Democratic German Workers' Party)
SED	Sozialistische Einheitspartei Deutschlands
SJGVV	*Schmollers Jahrbuch für Gesetzgebung, Verwaltung und Volkswirtschaft*
SM	*Sozialistische Monatshefte*
SPD	Sozialdemokratische Partei Deutschlands (Social Democratic Party of Germany)
SR	*Social Research*
SS	Schutzstaffeln (Elite para-military terror organization of NSDAP, i.e. Nazi Black Shirts)
SovS	*Soviet Survey*
TH	*The Historian*
USPD	Unabhängige Sozialdemokratischc Partei Deutschlands (Independent Social Democratic Party of Germany)
VDA	Vereinigung der Deutschen Arbeitgeberverbände (Union of German Employers' Associations)
VFZ	*Vierteljahreshefte für Zeitgeschichte*
WP	*World Politics*
ZAG	Zentralarbeitsgemeinschaft (Joint Industrial Alliance)
ZFG	*Zeitschrift für Geschichtswissenschaft*

CHAPTER ONE

Conflicting Theses: The Assessment of the Trade Union Role in German Politics 1890–1933

Since history has very much to do with promulgating views of the past to suit the current political needs of a particular school of thought or political party, it is necessary at the outset to examine the conflicting opinions now circulating about this subject. Such an exercise is designed to show that we have here to deal with a very vexed question: this is true not only as far as the rival schools of history in East and West Germany (i.e. Marxist–Leninist versus liberal, social democratic or conservative etc.) are concerned, but also because of the wider issue concerning the nature of historical truth. And beyond this we have the perennially fascinating question as to what the outcome in Germany would have been had the unions acted differently in the two crises in which it appeared as though history or fate had singled them out to assume a particularly critical role. These comprised the July–August crisis of 1914 when a general strike to prevent the outbreak of war might have been expected, and the governmental crisis of January 1933 when Adolf Hitler was named Chancellor of Germany. Again on this occasion the unions might have been expected to exert their strength to preserve not only democratic institutions in Germany but also to save Europe from the scourge of fascism.

With such crucial questions involved, it is little wonder, depending on the political sympathies of the writer, that such a variety of answers are being proffered. To facilitate the present task, it will be convenient to discuss the conflicting theses by dividing the period into two sections: the Wilhelmine Reich and the Weimar Republic, i.e. 1890 to 1918, and 1919 to 1933 respectively. Of course the problem of conflicting theses arises largely because of Marxist–Leninist writing on the subject. Since the Communists have always tried to force labour history, in particular, into the Procrustes bed of their own theory of history, the politics of the German free trade unions and the Social Democratic Party (SPD) have been generally regarded as a betrayal of the true goals of the revolutionary working class. In examining, then, the conflicting theses the method will be to juxtapose the findings of research from both sides of the Berlin Wall.

As Hermann Weber has pointed out, East German historiography is always subordinated to the ideology of the Marxist–Leninist party which rules that country.[1] Historical scholarship there on the labour movement has not only the task of justifying the party's sole claim to leadership but also of showing that this is an historical necessity. The party is always right and *was* always right. The historian has to depict the facts and evaluate them in such a manner as to justify the political line of the genuinely revolutionary party leadership at all times.[2]

For the non-Marxist historian, this results in a somewhat one-sided account which (while providing much valuable information) tends to distort or over-simplify what is, in reality, a very complicated historical problem. It is nevertheless considered by East German historians as an essential part of the ideological class struggle against the West to direct polemics towards their colleagues in the Federal Republic.[3]

In recent times, these 'bourgeois historians' have been subjected to heavy attacks from their East German counterparts. Although the latter have now abandoned their earlier Stalinism, they have not relaxed in their efforts to portray the labour movement exclusively as the historical process by which the SED regime emerged in the German Democratic Republic (GDR). An example of this is provided by the recent East German critique of bourgeois historiography of West Germany in which all schools of history there are taken to task.[4] In particular, those writing on labour history are castigated. The intensity of the polemics is a measure of the political importance attached to the question. For the period under consideration, their main concern is to show that the labour movement consisted essentially of a revolutionary party within the national framework. By implication, any movement that worked against the revolutionary core is regarded as virtually traitorous to the working class. It is confidently asserted that the main characteristic of the German labour movement in the final third of the nineteenth century was the triumph of Marxism in the struggle with, on the one hand, the ruling classes of the Prusso–German military state, and on the other, with the various forms of opportunism within labour ranks. Indeed, by the acceptance of the Erfurt Programme in 1891, the 'class party' had fully emerged. The SPD then had the task by means of gathering, schooling and organizing the proletariat, of systematically preparing this class for a political power struggle.[5]

Having projected this role backwards on the SPD leadership, Communist historians must today condemn all trends within the German labour movement which clearly weakened any revolutionary drive the SPD may have had. The condemnation of the trade union wing's activities 1890–1918 is particularly severe because of its eminently successful attempt in escaping from party tutelage to become what was virtually an autonomous section of the overall movement. This highly ideologically coloured dismissal of the union movement as somewhat 'heretical and schismatic' fails to do justice to the complexity of its history. On the other hand, West German writing on the subject has tried to present a far more differentiated image.

Dealing with the key West German studies on the 1890–1918 era chronologically, the first is from Heinz-Josef Varain who in 1956 set out to plot the course of the trade union leadership's struggle to establish its separate existence from the SPD; and then to assert its gradually acquired strength against the oppressive Wilhelmine state in the interests of its members.[6] In his discussion of the war years, Varain accounts for the patriotic stance of the union leadership (the General Commission under the chairmanship of Carl Legien) as being mainly due to their determination to preserve their organizations intact. Their hope was that by so doing they would have a better chance of extracting legislative

concessions from a virtually unassailable militaristic state. When
the war was lost and the revolution came, Varain shows how the
unions were one of the central factors in shaping the character of
the Weimar Republic—a state with which they essentially identified as their rescue action at the time of the Kapp *Putsch* (March
1920) indicated. At that time, the unions triumphed over the
enemies of the republic by staging a highly successful general
strike to restore the constitutional government.

Varain's relatively early account presents not so much a thesis
as a chronicle of events in party–union history that had not previously been surveyed with any precision or depth. It is written
clearly from a liberal point of view to show as objectively as
possible a process which had taken on a new relevence in the
political life of the new West German state. That is to say, there
had emerged for the first time among academic historians a concern to research the origins of the essential pillars of the radically
restructured West German social, political, and economic order.
There would have been clearly no interest in these things had
Germany remained a military monarchy or a fascist dictatorship.
But since the Federal Republic harked back to the Weimar Constitution and to an even older liberal–democratic parliamentary
tradition, there was a pressing need to examine the origins of that
tradition. Varain's work represents an attempt to rehabilitate a
once rejected tradition and to make it understandable if not
acceptable to bourgeois elements in the Federal Republic. If one
thing was certain, very few of these elements in the past had
regarded trade unionism and social democracy as pillars of the
'state'. Now post 1945 they are more than ever just that.

If Varain's book was written more with a view to explaining
the importance of trade unionism in the pluralist society to a
bourgeois public unaccustomed to that concept, the next piece to
consider was written by Heinz Langerhans (1957). This set out to
account for the socialist trade unions' achievement of virtual
autonomy within the labour movement.[7] Langerhans' analysis is
scarcely calculated to impress the Marxist–Leninists although
there is absolutely no polemical content in it. He approached this
question as a social and economic historian familiar with the general effects of industrialization on the various European coun-

tries. The process by which the German unions came to conflict with the party, and ultimately subject it to their policies, is seen by Langerhans as the result of Germany's comparatively late industrial takeoff. The subordination of the unions to the party took place at a time (i.e. in the 1860s and 1870s) in which Germany, in contrast to Britain, was industrially underdeveloped. The reversal of this situation in which the German experience parallels that of Britain—where the unions dominate the political wing of the labour movement—came about with Germany's full growth as an industrial nation.[8] Indeed, Langerhans is arguing that where industrialization occurs, trade unions tend to create a party to represent their cause in parliament. There is a primacy of union demands over party-ideological considerations implicit in this process.

In Germany, however, this process was complicated by the Anti-Socialist Law of 1878–1890. When this came into force, the movement by the unions to create for themselves a centrally coordinated leadership was made illegal and all unions in 1878 (except the printers') were actually dissolved by the police. Indeed, the Anti-Socialist Law had been from the beginning directed against the union movement. The party organizations, too, were dissolved leaving the parliamentary party or *Fraktion* as the only legal socialist institution in Germany. The effect of this was to force the workers to abandon all ties with the socialist party and to reconvene their craft organizations into strictly non-political economic pressure groups. This was necessary in order to comply with the Anti-Socialist Law and existing laws of association and assembly, and the effect of this enforced non-political reorganization was the renaissance of unionism in the latter part of the 1880s. In 1877, before the Anti-Socialist Law, there had been only 50,000 unionists in Germany. In 1890 when the law had lapsed, there were seven times that number. In the changed political climate brought on by the parliamentary events of 1890 the unions took up where they had left off in 1878 and tried to create a centralized or coordinated leadership. The drive for this came from within their own ranks, not from the SPD which in the meantime had grown accustomed to being the only mouthpiece of the working class. The party leadership consequently began to look with suspicion on the high-flown plans of the unionists to regiment their many fragmented sections under an umbrella organization separate from the party.

The resultant dispute for the primacy of the party over the unions dragged on until 1896 when an upturn in the business cycle that had been depressed for so long suddenly occurred. This observation led Langerhans to draw up the following periodization for party–union relations during the Wilhelmine period. It is of central relevance to the thrust of the present study.

1890–1895: These were the years when the centralization movement of the unions was revitalized. This provoked a sharp reaction from the SPD which had striven to maintain its tutelage over the unions. The reason why this had been possible was the economic depression which kept unions relatively weak.

1895–1900: Owing to the upturn in general prosperity the unions were able at least *de facto* to establish their autonomy.

1900–1907: The continued expansion of the unions and their determination to act independently of the party was gradually recognized by the party, and furthermore indicated the actual limits of party initiative and action.

1907–1914: The party and union leaderships finally agreed to a programme of action which was in effect determined by the unions. The bureaucratic leadership simultaneously alienated themselves from the mass support, while the existing challenge to orthodox Marxism caused an ideological split in the labour movement. This enabled the left wing at least to escape the strictures imposed on it by the extensive unionization.[9]

Langerhans' thesis is, then, that the party was forced to acknowledge the unions as an autonomous wing of the labour movement because in periods of economic prosperity the growth of unions was completely beyond the control of the party. Unions followed their own laws of development quite apart from any theoretical considerations held by the party that it must always exert the primacy of leadership in the overall labour movement. What Langerhans teaches is that unionism is the logical offshoot of industrialization and that labour parties are *de facto* the agencies by which the unions seek to get the parliament of the day to legalize their position as economic fighting organs against capital.

The implication is that the Marxist-revolutionary element in the German movement very much confused what otherwise would have been a rational or natural development, uncomplicated by theoretical dogmatism.

Such a view, understandably, conflicts strongly with the Marxist–Leninist analysis. But before looking more closely at this, it would be profitable to investigate another West German authority on party–union relationships during the Wilhelmine period. The work of Gerhard A. Ritter, dating also from 1957, indicates a greater awareness of the problems than that of Varain and it is similarly written from a mildly liberal standpoint. The date of these works is, as already indicated, instructive in itself. They were the products of doctoral dissertations begun in the decade after the Second World War when the West German professors, trained in more conservative days, first began to direct their attention to the origins of genuinely democratic movements in Germany. It is asserted in the GDR that this sudden concern on behalf of conservative professors to direct their students to the study of the labour movement took the form of a tactical man-oeuvre in the ideological cold war. For the first time they had found it necessary to confront this historical phenomenon seri-ously since it was necessary to falsify the course of its develop-ment as a means of destroying the justification of the rise to power in East Germany of the SED. It had therefore become a political task for the West German historians to focus on the labour movement (as part of the overall campaign to combat the spread of communism) to show that the German labour move-ment was not in effect a revolutionary movement of the pro-letariat but rather a reformist, state-friendly movement with a petit-bourgeois core.[10]

Whether or not this is an accurate characterization of the motives of West German professors, the work of their students certainly presents an image of a labour movement that scarcely conforms to the requirements of Marxist–Leninist historiography. In the case of Gerhard A. Ritter, who focuses on both wings of the labour movement from 1890 to 1900, we have a portrayal which coincides essentially with that of Langerhans. The unions are shown to be mainly concerned with, not revolution, but autonomy and reforms in social policy. Again, the point is that the broad movement was not out to destroy the Wilhelmine State but rather to secure a more tolerable position within it. Obviously, to affirm such a tendency is to repudiate the Marxist–Leninist line that the genuine labour movement was at the core revolutionary.

The most authoritative East German writer on the subject of party–union relationships is Wolfgang Schröder. He describes in great detail how the emergence of the potentially powerful trade union movement during the 1890s established its rival leadership organization beside that of the party. This, Schröder, however, ascribes not to any inherent incompatibility between the aims of both wings of the movement, but to the result of the triumph of opportunism over Marxism within the union movement. This is curious because the union drive towards centralization was merely a continuation of a much earlier tendency. If the champions of centralization and autonomy during the 1890s were opportunists, so must have been the earlier champions of this prior to 1878. But these are regarded as great forerunners of the revolutionary party.[11]

The motives for centralization in the 1890s, furthermore, were essentially the same as those in the 1870s. What had happened to make the new men of the 1890s opportunists when their forerunners were heroes? The answer must be the alleged triumph of Marxism in the German labour movement by 1891, when all ideologically reliable union leaders should have voluntarily subordinated themselves to the party leadership. It was not that Schröder objects to the fact that a separate union-coordinating body had been established in the 1890s, but rather that this body refused to acknowledge the primacy of the party and instead sought to impose its will on the entire movement. As Schröder maintains, there was no irreconcilability between party and unions in principle, only between Marxism and opportunism or, to employ the communist terminology, 'trade-unionism'.

By the 1890s the German trade union leadership had already succumbed to the temptation of putting partial gains over capital above the higher goal of destroying both the class system and the exploitative state.[12] As a result, the self-willed unions crippled the effectiveness of the spread of Marxism within the entire movement.

The value of Schröder's detailed research lies in the fact that he very carefully delineates the policies of the union leadership from that of the SPD, so that the basic rivalry and irreconcilability of the goals of the two organizations are clearly brought out. The conclusions drawn distinguish it as a conflicting thesis in the tradition of the earlier Marxist–Leninist studies of Richter and Merker who trace the deviation of the trade union leadership up to and including the First World War.[13]

To balance these ideologically restricted works it is necessary to consult the work done by the West German historian, Dieter Groh, on the labour movement prior to 1914.[14] Part of this compendious study deals with party–union relations and especially the socialists' assessment of the Wilhelmine state. His main theme is that although the polarization process between the classes had become very intense before 1914, the Social Democrats—both party and unions—had become 'negatively integrated' into the Wilhelmine state. The concept means that despite the class struggle which was quite bitter, neither side wished to risk a head-on collision which would result in revolution and the destruction of the old order. The bourgeoisie for their part feared the SPD and the unions but were powerless to institute the measures necessary for stamping them out. Bismarck had tried and failed. Now that they had become even more numerous and powerful, a repetition of the Anti-Socialist Law was unthinkable. On the other hand, it was recognized that the German economy needed the well-disciplined work force that the social democratic electorate had become.

From the organized workers' point of view, while the Wilhelmine State was oppressive, bureaucratic and authoritarian, it still allowed sufficient freedom of movement for the workers to improve their living standards and to extend (albeit under difficulties) their trade union organizations. The state was recognized and feared, however, above all as a military state which would not shrink from destroying the unions if they gave signs (e.g. a general strike) of threatening the state. In short, stalemate had evolved with each side highly suspicious of the other, but each powerless to do anything about it for fear of the consequences or cost to themselves. Expressed in another way, the Social Democratic organizations, although hostile to the Wilhelmine

State, had in the course of time become part of the political and economic structure and could not be eliminated. It was better therefore to speak, in this case, of a 'negative' integration rather than a 'secondary' integration.[15]

This model is most illuminating and is explained to a large extent by Groh's concept of the 'trade-unionization' of the German labour movement. By this he means not only the numerical superiority of union over party membership, but also the concomitant ability of the unions to prevent the party from embarking on courses which the unions believed to be disadvantageous to them. Groh does not, however, venture so far as to assert that the unions, especially since 1906, had won an absolute veto right in party–union negotiations or had usurped all initiative from the SPD. What he does maintain is that in the overall movement the unions had become so preponderant, that exclusively Marxist-revolutionary goals could hardly be pursued. As a result of this trade-unionization the social democratic movement took on the appearance of being merely reformist.

The value of Groh's work for the present theme lies in its differentiated picture of the unions and the party within the total social–political structure. Whilst one sees union strength dependent upon the condition of the economy, as Langerhans already observed, one also sees how party membership improved as did election results when the economic situation worsened for the workers. We thus see how a structural divergence existed in the fortunes of both wings of the labour movement. The importance of this is that it brought about the so-called 'immobilism' of the SPD. That is to say, when the party felt confident of mass support as a result of election successes and showed signs of wanting to become more politically active, the unions hesitated to provoke both the state and the barons of industry. The result was that the party remained quiescent in practice.[16] And it is against this background that Groh explains the behaviour of the SPD at the outbreak of the First World War.

While Groh clearly employs Marxist models in his analysis, he is by no means a disciple of the accompanying dogma which accuses the SPD and the unions of betraying working-class interests in 1914. Groh is much more concerned to discover the precise structural limitations imposed by the Wilhelmine state within which the labour movement as a whole was forced to operate.

It is as a highly valuable complement to Groh's work, that the contribution of Klaus Saul must be considered.[17] He has examined the Wilhelmine state and its perception of the threat from the so-called 'forces of subversion', i.e. the social democratic movement. This involves a study of the ways and means employed by both state and industry to contain and, if possible, eradicate the deleterious influence of both social democracy and trade unionism. It is Saul's contention that the daily war of the bureaucracy, the legal system, the employers' organizations as well as general social discrimination did more than any governmental legislation to shape the attitudes of the working class towards the state. There emerged during the Wilhelmine era an embittered and hostile attitude of the workers that carried over into the Weimar period. For this reason Saul has examined the formation of the anti-socialist organizations of the employers and the efforts made to shelter the population from 'social democratic pollution'. Beyond this, he has focused on the question of 'class justice' to show how workers were disadvantaged by the judiciary.

Saul's study illustrates how effective these attempts by anti-socialist forces were to stabilize and secure the state in the face of the continuing class struggle. By so doing, he shows how realistic the chances of success on the part of the socialist labour movement actually were. In this way the behaviour of organized labour in that context can be more objectively assessed. Indeed, such a method of inquiry produces a sympathetic and more balanced picture than any doctrinaire approach. The essential character of the Wilhelmine state with which the working class had to contend, namely a rigidly hierarchical and fiercely anti-democratic structure thus emerges. Saul argues convincingly that to imagine that this structure might have developed peacefully into a parliamentary democracy in the liberal, Western sense would be to underestimate the virulence of the anti-democratic forces present in it. Like that of Groh, Saul's portrayal must conflict with the Marxist–Leninist line.

The Wilhelmine Reich did progress from its militaristic bureaucratic monarchical structure to become a parliamentary democracy, but only as a result of the stresses of the First World War. Paradoxically, as writers as ideologically diverse as Gerhard Ritter, Fritz Fischer and Dieter Groh have now shown, the Reich plunged into the war determined to preserve the traditional Bismarckian social–political order. Indeed, it was partly due to the threat to that order by democratic forces that the Reich leadership welcomed and indeed manipulated the outbreak of that war. This was done in order to create at home those social–political conditions which would be more favourable towards cementing the monarchy, thereby inhibiting the development of democracy. How the reverse of this came about is the theme of Jürgen Kocka's study on the impact of the war on German society.[18] Certainly he confirms Saul's contention that the transition of the military monarchy to a parliamentary democracy could neither be accomplished rationally nor peacefully.

In a pioneering piece of structural–historical analysis, Kocka demonstrates how the state was forced into making concessions towards the working class in order to maintain the war effort sufficiently to stave off defeat. This characterization of the state grudgingly adjusting to social–political realities under the threat of total extinction confirms again the degree to which the Bismarckian structure had become ossified. The role imputed by Kocka to the German socialist trade unions in bringing about change in the structure of the Reich is of crucial importance. Their decision to support the state unswervingly throughout the four-year struggle in the hope of winning constitutional and social–political improvements even at the expense of alienating the left wing of the SPD and some unions, certainly contributed significantly to the shaping of events which led to the November Revolution and subsequently to the foundation of the Weimar Republic. The very fact that the unions led by Carl Legien's General Commission wished to pursue a middle course between a swing to bolshevism and the possibility of a civil war in 1918–19 made them one of the essential midwives of the Weimar Constitution.

This observation is scarcely novel, but Kocka's analysis shows how, in the confusion of conflicting forces in Germany at the end of the Great War, the unions emerged as one of the chief pillars of the republic. The value of Kocka's work here lies in the structural analysis that accounts for the influence of the socialist unions at a time when their numbers were drastically reduced by the absence of so many workers in the armed services. Essentially, this was because first the army and then industry had come to see in the relative moderation and conservatism of the unions' demands for reform, the lesser of the two evils of democracy Western style and socialism of the bolshevik variety.

Kocka, who employs a Marxist model of conflict between the polarized social groups, nevertheless steadfastly refuses to be drawn into the Marxist camp. The conflict or class dichotomy which developed into fierce class tension during the war was far more complex because of the wide spread alienation of middle class groups as well as, paradoxically, industry from the anachronistic bureaucratic Wilhelmine state.

The Marxist–Leninists explain the transition from monarchy to republic as the outcome of a frustrated proletarian revolution. The chief sinners were those right-wing social democratic leaders supported by the trade union leadership. Their policy of collaboration with the army and industry respectively to salvage the national economy was the chief factor in preventing the revolution from developing along Russian lines. Because of this, the unions merited the wrath of the German Communist Party (KPD) which had emerged in opposition to the alleged opportunism of both moderate Social Democrats and unions during the revolution. Naturally, this thesis of another class-betrayal is not shared by the non-Marxist historians of West Germany. The revolution and the founding of the Weimar Republic are again subjected to far more differentiated analysis, although the tendency to portray these forces of moderation in a favourable light is undeniable.[19]

To begin with, it is necessary to examine the thrust of East German historiography on this aspect. It is now part of the East German paradigm that the November Revolution of 1918 was the first great anti-imperialistic uprising of the masses in a highly industrialized European state to take place under the influence of the Russian October Revolution. The latter formed the beginning of that historical process which began the transition from capitalism to socialism.[20] Fifty years of research had enabled Marxist–Leninist historians to assess the true place of the November Revolution in German history. It had emerged out of the real contradictions of the imperialist system, and expressed for the first time the objective necessity of overcoming the domination of German imperialism and militarism. The revolution was a power struggle, the chief characteristic of which was that the masses were led by the working class; the means and methods were proletarian.

Although the November Revolution suffered a defeat, it represented (by virtue of the democratic rights and freedoms won) a base from which the working class and its allies could wage a more successful struggle for power. It was out of these events that the KPD was formed, and this was to produce the decisive precondition for the future class struggle and the ultimate success of the party in establishing socialism in East Germany after 1945. In short, the November Revolution was the first act of a later triumphant democratic socialist revolution in the GDR. The November Revolution was thus a proletarian-led uprising under the influence of the Russian Revolution; but it was hindered from running its natural course until more favourable conditions were created in 1945 through the Soviet occupation of central Europe. The chief hindrance in 1918–19 was clearly the above-mentioned cooperation of the right-wing Social Democrats and the free trade union leadership with the forces of imperialism and capitalism expressly to prevent the triumph of bolshevism in Germany. Thereby they split the labour movement and furthered the cause of the counter-revolution. It is here, according to the Communist historians, that the logical connection between imperialism and opportunism during the November Revolution becomes most evident.[21]

It is recognized that the majority of the working class in fact supported the anti-working class and anti-national policies of the right-wing SPD leaders. They did not understand that the precondition for social progress and the solution of the vital national problems of the German people was the political and economic emasculation of imperialism and militarism; and that therefore, in the question of power—the basic issue of all revolutions—there could be no half-measures. That the November Revolution remained uncompleted was in fact due to the falsification over the decades of Marxist theory with regard to the state and revolution. The Marxist–Leninist writers now claim it was a tragedy of the German labour movement that the majority of the working class remained steeped in a bourgeois conception of the state, and as a result were unable to envisage how they should take the leadership of the state into their own hands.[22] Marxist–Leninist historiography further asserts that the elimination of imperialism and militarism can only be achieved when the working class are led by a revolutionary party and when the influence of opportunism is overcome.[23] In this respect the rightist SPD and USPD leaders as well as the union leadership frustrated the working class from realizing its historic role in Germany. For this reason, the November Revolution retained the character of a bourgeois-democratic revolution that to some degree was carried through with 'proletarian means and methods'.[24]

This model does not enjoy much currency among West German historians, not a few of whom have concentrated on aspects of this period.[25] Yet the role of the trade unions has been one aspect to have received to date only scant attention. Most writers have been fascinated by the formation of the KPD and the councils' movement. Only a few have drawn attention to the mass of workers who joined the existing union movement in 1918–20.[26] Admittedly, the explanation for the rise, flourishing and decline of the councils' movement involves a consideration of the unions' role. These were decidedly against the slogan, 'All power to the workers' and soldiers' councils' which was proclaimed during the revolution. This was because a total takeover by the councils' movement would have rendered the unions superfluous. They for their part were determined to remain viable in order to maintain above all a semblance of economic stability. To allow the social situation to deteriorate into 'Russian conditions' was considered by the unions to be nationally disastrous.[27] As Peter von Oertzen has shown, the unions were in general quite successful in keeping the political dispute between the communist and social democratic elements within their own ranks at a minimum. By avoiding political dispute they concentrated on the purely economic issues, and in so doing had the approval of the government of the Commissars of the People. Only in the large metal workers' union did the political dispute result in the formation of hostile party-aligned groups.[28] Overall, the free trade unions, by virtue of the unprecedented influx of members at the time, managed to steer a moderately conservative policy during the revolution. They prevented the elimination of their organizations by the councils' movement and thereby established the major precondition for the evolution of a parliamentary as distinct from a Soviet-type republic.

Understandably, the present day apologists of the SPD and free trade unions see this behaviour of the unions between 1918–20 in a most positive light because the SPD and the unions emerged as the champions of moderation, economic rationality and law and order. For the Marxist–Leninists this policy, as has been indicated, was 'statist' and essentially hostile to the true interests of the working class. Indeed, it was the precondition for the 'integration of the working class into the imperialist state'.[29] The chief lesson of the November Revolution for Marxist–Leninist historiography is, however, the legacy bequeathed at the end of 1918 by the example of the hard core of uncompromising revolutionary workers, soldiers and sailors. Their achievement lies in the fact that through their councils they had made the first serious attempt to win power on behalf of the working masses.[30]

In order to gain a perspective of the course of labour history during the Weimar Republic from the Marxist–Leninist standpoint, it will be profitable here to précis their main theses. It is very clear that their aim is to vilify the efforts of Social Democrats and trade unionists to establish a viable parliamentary democracy in Germany during the Weimar period. In so doing, the Marxist–Leninists are trying to destroy the credibility of the present day SPD and trade unions for the reason that these appeal very strongly to the tradition of those labour politics established by the moderate left during the 1920s.

The Marxist–Leninists see the history of the Weimar Republic as being characterized by the presence of a highly organized and politically active working class. Unfortunately, this was split into the KPD, SPD and the various trade union bodies. So, in spite of the vast numbers of organized workers, the working class suffered a shattering defeat—a catastrophe for all democratic forces and for the entire German nation. How could such a thing happen? Marxist–Leninists reply that the reason why the German working class failed before 1933 to triumph over the forces of imperialism and thereby failed to block the fascist attack of monopolistic capitalism is because of the opportunistic elements present. The right-wing social democratic policy of cooperation with the bourgeoisie and the split in the labour movement crippled the entire working class. As a result, any long-term success of the KPD policy of opposition to imperialism was frustated—to the lasting detriment of the German people.

Secondly, the Marxist–Leninists claim to recognize that the Weimar Republic was a bourgeois-parliamentary state, and then ask what the correct attitude of the labour movement towards it should have been. Their answer is that such a state was still in the control of monopolistic capitalism and, as such, was totally unable to solve any of the vital questions of principle in the true interests of the people. On the contrary, this state allowed the forces of reaction a breathing space once more to gather themselves. Indeed, the labour movement would have been obliged under these circumstances to exploit the democratic opportunities of this state and to strive for their expansion, as did the KPD. Unfortunately, however, the right-wing Social Democrats, blind to the historical necessities, tried to employ the bourgeois-parliamentarian republic so as to realize a so-called democratic socialism, and to integrate the labour movement into this state. They thereby subjugated the working class to the dominant bourgeois class.

Thirdly, Marxist–Leninist historians draw parallels between the Weimar period and the present Bonn Republic where the forces of opportunism still seek to frustrate the emancipation of the working class. One of their chief means of doing this (it is alleged) is to falsify the history of the labour movement during the Weimar Republic by asserting that its collapse was, to a large extent, brought about by the policies of the KPD. In order to refute such falsifications the Marxist–Leninist historians have stipulated that the main elements of labour history during the Weimar period were as follows: the development of the KPD; the adoption of Leninism by that party; the consequent evolution of strategy and tactics; the efforts to educate the masses for the struggle to subvert German imperialism; finally its tireless striving to achieve unity of action within the working class. The chief examples of these efforts consisted of the great struggles during the postwar crisis to preserve the achievements of the November Revolution; the continued efforts to overcome the revitalizing of German imperialism; and finally the bitter struggle against the nazification of Germany, i.e. for the national and social emancipation of the German people.[31]

West German historians of the same era are reproached for not addressing themselves to the history of the working class and its activity: namely for not recognizing that history is concerned with class struggle, but instead investigating 'structures and psychologies'. Indeed, West German bourgeois historiography on the labour movement dealt predominantly with the SPD, that is with the forces of opportunism. The integration of the opportunistic leadership into the state and the subjugation of the greater part of the working class to the bourgeoisie were considered wrongly to be the true content of the labour movement. The history of the KPD and the revolutionary workers was thereby played down and explained away as being the result of foreign interference and consequently deleterious in its effects on the true labour movement.

That many West German historians do find themselves in the role of partisans for the anti-communist social democratic movement during Weimar is not at all surprising. They do not share the same belief in the validity of the 'laws of history' held by their East German counterparts. Because of this, their task is rather more complex, as is their understanding of what a democratic society ought to be. Nowhere is this dichotomy of opinion more in evidence than when the history of the collapse of the Weimar Republic is considered, a phase in which the trade unions' role was again critical. From what has been stated, the Marxist–Leninist thesis about the collapse of the republic should be quite clear: the SPD and the unions with few exceptions were in the hands of opportunistic leaders who by their wrong-headed opposition to the Communists were seduced by the forces of imperialism and militarism into trying to come to terms with fascism and thereby betrayed their own class.[32]

In reply to this over-simplification, West German historians have sought to present a far more differentiated image on the basis of an ever-broadening field of evidence. It will suffice here to furnish a summary of their findings that will serve as a framework for the more detailed account in the concluding chapters of this book. In trying to explain the failure of the union leadership to take more dramatic action against the Nazis in the years 1930–33, a series of arguments is advanced which taken together exonerate the unions of merely seeking to take the less dangerous course of expediency. It is stressed in the first instance that because the unions had so identified themselves with the Weimar Republic and its constitution they were from the beginning chiefly concerned to make it work in letter and spirit. Indeed, they were so gratified by the fact that this constitution, in sharp contrast to the Bismarckian constitution, had anchored basic rights especially designed to guarantee the unions' existence that the constitution became for them the guarantee of progress to real socialism. They had sought on the basis of the rights of assembly and association (article 165 of the constitution) to expand in traditional manner the power of the working class against capital. In other words, they believed in continuing the class struggle and pursuing the end goal of socialism by legal constitutional and parliamentary means. This was in conformity with their practice ever since 1890. And because the constitution of 1919 appeared to hold great hopes for the achievement of this, the unions developed an extremely loyal and almost conservative attitude to the Weimar state.[33]

This rejection of violent revolution which also characterized union practice in the pre-1914 period created in the chaotic economic situation of the 1920s a political gap which was only too willingly filled by the KPD: the Communists thus emerged as the sole bearers of the ideology of proletarian revolution and were able especially in the period from 1928 to 1932 to double the

numbers of their electoral supporters.[34] Because of this, the final
years of the republic presented two 'dictatorship models', which
had to be confronted, namely the Nazis and the Communists. The
Social Democrats and their unions saw themselves as trying to
steer a course between the 'Scylla of fascism' and the 'Charybdis
of bolshevism'. Indeed, the unions came to regard the NSDAP as
a collecting bowl of those bourgeois champions of the 'class
struggle from the right'.[35]

It was really only from 1929 until the Reichstag election of 14
September 1930 that the unions finally attributed any significance to the Nazis. Yet they were still not regarded as a serious
threat, rather as the 'lunatic fringe'. Only after the election of
September 1930 was National Socialism seen as a possible
danger. Nevertheless, it was still only regarded as yet another
form of the several examples of right-wing radicalism among the
political groups to the right of the Centre Party. When the Papen
government fell in December 1932 the trade union attitude to the
Nazis was further transformed because their political leverage was
obviously increasing. It was deemed necessary by the ADGB to
initiate talks with the left wing of the NSDAP and to sound out
the new Chancellor, von Schleicher, about their future.[36] Further,
because the NSDAP propaganda was being directed strongly at
the working class, the unions at the beginning of 1933 began to
stress their history of patriotism and loyalty to the state.[37] The aim
here was to counteract the nationalistic appeal of the NSDAP.
But prior to this the ADGB had sought to counter the Nazi
appeal to workers by advancing new job-creating programmes.

The famous programme of the unions formulated in 1928 to
achieve economic democracy had of course lost its propagandist
effect in the economic crisis. They had been forced to accept the
deflationary economic policy of the Brüning government (the
lowering of wages and prices, control of foreign exchange etc.),
but this simply increased unemployment. To combat this the
ADGB produced in April 1932 an elaborate programme to
create work, the Woytinsky–Tarnow–Baade plan. This involved
government contracts and an increased circulation of paper
money and the guaranteeing of credit. Such a policy assumed
acceptance of some inflation and an increased government

deficit. Similar proposals came from the Strasser (left) wing of the NSDAP. Brüning, however, rejected the ADGB plan because of its inflationary tendency but later, ideas from it were actually considered by Papen and von Schleicher.[38]

The point is, the ADGB by then had become desperate to save the economy and the constitution. In the belief that the maintenance of strictest legality would achieve this, the SPD and the unions then held back from employing the general strike weapon even after the Nazis had been elected to form a government. Instead, a policy of adaptation to the changed political constellation was preferred. This came about because the unions now hoped, by sacrificing all political influence, to preserve the social-service system as well as their own organizations.[39] It was this genuine hope of continued recognition as the economic representation of the working class which imposed upon the unions their passive tactics. There could be no suggestion that they voluntarily submitted in anticipation of the Nazi takeover. Indeed, while the union leadership understood the content of Nazi programme and its theoretical, political as well as social consequences, they like other groups within Germany continued to believe that its practical execution was impossible simply because it was too grotesque.[40]

For this reason Hitler's first cabinet was considered to be just another in the series of presidial governments that had ruled Germany since 1930. Indeed, the more the NSDAP exceeded the limits of constitutional legality, the more the unions and the SPD insisted on the strictest legality of their own position, even when the SPD did so comparatively poorly at the elections of 5 March 1933. The trade union leadership did not realize until 2 May 1933 when their offices were occupied by the SA that they were the victims of uncompromising and unscrupulous outlaws. In their hope of maintaining the constitution the unions were misled into believing that their insistence upon legality would be generally understood and respected. They thereby delivered themselves defenceless to their executioners.

These theses which seek to do justice to the union leadership draw attention to the extremely limited room for manoeuvre they had. When this is appreciated there can be no reproach of failure of self-destruction. At the most they were guilty of a degree of political naivety which caused them to underestimate the true nature of the enemy as well as their own political strength. It will be the task of this study to show just how this situation arose.

CHAPTER TWO

German Trade Union Theory: Marxians Versus Lassalleans 1847–1869

That the role of trade unions in the struggle for socialism was evaluated differently by the rival German socialist camps of Marxians and Lassalleans is relatively well known. However, the long-term significance of the original debate on the issue is probably not so well appreciated. It is also widely accepted that both Marx and Lassalle were the dominating ideological authorities within German social democracy although, paradoxically, they championed contradictory theories, a fact which automatically poses the question concerning the precise function of ideology in any mass movement. It has now been ably demonstrated by Hans Josef Steinberg that the reception of socialism in the German social democratic movement was anything but uniform, and despite the fact that officially Marxism appeared to triumph with the adoption of the Erfurt Programme of 1891, one could hardly speak of the SPD as an unequivocally Marxist party.[1] Also, the fact that the same party repudiated revisionism at its conferences of 1899 and 1903, thus reinforcing its confession of faith in Marxism, did not by any means improve the ideological purity of the movement.[2] Indeed, German social democracy continued to be wracked by internecine disputes on a range of theoretical issues as it had been from the time when Lassalle founded the *Allgemeiner Deutscher Arbeiterverein* (ADAV) in 1863.

From that date onwards, perhaps the central issue was that of trade unionism and its relationship to the political wing of the movement. This chapter seeks to focus on this question as understood by Marx and Engels on the one hand, and Lassalle together with his followers on the other. This, it is argued, is an essential prerequisite for understanding the behaviour of German socialist trade unionism, not only in the period up to and including the First World War, but also during the crucial period of the ill-fated Weimar Republic to 1933. As they developed, trade unions came to constitute the broad basis of social democracy, and insisted upon the pursuit of policies of their own devising in isolation from the party. Indeed, they maintained a so-called neutral, non-political, independent stance which in practice made it impossible for the party to direct the unions in the class struggle along lines which, according to party ideologues, appeared more orthodox. This dilemma was present right from the beginning of the German labour movement, both in the Marxist and Lassallean streams, and continued to exert a stultifying influence on it until the Nazi seizure of power in 1933.

It was, of course, Friedrich Engels who first drew attention to the political potential of the trade unions. His study, *The Condition of the Working Class in England* which he wrote after a sojourn of almost two years in that country (November 1842 to August 1844), was published in German in 1845. It was the first expression of Marxist trade union theory. In it Engels depicted the trade union struggle as the logical outcome of the capitalist social order. He explained how the workers' resistance to capitalists developed from the first primitive stage of Luddism to the more sophisticated methods of trade unionism. The drive of workers to form unions to overcome the self-destroying competition of wage labourers among themselves resulted from their recognition of their common exploitation at the hands of capitalists.

Engels then described how unions were organized, what means they employed in their struggles, and in what respect their existence was significant. Above all, he explained how the trade union struggle was a *Kriegsschule*, a training for war, in the preparation of the working class for the overthrow of capitalism. His chief purpose was to show how the development of capitalism inexorably led to the socialist revolution which would be brought about by the working class, the revolutionary section of society.[3]

As far as his wages theory at that time was concerned, Engels was still under the influence of Ricardo, and so based his concepts on the law of supply and demand—in contrast to later Marxist wage theory. The limit of the minimum wage was determined by the competition of the workers among themselves; the maximum wage was determined by the competition of the capitalists in periods of stronger demand for labour. So the average wage corresponded to the balance between supply and demand. In this system, however, the unions only gained influence in so far as they could exert pressure on the level of the wages, since they tended to lessen the competition of the workers among themselves for jobs.

Although this was an ameliorating factor from the workers' point of view, both Engels and Marx regarded this degree of union influence on the wage level to be relatively slight. They were of the opinion that overall in the capitalist system, the price of labour corresponded as a rule to the wage minimum.[4] This view runs through all the works of Marx and Engels during the 1840s, but although they modified their wages theory the more they learned about political economy, they remained adamant concerning the essentially revolutionary role of the emerging trade union movement. Strikes were, after all, the best training ground for revolution.

Karl Marx, for his part, echoed this view in his famous polemic against Proudhon, *The Poverty of Philosophy*, which first appeared in French in 1847. *The Communist Manifesto* of 1848 also contains key statements about worker combinations, as does the pamphlet, *Wage Labour and Capital* which was published first as an article series in the *Neue Rheinische Zeitung* from 4 April 1849. The famous address, *Value, Price and Profit* presented in English in 1865 was written expressly to clarify the function of unionism in capitalist society. Further, volume one of *Capital* which appeared in 1867 also contains important implications for trade union practice. But in addition to these scholarly writings, both Marx and Engels made a number of *ad hoc* statements, not only in addresses to the International but also in correspondence and interviews with political and trade union leaders which were of immediate reference to trade unionism. All these need to be ventilated.

When writing *The Poverty of Philosophy* in 1846, Marx like Engels previously, was obviously impressed by the drive of workers to combine into unions so as to force up the price of labour. And in refuting Proudhon's assertion that strikes were counterproductive because they allegedly forced up the price of commodities as a result of increased wages, Marx averred that, 'the rise and fall of profits and wages expresses merely the proportion in which capitalists and workers share in the product of a day's work, without influencing in most instances the price of the produce'.[5]

Marx then went on to observe that in England, strikes had regularly given rise to the invention and application of new machines because machines were the weapons employed by the capitalists to quell the revolt of specialized labour. This tendency was, however, for Marx not a cause for despair since it promoted the extension of industry: 'If combinations and strikes had no other effect than that of making the efforts of mechanical genius react against them, they would still exercise an immense influence on the advancement of industry'.[6] And this in itself served to advance the labour movement. Combinations grew with the development of industry. Unions were, then, an automatic concomitant of industrial development.[7] But the next observation by Marx is even more significant:

> Large scale industry concentrates in one place a crowd of people unknown to one another. Competition divides their interests. But the maintenance of wages, this common interest which they have against their boss, unites them in a common thought of resistance—*combination*. Thus combination always has a double aim, that of stopping competition among the workers, so that they can carry on general competition with the capitalist. If the first aim of resistance was merely the maintenance of wages, combinations, at first isolated, constitute themselves into groups as the capitalists in their turn unite for the purpose of repression; and in face of always united capital, the maintenance of the association becomes more necessary to them than that of wages.[8]

This was a very acute observation by Marx at a time when trade union membership in Britain was only about 80,000.[9] Worker loyalty to their unions had actually cost them a great deal of material sacrifice—for example when strikes failed—so that workers looked upon their associations as something more than mere instruments for extracting higher wages from capitalists. Unions were clearly, already at that time, following laws of their own development with the aim of perpetuating their identity as rallying points for oppressed wage earners. Indeed, Marx's British experience had taught him to regard the wage struggle of the unions as a veritable civil war in which all elements were being united for the coming final battle. Once the unions reached this militant stage they took on a political character.

In the *Communist Manifesto*, Marx and Engels again allude to the fact that industrialization leads to pauperization of the workers who, in order to resist this, form what they called revolutionary combinations:

> The essential condition for the existence, and for the sway of the bourgeois class, is the formation and augmentation of capital; the condition for capital is wage labour. Wage labour rests exclusively on competition between the labourers. The advance of industry, whose involuntary promoter is the bourgeoisie, replaces the isolation of the labourers, due to competition, by their revolutionary combination, due to association. The development of modern industry, therefore, cuts from under its feet the very foundation upon which the bourgeoisie produces and appropriates products. What the bourgeoisie therefore produces, above all, is its own grave diggers. Its fall and the victory of the proletariat are equally inevitable.[10]

This is a statement of far reaching significance because it shows that Marx understood the formation of trade unions to be not only the natural and automatic consequence of industrialization, but also as the indispensable prerequisite of the proletariat for the class struggle against, and ultimate victory over the bourgeoisie. And in attributing this function to the unions, Marx immediately politicized them. That is to say he ascribed to them an essential and pre-eminently political role in capitalist society; but he added that this role had to be played out under the guidance of 'the most advanced and resolute section of the working class parties of every country, that section which pushes forward all others'. As far as theory was concerned, these groups 'have over the great mass of the proletariat the advantage of clearly understanding the line of march, the conditions, and the ultimate general results of the proletarian movement'.[11]

With this postulation of two indispensible factors in the class struggle, namely trade unions and a communist elite, Marx injected a tension in the labour movement which has never been overcome, because, as the history of German labour in particular illustrates, the goals of the union wing and those of the political wing could never be brought into full harmony with each other. At this early stage of their writing, however, there was no evidence of a clash between union and party goals since neither were sufficiently developed anywhere in 1848, or for that matter during the life of the First International 1864–1872.

In *Wage Labour and Capital* from 1849, the *Leitmotiv* of the continuing struggle between bourgeoisie and proletariat is most evident. Here, Marx affirmed that 'The more productive capital grows, the more the division of labour and the application of machinery expands. The more the division of labour and the application of machinery expands, the more competition among workers expands and the more wages contract.'[12] And although Marx in this text did not mention combinations of workers, it is clearly implied that the only way in which the growing helpless army of the proletariat can halt the contraction of their wages is by combining into unions.

Before the appearance of volume one of *Capital* in 1867, Marx had declared his stand on trade unionism on two significant occasions. The first was when he was invited to give the inaugural address at the founding of the International at the famous meeting in St. Martin's Hall, London 28 September 1864. E. H. Carr commented on this invitation by British trade union leaders to the German expatriate theoretician as 'a decision which determined the whole course of the International from its inception to its death'.[13] Marx himself had had little to do with the preparation of the historic mass meeting; the initiative had come, significantly, from the union men, a fact from which Marx must have drawn some basic conclusions about the nature of the proletarian class struggle.

In his speech, Marx praised the victory of the Chartist movement in forcing Parliament to pass the ten-hours bill in 1847, and other examples of worker self-help such as the Co-operative movement. Marx proclaimed that such initiative from cooperative labour with the goal of saving what he called the 'industrious masses . . . ought to be developed to national dimensions'.[14] This would be the prerequisite to workers conquering political power, the achievement of which had become the great duty of the working classes. Marx then observed that the workers possessed here one great advantage—numbers. However, he went on to warn that numbers only were effective when they were 'united by combination and led by knowledge'.[15]

When drawing up the provisional rules for the newly found organization, The Working Men's International Association, Marx stipulated that 'the success of the movement in each country could not be secured but by the power of union and combination'.[16] So thus far in the development of Marx's thought, there is a clear primacy of initiative imputed to the union movement. That is to say, the organization of those powerful unions on a national level throughout the industrialized world which were affiliated in the International was the basis from which workers would conquer political power for the emancipation of their class. From this, a doctrine of the primacy of union organization can readily be drawn. And that this was Marx's intention can be deduced from the fact that he was particularly displeased with the General German Workers' Association founded by Lassalle in 1863. This was set up as a purely political organization intending to rely solely on manhood suffrage to democratize the state with a view ultimately to setting up cooperatives with government aid. Thereby the workers were supposed to become their own employers; the trade union organization was in this system totally discounted as being of any help at all.

Ferdinand Lassalle had made his position most clear during his short agitation period in a speech at Ronsdorf on 22 May 1863.

Here he referred to a petition from Berlin printers' assistants demanding the right of association. Lassalle stated that 'this right only brought relief to certain types of workers in a few . . . exceptional cases; it could, however, never achieve a real improvement of the condition of the working class'. All that Lassalle would admit was that workers' combinations ought to be legalized since they were an excellent means of stirring up worker support for the party which must always remain of primary importance in his theory of socialism.[17]

Lassalle's socialism was founded upon the Ricardian doctrine of the iron law of wages. This he formulated as follows:

The iron law of wages, which under present day conditions, under the domination of supply and demand for labour determines the workers' wages, is this: That the average wage is always reduced to a level necessary for subsistence, i.e. a level which a people usually accepts as necessary for the eking out of an existence and the reproduction of the species. This is the point about which the real daily wage gravitates in the pendulum swing all the time neither being able to raise itself above the same nor being able to fall below the same. It cannot raise itself permanently above this average—because then there would arise, by means of the slightly improved conditions of the workers, an increase in the working class marriages, and thus an increase in the working population, an increase in the supply of hands which would force down the wages back to their earlier levels. Again, the working wage cannot fall permanently below the necessary subsistence level because then emigration increases, there is a reduction in marriages, a fall off in the reproduction of children, and finally a reduction in the number of workers caused by the general pauperization which thus reduces the supply of hands still more, and therefore brings back the wages again to the previous level. Thus the real average working wage floats in the movement constantly around its centre to which it always must sink back, circle around, sometimes above it (periods of prosperity in all or individual branches of industry), sometimes a little below it (periods of more or less general depression and crisis).

The restriction of the average wage to a level within the population which is required for maintaining an existence and for reproduction—that is, I repeat, the iron and cruel law which controls the working wage in today's conditions.[18]

According to Lassalle, this was the brutally unchangeable law of *laissez faire* economics, the result being that the working wage always hovered around the very limit of that which at a given time was necessary to basic subsistence, sometimes a little above the limit, sometimes a little below.

The iron law was a seductive argument, but if it were true, the cultural advance of the workers could not be explained; they would have remained in a constant state of immiseration. Lassalle only conceded that in instances of extremely high productivity many industrial products became extremely cheap. Thereby the worker as consumer enjoyed a temporary advantage. But this did not affect or change the fraction of the value of his labour that the worker received. Rather, it improved the general condition of all the population including those who did not participate in the work process. And the advantage which thereby accrued to the worker as consumer would be cancelled out by the iron law. Only when an increase in productivity occurred quite suddenly and coincided with a long period of demand for labour, would goods be produced in such quantities at such unusually cheap prices as to become items of basic necessity in a given society, i.e. those regarded as the minimum for a subsistence level. The workers' living standard always remained at this point, and so any real cultural advance was impossible.

If this were the case, Lassalle would have been right with regard to his repeated statements about the utter pointlessness of trade union activity. This brought advantages only for a small strata of workers in wage struggles, and such advantages could never become the norm for the mass of workers—because of the iron law. In the existing system of political economy, there was no way out of this vicious circle. Lassalle therefore proposed that workers should become their own entrepreneurs; they should set up productive cooperatives, and since they did not possess the capital to do so, the state should provide it. And to move the state to do this, it first must be democratized by means of manhood suffrage. The capturing of the state in this way was the chief task of the workers.[19]

Lassalle made the iron law not only the very persuasive basis of his agitation, but also the touchstone of real concern for the workers. It was, indeed, an infallible means of unmasking those politicians who were out to deceive the workers. If one spoke of the need to improve their lot, and did not recognize the iron law, he was either an opportunist or abysmally ignorant of the principles of political economy. And if one did recognize the iron law, he would have to say how he would go about remedying it. If he could not supply the answer, he was nothing but a turner of empty phrases. Such politicians could be ignored.

For these reasons, adherents of Lassalle could not be particularly sympathetic to the trade union movement. And it is an historical fact that his doctrine of the iron law remained an official part of the Social Democratic Party's programme until 1891. Lassalle's teachings, too, were still being read in the period of the Anti-Socialist Law of 1878–1890, so that they had a long-lasting effect well after his death in 1864 and the disappearance of his party in 1875. Further, they continued to be read by workers long after Marx had refuted the iron law in volume one of *Capital* where Marx demonstrated that it was not the rise and fall of the birth rate of the working class which determined wages, but the 'industrial reserve army' which was created by the accumulation of capital.[20]

Marx's ponderous refutation of Lassalle appeared three years after the latter's death. An earlier posthumous confrontation occurred when Marx debated with J.B. von Schweitzer, Lassalle's disciple (and later president of the ADAV) and editor of the workers' newspaper, *Der Social–Democrat* which had began publishing in December 1864. It was a time when the Berlin workers were agitating for the right of association. Von Schweitzer could not ignore the workers' demands and actually used his newspaper to promote them. However, he did this in such a way as to indicate that he regarded the formation of unions in exactly the same light as Lassalle. Indeed, von Schweitzer wrote in *Der Social-Democrat* that it certainly was not part of the platform of the ADAV to strive for the right of association. That could not help in liberating the workers from the yoke of capitalism. Nevertheless, von Schweitzer conceded that if the demand for the right of association served to rally the workers and make them politically aware, he would support it. But, he made it clear that this was only a concession to those workers 'who had not yet recognized that under the present system of production the interests of the factory–owner class and the interests of the working class were simply irreconcilable, and that for this reason their efforts within the present necessarily miserable condition only tended to achieve little relief'.[21]

By treating the question of trade unionism in this way, von Schweitzer was really suggesting that it was only a concession to the stupidity of the not yet enlightened masses. Karl Marx, who at that time was contributing to *Der Social-Democrat* was hardly edified to read this contemptuous view of unionism coming from the Lassalleans. He therefore took von Schweitzer to task in a letter of 13 February 1865 wherein he asserted:

> Combinations, with the trade unions which grow out of them, are not only of the most extreme importance as a means of organizing the working class to fight with the bourgeoisie—this importance shows itself in other things in that even the workers of the United States, in spite of their voting rights and republic, cannot do without it—but in Prussia and Germany at large the right of association, in addition to making a breach in the rule of a police-state and bureaucratism, destroys the master and servant regulations and the control of the feudal nobility in the country.[22]

In this way Marx corrected the Lassallean, von Schweitzer. Yet Marx's defence of trade unionism was not without certain important reservations. In his famous London address, *Wages, Price and Profit* communicated to the General International Congress in September 1865, with the purpose of refuting erroneous views about the purpose of unions, Marx concluded:

> Trade unions work well as centres of resistance against the encroachments of capital. They fail partially from an injudicious

use of their power. They fail generally from limiting themselves to a guerilla war against the effects of the existing system, instead of simultaneously trying to change it, instead of using their organized forces as a lever for the final emancipation of the working class, that is to say, the ultimate abolition of the wage system.[23]

For Marx, clearly, unionism was not an end in itself. Rather, it was the indispensable beginning of worker politicization without which the working class would not become a revolutionary force. This very same idea emerges in his instructions to the delegates of the Provisional General Council going to Geneva, Switzerland, for the First Congress of the International Association, 3–8 September, 1866. Here again Marx underlined the importance of unions:

Trades unions originally sprung up from the *spontaneous* attempt of workmen at removing or at least checking that competition [among themselves], in order to conquer such terms of contract as might raise them at least above the condition of mere slaves. The immediate object of trades unions was therefore confined to every day necessities, to expediencies for the obstruction of incessant encroachments of capital, in one word, to questions of wages and time of labour. This activity of the trades unions is not only legitimate, it is necessary. It cannot be dispensed with so long as the present system of production lasts. On the contrary, it must be generalised by the formation and the combination of trades unions throughout all countries. On the other hand, unconsciously to themselves, the trades unions were for many *centres of organization* of the working class, as the medieval municipalities and communes did for the middle class. If the trades unions are required for the guerilla fights between capital and labour, they are still more important as *organized agencies for superseding the very system of wages labour and capital rule*.[24]

Nothing could document more clearly that Marx regarded the

unions as the most effective aspect of the labour movement. They were obviously the most logical form to begin the class struggle in a way which could promise to lead to success. Unions were, in short, the beginning and central factor of the labour movement. However, they were not to satisfy themselves with winning wages struggles and limiting the hours of work; they must always keep in mind the end goal, the ultimate elimination of the wages system. This was because they were struggling against the effects of a disease, and only functioned as a palliative without being able to cure the disease by their own efforts.

What is noteworthy at this stage of Marx's theoretical development is his apparent change of attitude to the formation of a workers' party in Germany. In 1848 his view had been that the relatively few politically active workers ought only to support the more progressive elements of the bourgeoisie in order to help them into power. But in 1848, the liberals had capitulated in the face of the forces of reaction because they feared the political demands of the working class more than the existing conservative state.[25] For this reason both Marx and Engels came to the conclusion that, after all, the only truly revolutionary element in modern society was the working class. But this recognition only applied to an international organization of workers. Within the framework of the nation–state, the working class should continue its cooperation with the bourgeoisie.

It was precisely on this point that Lassalle performed his historical task by detaching the labour movement in Germany from the tutelage of certain liberal groups in setting up his ADAV as a purely worker's political party. 'The revolutionary mission of the bourgeoisie had come to an end through its failure in the revolution of 1848.'[26] Lassalle had seen, too, that it had become quite impossible for the liberals to create a state in the future. They would only concern themselves with the maintenance of state and society and above all their own power position in the economy. It was, therefore, necessary within Germany for the working class to have their own political identity. But the existing worker's political clubs either under the aegis of Wilhelm Weit-

ling or that of Marx and Engels exerted no influence worth men-
tioning among the workers of the early 1860s.[27] A more viable
organization was needed to harness the energies of the developing German labour movement. It was not Marx or Engels, but
Lassalle who provided this. In so doing, he anticipated developments and forced Marx to accept an accomplished fact. Indeed,
the attitude of Marx and Engels to the ADAV was at first cau-
tiously reserved, but then critically hostile. Nevertheless, Marx
paid a tribute to Lassalle posthumously when he conceded in a
letter (13 October 1868) to von Schweitzer that Lassalle's
immortal contribution had been to arouse the labour movement
to action, in spite of the large mistakes he had made.[28]

Events in Germany between 1863 and 1869 within the labour
movement saw developments upon which Marx could exert no
direct influence. The Social Democratic Workers' Party of Germany which was founded at a congress in Eisenach (August
1869) by August Bebel and Wilhelm Liebknecht has been shown
to have associated itself with the First International purely out
of tactical considerations. There can be no suggestion that the
Eisenach group which was set up in rivalry to the Lassalleans and
also to escape the tutelage of the bourgeoisie, was in any way
motivated by exclusively Marxist ideological considerations.[29]
The emergence of this party was essentially a by-product of an
internecine struggle between those German workers who wished
to endorse the Lassallean formula of support for Prussia, and
those who preferred an alternative solution to the question of
German unity.[30] The situation again, however, presented Marx
and Engels with an accomplished fact. It is untenable to assert, as
for example East German historians do, that the SDAP was
founded under the guidance of Marx and Engels who had at last
recognized the time had come for the establishing of a revolutionary party in Germany.[31] The evidence is rather that Marx
believed at the time that purely political parties would be only
transitory in nature.[32] Indeed, Marx's most emphatic encouragement to German trade unionism shortly after the Eisenach Congress certainly appears to confirm that he had doubts about the
viability of the newly founded workers' party at Eisenach in
August 1869, particularly as significant numbers were still, as far

as socialist theory is concerned, disciples of Lassalle. Marx had already in the month after the Eisenach Congress made un-equivocal statements to the German trade union leader J. Haman of Hanover who sought in September 1869 Marx's advice on the role and function of trade unionism. On that occasion, Marx affirmed:

> Never should the trade unions be brought into connection with a political association or made dependent upon one if they are to fulfil their task; if this happens it would mean giving them a death-blow. The trade unions are the schools of socialism. In the trade unions workers are daily confronted by the struggle with capital. All political parties whatever they are without exception are able to enthuse the mass of workers for a limited period; only the unions, on the other hand, are capable of representing a real labour party and of opposing a bulwark to capital. The large mass of the workers has decided that their real material position must be improved whatever party they wish to belong to. When a worker's material condition is improved he can then devote himself more to the rearing of his children. His wife and children no longer need to work in the factory and he can educate and look after himself more; he then becomes a socialist without suspecting it.[33]

This relatively obscure statement by Marx was made at a time when there were two rival social democratic parties in Germany competing for the loyalty of the workers. The Lassalleans' con-cept of the labour struggle clearly discounted unionism but sought nevertheless to exploit the drive to organization by artisans for the benefit of the party. Von Schweitzer had experimented with the idea of creating a nationwide workers' mutual aid society to replace existing craft unions but this had been a dismal failure.[34] Marx had obviously seen his concept of unionism confirmed. It was doubly essential in the German situation that unions go on pursuing their historic task independent from either party. On the other hand, it must have been clear to Marx that Bebel and Liebknecht had no alternative but to go ahead and found their party in opposition to the Lassalleans. Their motivation for this step was chiefly their hostility to von Schweitzer and his pro-Prussian tendencies, not necessarily because the workers had outgrown the influence of Lassalle's ideology.[35] Nevertheless, from Marx's view point the need to form a new party which would encourage the growth of unionism must have been obvious, although the formation of a revolutionary elite before the unions had time to school a broad basis of mass support was clearly a premature step. The necessity of the situation, however, demanded it.

After the SDAP was founded at Eisenach with the help of leading ex-Lassalleans such as the union champion, Theodor York, one might have expected the debate over the usefulness of unionism in the class struggle to have subsided. On the contrary, it continued quite virulently in the pages of *Der Volksstaat*, mainly because the Lassallean iron law doctrine was still held by many to be valid. It was even retained, much to Marx's disgust, in the Gotha Programme which united the remnant of the Lassalleans with the Eisenachers in 1875.[36] And in the entire period between the founding of the SDAP and the Anti-Socialist Law of 1878 it had not been possible, despite repeated attempts, to establish a centralized trade union federation in Germany. This had to wait until the fall of Bismarck's infamous legislation against the Social Democrats in 1890. Even then, however, the usefulness of unionism was still being questioned. The adoption of the Erfurt Programme in 1891 did little to stifle the deeply engrained hostility of certain party leaders to encouraging separate union organization. Indeed, the trade union issue remained a crucial one throughout the history of German social democracy, at least until 1933.[37]

Although by 1891 Lassalleanism had been officially replaced by Marxism as the ideology of German social democracy, the effect on the union issue was surprisingly limited in view of Marx's unequivocal statements on the prime importance of unions. It appears that trade union leaders themselves remained aware of Marx's doctrine regarding them, but party leaders had by the 1890s come to the view that now the elite had to establish the primacy of political leadership. The history of German labour thereafter shows very strongly that the union movement, despite their confession of faith in Marxism, refused to accept this primacy.[38] From their view point, there was still the need to organize many more millions of workers before it was time for the elite to make the decisive steps to realize socialism in Germany.

This tension within German social democracy is evidenced by the fact that union champions right up to Hitler's seizure of power again and again insisted on maintaining an independent stance from that of the party leadership, especially at times of internal or national crisis. In doing so, they could always appeal to Karl Marx to justify their position. It was indeed an open question whether the time was ripe for a general strike or rebellion, or again whether one should cooperate with the state or confront it. That the German unions always played a wait-and-see game until it was too late, that is until January 1933, turned out to be a miscalculation of immeasurable effect. It was all the more a tragedy since their motivation throughout had been to spare the working population all unnecessary hardship—a consideration which certain party intellectuals in the period 1890 to 1914 in particular failed to understand.[39]

A footnote to this problem is provided by the writings of the trade union leader, Hermann Müller-Lichtenberg (1868–1932), who like many of his contemporaries during the First World War and the Weimar Republic sought to justify SPD and trade union policies at that time by appealing to the writings of Marx referred to above.

Müller affirms that Marx intended the unions to remain party–politically neutral as he had explained in the famous interview with Haman. Müller also alludes to the fact that Marx approved of the setting up of the SDAP in 1869 as a separate workers' party in opposition to the Lassalleans on one hand, and removed from the tutelage of the bourgeois parties on the other. Although such a move must have appeared unorthodox in Marxian terms since the unions were at that stage very undeveloped in Germany, Müller asserts that Marx was not being inconsistent in supporting the tactics of Bebel and Liebknecht. These two went ahead, as is well known, and set up a party virtually on their own initiative. And when at the Eisenach Congress J. P. Becker, the chairman of the German-speaking section of the International from Geneva, tabled a resolution requiring that the new labour movement in Germany be based exclusively on trade unions, it was rejected. Instead, a resolution was passed that the new party *encourage the formation of trade unions.*[40]

Hermann Müller reports that Marx knew of Becker's resolution to make unions the central factor in the labour movement, and he disapproved of it![41] How, inquired Müller, is one to understand Marx's blatantly inconsistent attitude? Was Marx the socialist theorist different from Marx the politician?

The answer supplied by Hermann Müller is as follows: Marx was not being at all inconsistent; he was merely taking the peculiar circumstances of Germany into consideration. First of all, the German combination laws did not allow for the formation of trade unions on a national basis, although these regulations were repealed in 1869 within the North German Confederation. This meant, that up until the time of the Eisenach Congress, any labour movement based exclusively on trade unions in Germany would have been illegal. It was, therefore, only possible to form a new political party.

In any case, the various existing local craft unions were divided in their loyalties. Some were Lassallean while others leaned towards the Bebel–Liebknecht movement. It would likewise have been impossible to base the new organization on a divided trade union movement. In addition, both Bebel and Liebknecht were already members of the Reichtag as representatives of the Saxon Peoples Party.[42] It had become clear by 1865 that they needed their own party organization for an operational base. A further factor adduced by Müller to explain Marx's apparently opportunistic attitude in 1869 was the fact that workers had already developed political loyalties having been wooed in the past by the bourgeois parties. Here, both historical and religious tradition had been determining factors; the workers had not yet developed a class consciousness. For these reasons it would have been all the more impractical either to base a workers' party on the unions as they then existed or to subjugate the unions to one political party. The task of unionism was to organize all artisans and labourers without concern for their political or religious sympathies.

Yet another factor made for a separation of the political and industrial wings of the labour movement in Germany: this was the law which forbade craft unions taking part in political activity.[43] In other words, not only the industrial situation, but also the party–political and the legal conditions prevailing in Germany demanded that trade unions be kept strictly neutral and independent from the party organizations. This necessity was underlined very strongly at the Eisenach Congress of 1869 and repeated at the subsequent conferences of the SDAP prior to the complete banning of socialist political activity in Germany in 1878.[44] At that time the debate as to the usefulness of unions was carried on with great intensity. What is remarkable is that the union champions within the party appealed neither to Marx nor Lassalle as a basis for their organizational practice. Rather they were following a pragmatically observed need. Workers had to be organized into unions so that the struggle for better wages and conditions there and then could be more efficiently carried on.

CHAPTER THREE
Trade Union Thinking in
Bismarckian Germany to 1878

Although the German artisan had inherited from the Middle
Ages a long tradition of guild-consciousness, namely of belong-
ing to the journeymen's organization of his trade or craft, a modern trade union movement did not emerge until the 1860s.[1] This
is not to deny that the Workers' Brotherhood organized by the
Berlin typesetter, Stephan Born during the 1848/49 revolution in
Germany had certain trade union characteristics. It was, however,
more in the nature of a workers' pressure group articulating the
political as well as economic grievances of artisans who had
endured great legal disabilities in addition to appalling labouring
conditions in a period when industrialization was having its worst
disrupting social effects.[2]

The Workers' Brotherhood of 1848 had, despite its short-lived
existence, a long term impact. It was the first German labour
movement as distinct from a socialist club and as such the most
significant attempt hitherto by workers to organize themselves
for the purpose of improving both their social–political and
economic rights within the existing state. Indeed, it was well
remembered long after it had ceased to function, and since it
consciously dissociated itself from Marxism, it was far from being
a revolutionary organization. In the understanding of its leadership it was a rational, non-violent response to the new social
conditions with the aim of emancipating tradesmen from sub-
human working conditions. The German governments of
1848/49, however, and particularly those after their reactionary
swing during 1850, were totally unresponsive to what the articulate tradesmen regarded as reasonable demands for reform. Even

the right of association which had been granted during the revolutionary year had not applied to trade unions. During 1848 the relaxing of the laws of association in the Germanic states had led to widespread party–political activity, but not to combinations of workers in the accepted trade union sense. As Frolinde Balser points out,[3] German law made a distinction between *Vereinsrecht* (the law governing the right of association) and *Koalitionsrecht* (the law governing the right to combination). The former affected the emergence of party–political organizations whereas the latter had considerable influence on the organization of trade unions. During the revolutionary period of 1848/49 unrestricted right of association had been established in all German states. This led to the well-known spread of party–political activity. On the other hand, the right (or lack of it) of combination, which regulated the sphere of labour–management relations (*Arbeitsrecht*), did not allow the completely free development of trade union organizations. In Prussia, by far the largest German state, the *Gewerbeordnung* (the Industrial Code) of 1845 expressly forbade labourers, artisans and factory workers from organizing themselves to strike for higher wages, to engage in picketing or to form any associations among themselves without police permission. Indeed, the regulations stated specifically that the fixing of wages for artisans, labourers and apprentices was a matter of individual agreement between master and servants. But, under the prevailing conditions, this meant simply that the employers had an unrestricted right to exploit their workers.

The interlude of the revolution did not bring any modification here, and after 1850 the same restrictions continued to apply to the right of combination.[4] And considering the situation regarding *Vereinsrecht* after 1849 (during the period of reaction) in the various state constitutions, even the right of association was virtually meaningless. W. H. Dawson, writing as late as 1894, observed that the totally unrestricted right of combination and of public assembly had hardly yet been legalized in most German states. Admittedly, the post 1848 constitutions accorded the nominal right, but the law had hedged it around with so many restrictions that, as Dawson comments, 'this first condition of civil and political freedom has never been enjoyed in its integrity.'[5] So then, from 1848 onwards, while a certain degree of political freedom, namely the right to form political parties was in evidence, the right to form trade unions was severely limited by the Industrial Code. Again as Frolinde Balser summarized the situation:

In 1848/49 there was an unrestricted right of association in Germany—this enabled party–political activity; in 1850 this right of association was in many states considerably reduced again for political associations. The freedom of combination and therewith the beginning of trade union activity was granted first in 1861 in the Kingdom of Saxony, 1867 in the Grand Duchy of Baden, in 1869 in the North German Confederation and then in the German Reich.[6]

This meant that modern trade union activity could only really begin in the 1860s, but as Dawson has noted, a completely unrestricted right of combination was not even evident in the 1890s. This was not only because the Masters and Servants legislation prohibited certain categories of workers altogether from organizing, but because the Industrial Code was interpreted in an anti-trade union manner by the police and judicature. Indeed, German labour history from the Industrial Revolution onwards is the history of the workers' struggle for an unrestricted right of combination.

The industrial legislation of 1869 in the North German Confederation which after 1871 applied to the entire Reich admittedly guaranteed the right of combination to most German workers, but the wording of the regulations immediately negated the right as soon as it was invoked. Whereas paragraph 152 of the *Gewerbeordnung* of 1869 allowed the right of combination to most categories of workers, paragraph 153 foresaw penalties for the misuse of this right. The wording implied that any person who tried to persuade others by means of physical force, threats, defamation or libel to join a union or to conform to its actions, or on the other hand likewise sought to hinder a member from voluntarily leaving a union, could be imprisoned for up to three months.[7]

Clearly, a hostile police chief or judge was allowed a very wide freedom of interpretation under this regulation. And since the attitude prevailing among employers and police alike was decidedly unsympathetic to unionism, the movement experienced great organizational difficulties. Workers who were organized in trade unions automatically aroused the suspicion of the state because of the association of the union movement in the bureaucratic mind with social democracy. The enmity of the Bismarckian state towards the politically articulate industrial proletariat gained expression in the legalistic persecution of what were in the opinion of state officials socialist-inspired worker organizations.

An illustration of this hostility can be seen in the attempts by the Reich government in 1873 and 1874 to make the industrial regulations even more draconic by increasing the penalty for industrial action to at least six months imprisonment. Beyond this, the number of possible offences listed in the draft regulation was also considerably increased. Having debated the draft, the Reichstag committee rejected it with the reasoning that 'the social danger would not be lessened by declaring one section of the population punishable for activity which for other sections continued to be legally permissible'.[8] However, four years later, in 1878, the infamous Anti-Socialist Law virtually achieved what the Industrial Code had as yet been unable to do.

But before an idea can be gained of the effect of the Bismarckian Anti-Socialist Law on socialist and trade union organization, some knowledge of the pre-1878 movement is required. What was the relationship to the Social Democratic Party of the trade union movement, and to what extent was this movement centralized in a nationwide organization? The answers to these questions have an important long-range bearing on the future of social democracy in Germany.

It is well known that the social democratic movement in Germany from its very beginnings was by no means ideologically unified either in Lassallean or Marxist terms. The original drive for workers to form a nationwide combination under Stephan Born was motivated by a pragmatically recognized need to improve their working conditions, as well as the legal status of their organizations within the existing state. Ideology played a distinctly minor role in this drive although the leaders were individuals who had certainly imbibed socialist concepts. Still, the purity of the ideology, whether it was Lassallean or Marxian, was scarcely the main concern of those early agitators for worker organization and social reform. This is borne out by the history of the trade union organization's efforts prior to 1878.

Not even the Lassalleans, who of course had virtually no place in their theory for trade unions, could in practice dispense with or ignore them. Indeed, the experience of the Lassalleans, from 1864 until they merged with their rivals at Gotha in 1875, was that the party really could not exist without responding to the workers' drive to be organized into craft unions. This response was admittedly a cynical one insofar as the Lassallean party leadership (especially Johann Baptiste von Schweitzer) only wished to exploit the workers' organizational drive—particularly intense in 1868—to encompass them within his party, the *Allgemeiner Deutscher Arbeiterverein*.[9] As always with the Lassalleans, the primacy of the party had to be asserted in order to conform to the theory of the iron law of wages.

With this end in view, a gathering of representatives of local Lassallean craft unions was held in Hamburg, 23–26 August 1868. This decided to found a centralized union organization in order to prevent the Workers' Educational Association sponsored by Bebel and Liebknecht from stealing a march on them and doing the same. The Lassalleans, however, enunciated the following principle:

Strikes are not a means by which the bases of present day production can be changed and thereby to improve radically the condition of the working class; they are only a means of promoting the class consciousness of the workers, to break the tutelage of the police and, presuming correct organization, to remove individual abuses of the most oppressive kind such as excessive hours of work, child labour and the like from present day society.[10]

Then, after initial opposition, the meeting conceded that the chairman of the ADAV, von Schweitzer, should convene a General Workers' Congress. Von Schweitzer was not content to be just party chairman, he also demanded the right to be union leader as well. Theoretically, in the Lassallean *schema*, this was an understandable demand; the primacy of the party had to be maintained. Union activity was useful, after all, only for recruiting members to the party.

Von Schweitzer and his lieutenant, Fritzsche, on being informed that their rivals Bebel and Liebknecht would soon be founding union organizations of their own, lost no time in arranging a General German Workers' Congress planned to take place in Berlin on 27 September 1868 with the purpose of creating an all-encompassing organization of the entire German working class. Its declared aim was the coordination of strike activity.[11] This apparently contradictory purpose for Lassalleans is of central significance. The leaders did not believe that the strikes would achieve any lasting good because of the iron law, but they were loathe to ignore the drive of workers to organize for this goal because, through conceding to the workers' will to stage frequent strikes by setting up unions, they hoped to win them as voters for the party. The point here is that the party leadership could not dispense with the unions as a means of recruiting supporters. Indeed, the anti-union Lassalleans found themselves compelled to envisage the formation of unions in order to survive as a party.[12]

This first Lassallean attempt to establish a nationwide union was frustrated by the police department in the city of Leipzig where the party headquarters were located. The party was simply dissolved for having violated the combination laws of the Kingdom of Saxony.[13] But this setback did not prevent the wily von Schweitzer from very quickly planning a future congress in another German state. This was announced in the Press on 30 August 1868, and then actually took place in Hamburg on 26 September 1868 where a so-called *Allgemeiner Deutscher Arbeiterschaftsverband* was set up.[14] It was important because it was the first viable attempt to encompass the existing craft unions into a strong centralized organization. The constitution made the strike issue the responsibility of the member unions who could, if they so decided, transfer this responsibility to the central body. The tendency was to concentrate the key decision making power in the hands of the president, von Schweitzer, since the central executive had the right to advise all the individual unions.[15] This principle of strong union centralization was to have far-reaching consequences in Germany.

While von Schweitzer was busy getting his union established, the rival group of socialists in the *Arbeiterbildungsverein* led by W. Liebknecht and August Bebel had gone ahead and planned to set up a union body, though on significantly different principles from those of von Schweitzer. On 28 November 1868 Bebel had published his 'model statute' for union organization, but only after he had made a bid to exhaust all possibilities of reconciliation and cooperation with the Lassalleans.[16] Von Schweitzer, though, brusquely rejected this gesture, preferring to cement his dictator-like control of his party and unions, with the result that German workers from then until the famous Gotha union of 1875 had the choice of two kinds of socialist trade unions as well as political parties.[17]

As has been noted, Bebel's organizational principles for trade unions contrasted sharply with those of von Schweitzer. Instead of being centrally organized from the top downwards, Bebel preferred to see so-called local unions formed among the various trades which would then coalesce in the one district into an *Ortsverein* (literally a local union). This would thus produce a series of local associations throughout the country. There was, of course, to be a central committee acting as the executive of a federation which could function as an arbitrator in disputes between workers and the local association. Here the federative principle in contrast to the monolithic organization of the Lassalleans was strongly emphasized. The two principles were, however, modified in actual practice as events later proved.

When in 1869 the Social Democratic Workers' Party of Germany was formally established at the famous Eisenach Congress, Bebel's trade union concept was debated anew.[18] The key issues were the relationship of the new party to the union movement and the internal union organizational question. These problems had to be confronted because the International had recommended that the labour movement be actually based on trade unions as the British experience had indicated. A further reason for the confronting of the issue was the existence of the Lassallean and the Hirsch–Duncker organizations which constituted in theory dangerous competition for the Eisenachers. In practice, though, the Lassallean organization experienced a series of crises which cost it numerous members, while the Hirsch–Duncker unions fostered by the Progressive Party appealed only to a limited number of highly skilled craftsmen.

As a result of the dispute among the leaders of the Lassalleans, already in June 1869, a number of their most active members resigned and joined the Eisenach group. The chief reason for this dramatic defection was the general revulsion towards von Schweitzer's dictatorial control over both party and union. The most outstanding defector was the chairman of the German wood workers' union, Theodor York, a man destined to become the first party secretary of the SDAP.[19] As an experienced champion of the union movement, York had developed grave misgivings about von Schweitzer's requirement that union members were obliged to become members of the ADAV and to follow its leader's directives. This, York argued, when he was putting his views on the subject at the Eisenach Congress, would inhibit the spread of the union movement which should be independent of all political parties.[20] He therefore preferred to join the more democratically organized labour party which he served with great merit until his untimely death in 1875. York's principle (like that of Marx) that trade unions should impose no political conditions for accepting new members was one which was gradually accepted in the SDAP; and it is the reason why it was legally possible for the unions to reconstitute themselves after the initial mass dissolution resultant on the Anti-Socialist Law of 1878 coming into force.

York's organizational concepts as enunciated in the years 1869 to 1875 merit closer attention because they also formed the basis for the reconstituting of the central union organization after the lapse in 1890 of the Anti-Socialist Law. As has been noted, this former Lassallean, one of whose chief motives for joining the Eisenach group was his opposition to von Schweitzer's policy of eventually incorporating all unions into the ADAV party organization, championed the idea of an entirely separate, non-political union organization. All this emerged at the Eisenach Congress which founded the SDAP.[21] Trade union leaders of York's persuasion saw clearly that the von Schweitzer concept would scarcely win support among the workers not only because of the latter's autocratic tendencies but also because the individual craft unions would have lost their identity by being merged into one big anonymous strike insurance organization.[22]

On the other hand, the Bebel concept of local unions, which in a real sense he was forced to promulgate to counter the separate organizational efforts of both von Schweitzer and Max Hirsch, was only a tentative attempt by the anti-Lassalleans to win the allegiance of workers to the new socialist party of the SDAP. All rival groups were able to perceive the importance of harnessing the organizational drive of workers: this had been gaining particularly dramatic expression in the strike waves of the 1860s.[23] Nevertheless, as already seen, Bebel and Liebknecht for their part were mainly concerned with establishing an exclusively workers' party which stood neither under the tutelage of the bourgeois liberals nor under the one-man dictatorship of von Schweitzer. This, indeed, was the main reason for concentrating on forming a party before the centralization of the trade union movement in Germany really had time, or legal opportunity, to get launched. The peculiar circumstances prevailing in Germany made it necessary for the workers' party to be formed before a viable trade union movement existed. This, as has been indicated, was a reversal of Marx's observation (and then prescription) that first, workers combine into unions, and out of these emerge the leaders who will form the political party.

The direction taken by Bebel and Liebknecht in Eisenach appeared to them, under the circumstances, as the only practicable one. They needed to provide an alternative to the union organizations of the Lassallean and Progressive Parties in order to remain viable. But to confuse the issue further, there were factions still present in the Eisenach group who remained unconvinced of the usefulness of trade unions in the overall labour movement. This was due to the fact that the belief in the Lassallean iron law of wages remained widespread—even among those who were attracted to Marxism. As Hermann Müller has pointed out, the Eisenach Congress had not been convened because socialist workers in Germany had outgrown Lassalle's doctrines but because of their opposition to the personality of von Schweitzer.[24] Indeed, the question of ideology was extremely fluid then as later. For this reason the SDAP in Eisenach was unable to solve the trade union question either in a Lassallean or Marxian direction. Theodor York and his fellow union champions did, however, manage to get a resolution passed which stated that:

> The Social Democratic Workers' Party considers it the duty of every party member to work with all means available for the unification of the trade unions but makes it a firm condition that the trade unions detach themselves from the workers' presidium of Herr von Schweitzer. At the same time the congress recommends the continued extension of trade unions on the basis of the International.[25]

This motion expresses the then prevailing sentiment of the party leaders towards the trade union issue. Bebel had wished to align the entire labour movement with the directives of the International as far as possible; and at that time, this body regarded trade unions as the basic components of the party organization.[26] Since, however, the trade union movement was already so fragmented with different party loyalties, it would have proved totally impracticable to have constructed the party with only those unions sympathetic towards the International. It was a question, therefore, of first establishing an independent Marxist-oriented labour party and afterwards of trying to solve the all-important trade union issue.

A further reason for not making the unions the basic units of the new party was to be found, as has been seen, in the existing combination laws which forbade craft organizations becoming involved in politics—a fact which was not altered by the new industrial regulations of October 1869.[27] In short, circumstances in Germany militated against a formal organizational connection between the trade union movement and any political party. Theodor York was the first union spokesman to draw practical conclusions from this situation. Being firmly convinced that unions were nevertheless the backbone of any labour movement, he devoted the remaining five years of his life to propagating the idea of an independent trade union federation beside the party and totally independent from it. But, with so much residual hostility towards this concept within the general movement, as well as bureaucratic persecution, Theodor York was to encounter many obstacles.

He had brought with him the well-established Lassallean concept that trade unions functioned as a means of political agitation, but saw accurately that to weld all the various trades together into one single agency for agitation (as von Schweitzer had envisaged) would alienate many thousands of craft-conscious artisans. York therefore emphasized the necessity of exploiting the average artisan's traditional association with the craft organization of his particular trade. These bodies, which as a result of the Industrial Revolution had developed out of the earlier journeymen's organizations into more modern workers' combinations, were the logical starting points for the new style of union federation. On the other hand, because these bodies were so very numerous, there would have to be some means of linking kindred trades together in order to achieve some unity of purpose. Out of these considerations York evolved the concept of mixed unions. That is to say, all trades involved in working with one particular material, for example wood, were to be united into one large woodworkers trade union—the basis in fact of the modern idea of the industrial union in West Germany. Nevertheless, York's appeal to the craft union is witness to the fact that guild-consciousness rather than class-consciousness must still have been very strong in the Reich as late as 1870. It was therefore only common sense to exploit traditional links in attempting to mobilize workers into the modern labour movement. Once these mixed unions were viable York envisaged the setting up of a central coordinating body to mediate relations among them.

This basic concept gained the approval of the 1870 Stuttgart Congress of the SDAP[29] but it was not acted upon. At the next year's congress in Dresden, York emerged again as the champion of a new union organization. As such, he was acting as the practical agent of socialist theory as he understood it. The theory had clearly made him aware of the causes of worker immiseration—he believed in the iron law of wages—but on the other hand, York had experienced that workers were compelled to undertake some direct action against the apparent source of social injustice, and that meant the use of the strike weapon. And to employ this most effectively there had to be cooperation among the existing combinations of workers, hence the need for a central union body.[30]

Underlying York's rationale was an essentially common sense insight: 'The workers want to win the shortest possible hours of labour so that they can feel themselves as human beings, so that they can live as human beings, and are not unnecessarily forced to spend half their lifetime under the yoke of slavery, but rather learn to appreciate their dignity as human beings.'[31] This formulation by York regarding the primary motivation of workers and industrial action has retained its validity down to the present day. And in the Germany of the 1870s the practical successes of the better organized trade unionists in Britain and the United States were beginning to gain notice.[32]

In 1872, York's conceptions appeared to have a chance of being clothed with reality. A trade union congress was planned for Erfurt to take place in June of that year. Party chairman, Bebel, warmly supported the project in the SDAP organ, *Der Volksstaat*.[33] Indeed, he wrote that the unions were the means of overcoming the fragmentation among the workers. In the union movement lay the future of the working class. It was there that the masses acquired their class-consciousness and learned how to conduct the struggle with the power of capital. As union members, in actual fact, workers developed into socialists without any further indoctrination (*ohne äusseres Zutun*). Bebel's indebtedness to Marx's earlier statement to Haman (published in *Der*

Volksstaat 27 November 1869)[34] is more than obvious. He then went on to make practical suggestions as to how the future union body ought to be constituted. What Bebel called 'Die Union' meaning the umbrella organization, was to be, 'a healthy federation of all existing trade unions' which had set up their own central coordinating body. This in turn would convene, in agreement with the individual organizations, an annual congress. The main function of the congress, apart from collecting statistical material from individual unions, would be to determine whether or not, and to what extent, a strike in one organization merited the support of the others. Beyond this, the congress would assume responsibility for the general agitation necessary in expanding the overall movement; and to administer mixed unions (in York's sense) in areas which were as yet too weak to organize themselves.[35]

This advanced plan which reveals a high degree of cooperation between the party leadership and the champions of the 'Union' idea, was the basis for a congress held in Erfurt, 15–17 June 1872. There were, however, only 49 delegates representing 11,358 members of various craft unions.[36] This weakness was only in part due to the splits within the trade union and socialist movements; it was also due to the low degree of political awareness of the vast majority of German workers at the time. That the congress was fully conscious of this weakness is evidenced by the following resolution which was unanimously passed:

> In consideration that the power of capital oppresses and exploits all workers regardless of whether they are conservative, progressive liberal or social democrats, the congress declares it to be the sacred duty of workers to put aside all party disputes in order to create on the neutral basis of a unified trade union organization the precondition for a successful, strong resistance, to secure our threatened existence and to strive for an improvement in our class situation. In particular, however, the different sections of the Social Democratic Workers Party have to promote the trade union movement as forcefully as possible, and the congress expresses

regret that the General German Workers' Association has passed a contrary resolution.[37]

This resolution gave expression, for the very first time at a congress, to the idea that trade unions should be politically neutral. It was a concept which re-emerged again and again in the history of social democracy. It was an indication that at least the party leaders had recognized the necessity of achieving a centralized union organization on a separate plane. On this occasion, York's draft plan was adopted, though modified in two respects. Originally he had wished that all local craft unions in the same general industry coalesce into centralized mixed organizations. He did not see the point of allowing the separate representation of a local union of a particular trade alongside a centralized union of that trade. The congress saw fit to allow this as well as to stipulate that the official trade union newspaper—which York wished to be separate from that of the party—be published as a supplement to the party newspaper.

With the decision, then, to set up headquarters in Leipzig, it appeared that the essential basis for the takeoff of a modern trade union movement in Germany had been established. But again, despite the new Industrial Code, the Saxon Ministry for Police managed to frustrate all union efforts by repeatedly challenging the legality of the new union statute.[38] It was indeed a great problem to locate the headquarters of such a movement in a city which would be more or less amenable to the presence of such an organization. All that could be achieved in 1872 was the convening of a provisional committee in Hamburg to encourage the cooperation of craft unions and to discuss the form of the future union body.

Not even these interim arrangements were rewarded with any success. The entire discussion of the issue tapered off, not only because of legal obstruction but also because of suspicion from many union men that York was trying to establish a monolithic organization under his dictatorship in the mould of the Lassallean, von Schweitzer. Nothing significant is heard again of the Union plan until May 1873 when unemployment had become acute.[39] In a series of articles in *Der Volksstaat* (beginning 17 May 1873) Karl Hillmann, who shared York's organizational concepts, urged the creation of a centralized union body. Hillmann's argumentation is an interesting revelation of the politicized worker's state of mind in 1873. He firmly rejected the apparent widespread Lassallean view that only an organization devoted to political agitation would help the working class. It had to be grasped that the social programme of the unions could also have in the long term an effect on legislation. Indeed, there were two ways to emancipate the working class: through the trade union movement *and* through the workers' political party. Under the circumstances then prevailing in Germany, the unions were especially called to put aside all political disputes dividing them as a preliminary step towards the social and political emancipation of the workers. For this reason it was disastrous to subjugate the unions to any purely political party.

Hillmann argued exactly as did York. It was a matter of regret that the iron law still held workers back from joining unions. This law was no reason to abandon efforts at organization. For a successful strike achieving higher wages would, in spite of the iron law, automatically raise the expectations of the workers for better conditions. This in turn effected an increased political awareness and an extension of the will to break the class domination.

Hillmann stressed in the continuation of his article series in *Der Volksstaat* 24 May 1873, how political power was essential for the achievement of full equality for the working class and the abolition of class rule. However, he reiterated, the consciousness of the people for the emancipation of the 'fourth estate' had to be aroused above all. That was the essential precondition.[40] For Hillmann, the drive of the working class for emancipation was an inescapable fact everywhere in evidence where there was political agitation, where workers attempted to abolish existing factory conditions, either to shorten the working day or to regulate the labour market. The total movement was aimed at achieving independence for the working class. Therein was encompassed the entire content of the social question.

The social analysis which this early champion of trade unionism made provides insight into the world of ideas of German labour leaders in the age of Bismarck. They saw themselves in a condition of virtual slavery which had to be removed. All means to serve that end such as trade unionism were regarded as defensive. The unions themselves functioned as the preparatory school and training ground for the proletariat. They opened the eyes of the working class to its own miserable condition. Indeed, they waged a veritable war of independence against exploitation. Also, in contrast to purely political parties, trade unions enjoyed the trust of the masses. The latter had often been misused and deceived by the parties, and beyond this, workers had greater understanding and practical insight into questions which affected themselves directly, such as shorter working hours, better wages and the removal of unacceptable factory conditions. By setting itself such goals, the movement was exerting a constant and growing pressure upon legislation and those in power. In this context, trade unions were political, if only in a secondary respect. However, the establishment of a free 'peoples state' by virtue of the economic, social, political and intellectual liberation of the working class would only then result if the workers were sufficiently informed and trained. And this process of education was a function of the trade unions. Their efforts at organization brought the idea of emancipation of the working class to maturity, and for this reason these natural organizations should be accorded equality of status with those of purely political agitation.

Hillmann argued that from these observations the tactical behaviour of the party towards the unions should be derived and determined. There should be independent trade unions organized. By the winning of better wages and shorter hours, trade unions helped not only in beating hunger but also taught the worker to appreciate the usefulness of shorter working hours. But more significantly still, the value of labour was increased: with the worker protected from over-production and busines crises, he improved his social–political and economic education and was not alienated from his family. Finally, the trade unions placed in the hands of the proletariat the most effective of all weapons, namely statistics and mass discipline. When this was supported by organization and agitation the bourgeois world would be shattered and the new society would emerge.[41]

The opinions of leading trade unionists in this early period had a long life. They re-emerge very soon after 1890 seemingly unmodified—and for very good reasons which will become apparent. In the 1870s, the union champions had been at pains to overcome the scepticism of many Social Democrats as to the usefulness of unions. They were attempting to show that there was no contradiction between the goals of the unions and those of the party programme. It was maintained, for example, that there could be no international organization of trade unions if there were first of all no national bodies set up. And beyond this, experience indicated that unions were a historical and natural necessity and these had to be independent from, and equal to, the party. Indeed this early claim to independence and equality by the unions foreshadowed the long-winded debate on the subject after the lapse of the Anti-Socialist Law. The problems which York and his colleagues in the 1860s and 1870s perceived had still to be confronted in the 1890s. Indeed, the persecution by the police and administration, the hostility of the bourgeois press as well as the suspicion within the Social Democratic Party itself were already in the pre-1878 era the principle obstacles for the trade union movement.

Already, at that time, the view was being promulgated that the trade unions only needed to be encouraged and expanded to be able in time to replace the 'dying organism of the state'.[42] In practical terms the unions were considered as indispensable instruments for the solving of the social question. They were the prerequisite for a successful party. Thus, in moulding the political awareness of the workers, the unions played the decisive role.[43] This view, however, was not shared by certain social democratic journalists, who like Bruno Geiser of Breslau, would concede only that the trade unions were useful for the party because they stirred up indifferent workers to solidarity by illustrating to them the hopelessness of their position in the economic system. The petty achievements of unions merely served to underline their essential inadequacy to change the system. On the other hand, unions were a definite disadvantage to the labour movement whenever they pretended to be able to solve the social question by the limited means available to them. It was an error to suggest to the workers that they could achieve economic emancipation by means of the slow and steady trade union struggle. Geiser saw a great danger in the trade union demand to be allowed to pursue their role independently from the party because of the possibility of them falling under the influence of a non-socialist party.[44]

The notion of the primacy of the party was, it seems, well established in the 1870s in Germany. As a result, the plan of some unionists to set up a trade union federation independent of the party executive was an idea which the latter regarded sceptically.

There was, too, a degree of suspicion on the part of some craft unions with regard to the union federation. They felt that such a body would rob them of their right of self-determination. For these reasons, then, the Erfurt resolution to set up a union federation was not acted upon. In the meantime, Theodor York as chairman of the wood workers' union took up the cause in his own trade union newspaper *Union*. His conviction that the class struggle could be most effectively carried on by a viable union federation remained unshaken,[46] and the agitation he stirred up was reflected in the pages of *Der Volksstaat*. In an article 'Do we want a trade union federation or not?' (22 May 1874) the union champions sought to refute the party critics. The criticism from certain party quarters that the projected federation would be another kind of dictatorship was answered by maintaining that there would be no success without a concentration of forces and means. It was explained that a politically independent trade union federation would be a corporation under a central leadership functioning parallel to the local bodies of a particular branch of industry. The continued existence of individual unions would not be jeopardized by the existence of a federation. Only by proceeding like this could the counter-productive fragmentation caused by three different union federations be overcome, namely the Hirsch–Duncker, the Lassallean and the SDAP dominated trade unions. Clearly the sterile disputes about theory among them were seen as a great bar to progress by the socialist union advocates. They bitterly observed that an 'ounce of organizational force was better than a hundred-weight of theoretical phraseology.'[47]

This view of many important trade union leaders runs like a red thread through the subsequent history of the movement. But it would be an error to assume that such men worked entirely without theory of some kind. For such leaders as York and Hillmann are quite inconceivable without their having been exposed to theory; only with this equipment were they able to make the analysis of society which they did. York, for example, had come to the conclusion that the theory had to conform to practice. In other words, an understanding of the theory meant encouraging, harnessing and exploiting the natural and historically necessary drive of the workers to organize themselves. It was an error to hinder this while disputing over theoretical niceties. The lack of understanding even among leading party personalities was for the trade unions highly disturbing. They were aiming at a central body staffed by full-time officials after the English model. Such an organ with a coordinating function was considered even at that time to be the essential prerequisite for progress. Inadequate, sporadic and badly directed agitation only hindered development. Organization and still more organization was the essence of success in all agitation in the trade union movement and this had been sadly neglected.[48]

The degree of impatience on the part of the trade union advocates with regard to their critics in the SDAP is evidenced by the following statement: 'With the phrase "workers of the world unite" in the mouth and the hands in the pockets nothing in the slightest is achieved for the association, i.e. for the organization'.[49] It was observed that the Progressive Party was supporting the Hirsch–Duncker unions and so the SDAP was urged to get behind the trade union agitation for a centralized body. In order to lend emphasis to their position the advocates stated:

Those members who have recognized their class status as workers and are serious about wanting to improve it are the driving force. Those members who are aware that the liberation of the proletariat from wage slavery is the end goal that must be reached, hold out the longest. Those members are the keenest and stand at their posts in spite of all the failures even if they have been defeated ten times; they are the ones who have grasped that a change in their condition will not be achieved by small temporary material advantages, but rather only through the complete restructuring of economic conditions. . . . In a word, it is the few who are completely clear about the ways and means, about the nature and purpose of trade unions who form their core, and as enthusiastic and firmly convinced comrades, standing loyally and unshakeably by the flag, promote the trade union movement.[50]

The elitist conceptions of these early unionists and their self-image as pioneers of the labour movement are very clear, as too is their virtually schizophrenic relationship to socialist theory. Although in the latter respect it would be difficult to maintain that those in the party who claimed to understand the theories were really any clearer in their own mind than the union advocates. York, Hillmann and the others of their persuasion were not to be put down. At a congress in Magdeburg (23–25 June 1874) a central body for the trade union movement was set up again. It was described as 'an association of the trade unions for the mutual preservation and the common promotion of their efforts.'[51] These goals were to be achieved by strengthening and extending all of the established insurance and assistance funds of the united trades organizations as well as arranging for the unrestricted availability of these funds to members wherever they might be throughout the country. In addition there was to be a labour exchange established together with an office for the collecting and collating of those statistics concerning wage and labour conditions and living standards of workers. Finally, there were to be separate newspapers established for the various unions with the central body acting as the media for union demands.[52]

Beyond all this, an annual conference of the federation was to be held and this would be the governing body. A standing and a central committee were to take charge of current business. The historian of the German trade union movement, Hermann Müller, considered it important to note the differences between this programme and that of Erfurt in 1872. At that time the question of strike money had been precisely regulated, but in Magdeburg the issue was not raised. Even when the purposes of the organization were listed the strike was not included, although it was clearly assumed in paragraph 20 that the federation would provide money during strikes.[53] Apparently the strike question was left in the background so as not to startle those of Lassallean persuasion. Nevertheless, the new *Union* was supposed to raise contributions of two pfennigs per month per member as well as collecting the annual subscriptions of the associated unions. The standing committee was also entrusted with the management of the central or federal committee.

In this regard, the Magdeburg Congress realized to a great extent York's original conceptions; he was named editor of the central newspaper, *Die Union*, and his own organization, the wood workers, assumed the function of the standing committee. York himself was naturally the chairman, and as such chief of the first socialist–oriented trade union federation on modern lines in Germany.[54] Everything now appeared to favour the firm establishment of the body. This however was not to be. The attempt to stimulate a common will among workers to join the union of their trade and to focus this will on the federation was clearly premature, but the tireless York continued to struggle for trade union unity. His efforts were, however, crowned with success in one very important respect. On his death at the age of 45 on 1 January 1875, the Lassalleans and the Eisenachers became reconciled, and as Hermann Müller reports, at York's funeral in Hamburg, the banners of all socialist associations could be seen.[55] This event, attended by 7,000 workers, was a mighty proclamation of solidarity and was the signal for the actual fusion of the ADAV and the SDAP, with the result that the trade unions of both loyalties also abandoned past rivalries. This reconciliation of the industrial wings of the two parties had, however, been practically prepared at an earlier conference in Hamburg in April 1875. At that time a group of leading trade unionists from both camps had met and proclaimed in both party newspapers that a unification on the union level would automatically follow that of the two socialist parties.[56]

The trade union conference which took place after the more famous party conference at Gotha in May 1875 represented virtually a new beginning. Nevertheless, it was not possible to ignore existing achievements in the sphere of organization as well as in that of theory. On the other hand, it was not possible to carry on in the expectation that the ex-Lassalleans would adapt themselves forthwith. First there had to be reconciliations between individual groups before a future trade union congress could be planned. And in order to accelerate this, the Gotha Congress appointed a five-man committee.[57]

Circumstances in the Reich, however, militated against the establishment of a viable trade union federation before Bismarck's Anti-Socialist Law of 1878. This was partly due to the intensity of police surveillance which made legal difficulties harder to overcome, and partly due to the scepticism with which the former Lassalleans approached the fusion of the two previously rival parties. Nevertheless, the entire exercise had raised the trade union issue into the foreground at the Gotha Congress where it was resolved that while it was the duty of union men to keep politics out of the trade union organizations, they were obliged to join the SDAP because, as it was stated, it was the only one capable of elevating the political and economic status of the worker to a level commensurate with human dignity.[58]

This was the definition of party union relations as laid down in 1875 and it remained so in practice. Whilst the trade unions had to maintain political neutrality, they urged their members at least to support the Social Democratic Party. Ideologically, the unions saw themselves as unable to change the condition of labour permanently but were nevertheless in a position to elevate the material condition of workers for limited periods, to advance worker education and to stir up class consciousness.[59]

The concepts appearing here at this time are a remarkable mixture between Lassallean and Marxist components, although the notion that trade unions on their own could not permanently change conditions is available in both theoreticians. The difference lies in the fact that Marx imputed a far greater significance to trade unionism as propagators of socialist ideas than did Lassalle. But beyond this Marx postulated a primacy of trade union action out of which the political action of the working class was to emerge.

One thing is clear and that is Lassalle's iron law of wages had by no means been overcome in the 1870s. This fact demands that one queries the motivation of such pioneers as York. How could they justify their aims of creating a trade union federation? Certainly they had been influenced by Marx's trade union conception and by the achievements of the British trade unions. For these reasons Lasalle's doctrine, which presumed the primacy of the party and underrated the tacit 'recruiting–agency' function of the unions, was unacceptable. Under York's leadership the self-image of the unions as an independent element within the social democratic movement became established. Carl Hillmann who carried on York's policies after the latter's death proclaimed in *Der Volksstaat* that the trade unions were the beginning of the social–political organization of the working class. They were not there just to fulfil their immediate economic goals and then turn themselves into political clubs. Rather, they were the very basis itself of the social and economic organization of the people's state. They were the pillars of the yet-to-be won rights of the workers.[60]

Clearly, already in the mind of the early champions of trade unionism in Germany was the notion that unions would enable the socialists to realize the theory of the socialist state in practice. Indeed, they had an indispensable role to play in the emancipation of the fourth estate. It was even maintained by Carl Hillmann that the true socialist acted rather than talked; deeds spoke louder than words. Turning fine phrases was no characteristic of the genuine socialist, whereas trade union action was.

Such argumentation is the result of the reciprocal action between theory and practice as it developed in the thinking and experience of the politicized labour leader. These men had very early recognized that the social democratic movement could not dispense with the trade union base, indeed that this was the precondition for a viable political party.

In the midst of their efforts to regulate the party–union relationship, namely the question of whether or not to establish a trade union federation, Bismarck's Anti-Socialist Law was enacted. Since the Gotha unification of the ADAV and the SDAP, the discussion on centralization of the unions had flagged until it was revived late in 1877 at a conference to improve the effectiveness of the trade union press. The outcome of these deliberations among the chairmen of most of the existing unions was that a full trade union congress to establish a viable federation was planned for Whitsun 1878. Although the Anti-Socialist Law only came into force on 21 October 1878, it had long since been fore-shadowed by Bismarck—indeed since the second assassination attempt on the Emperor on 2 June.[61] The outcry in the patriotic press against Social Democrats stimulated a persecution against them which anticipated the conditions imposed by the actual bill. Under these conditions the police in Magdeburg where the trade union congress was to take place refused to grant permission for the meeting. A second attempt was made to convene at Hamburg but the same difficulties were encountered. The organizers had then to postpone their congress indefinitely.[62] However, then the Anti-Socialist Law came into full force to usher in an era of overt persecution against trade unionism. The goal of setting up a trade union federation was not quite illusory. As far as the workers of social democratic persuasion were concerned the Bismarckian Reich had become nothing less than a police state.

CHAPTER FOUR
Trade Unionism under the
Anti-Socialist Law 1879–1890

The effect of Bismarck's notorious anti-socialist legislation was to frustrate all attempts at overall trade union federation such as had been projected by Theodor York. At the end of 1877 there were twenty-six socialist-oriented trade unions in Germany with some 50,000 members in close on 1,300 branches.[1] The Anti-Socialist Law came into force on 21 October 1878 and by the end of that year police action had either officially banned or forced virtually all unions to cease activity. The SPD itself was forced to abandon all efforts at open political agitation and to transfer its organizational meetings outside the Reich.[2]

Bismarck had declared in the Reichstag that the law was not directed against the trade unions, but in practice this claim was by no means borne out.[3] Without doubt the law was directed against the trade-union organizations although they were, legally speaking, not part of the SPD. While the law was explained as having being designed to deprive this party of the means of publicly making propaganda, it did not limit itself to merely banning the socialist press but also attacked the right of association and combination.[4] In this way it was not just the ideology of socialism that was to be suppressed but also the economic self-help organizations of the workers' agencies that were designed to protect them from the worst effects of capitalism. Indeed, the mode of application of the law indicated to the workers that the new German fatherland was really functioning chiefly in the interests of reaction and capital.[5] Within a few weeks at the end of 1878, seventeen centralized unions and some sixty-two local organizations had been dissolved by the police.[6] The legal justification for such widespread action was generally that the unions were functioning as social democratic or communist agencies for the subversion of the social–political order and were disturbing the peace in a dangerous way. As evidence for this the police pointed to the constitutions of the various unions, the minutes of their proceedings, congress reports together with their newspaper articles.[7]

Even where the constitution of a union emphasized its purpose as being only the material improvement and intellectual elevation of its members with all available legal means, it could still be dissolved. This was because the shortening of working hours, the increase in wages, the abolition of overtime and female and child labour were interpreted as dangerous to the common good within the meaning of the act! But beyond this extraordinarily elastic application of the law, many police officials simply nominated as grounds for the liquidation of a union the political views of the executive members or the appearance of a known Social Democrat to address a union meeting. Additional grounds would be the obligation on members to subscribe to the union newspaper, the existence of Marxist literature in the union library or the activity of a so-called agitation committee in the union.[8] So extensively was the ban carried out that even isolated local unions which had severed official connections with the central body and were strictly within the letter of the law were dissolved. By the end of 1878, then, there were only very few of the free trade unions in existence with a membership so small that they could have had little influence on the mass of the workers. These minor organizations were not led by socialists, while their constitutions emphasized their mutual help character and their intention to pursue their aims with strictly legal means.[9]

A notable exception to the spate of dissolutions was one of the strongest trade unions, that of the printers. They protected themselves by changing their constitution to become the mutual help association of German printers. Thus, by shifting the emphasis of the organization away from traditional trade union activity, especially by experimenting with wage agreements with management, the printers were able to preserve their organization intact, although at the price of denying the class struggle.[10] It was this kind of behaviour (i.e. that of worker quiescence and submissiveness) that the Bismarckian state wished to achieve. Indeed, it would have been most desirable from the state's viewpoint to see an extension of the liberal and non-militant Hirsch–Duncker unions which of course remained unscathed.

It is of great importance historically, however, that the socialist trade union movement was not permanently suppressed under Bismarck's Anti-Socialist Law and that it was able to recover its dynamism and set about reconstructing itself. This is significant on two grounds. It showed that a hostile state could not prohibit over a length of time the emergence of the defensive organizations of labour, especially in a time of industrial expansion. In the decade after 1878 the number of workers employed in large factories doubled. The Anti-Socialist Law could not eliminate the economic and social factors which force workers into a position of having to defend themselves from exploitation.[11] Secondly, following from this regrowth of craft unions is the fact that the unions functioned unofficially as organs for sustaining and propagating socialist ideas while the SPD, in virtual exile, was unable openly to do so.

Whether it is possible to argue, as Marxist–Leninist historians do, that the period of the Anti-Socialist Law was the time during which the revolutionary training of the German worker was completed is a moot point indeed. Friedrich Engels had in 1879 prophesized that this would be the effect of the law on the consciousness of the workers,[12] but it is scarcely possible to argue that the twelve years oppression saw more than a partial reception of revolutionary Marxism among the ranks of the workers. Nor is it reasonable to assert that those active organizers among the unions who at that time did not fully accept Marxism were simply opportunists. Many class-conscious party and union men worked for the reconstruction of the movement clearly without the intention of overthrowing the state in accordance with the Marxist model. And as future developments showed, these formed by far the majority of the movement.[13] For these reasons it is important to gain clarity regarding the trade union movement during the era of overt oppression from 1878 to 1890, a time when the issue of the political–ideological colour of the trade union movement became a subject of struggle between socialism and anti-socialism. It was, however, not only a struggle between working class and ruling class, but also a struggle between those claiming to possess ideological orthodoxy and those for whom ideological conformity was of very much secondary consideration.[14]

After the destruction of the free trade unions already referred to, there arose the so-called craft union (*Fachverein*) movement. As Wolfgang Schröder relates, this came from a relaxation of the initial severity of the police persecution that was noticeable after the Reichstag election of 27 October 1881. On that occasion the SPD had gained 311,961 votes and won twelve seats. This was eloquent testimony that, despite the Anti-Socialist Law with its ban on open-party activity, the working class responding to what the embryonic party stood for. The election results also made clear that the law had failed in its intention to stamp out social democracy as a political power factor. Once this was recognized by the authorities, a new tactic in the struggle to eliminate socialism from the body politic had to be devised.[15]

This was the background to Bismarck's famous social-service legislation, the aim of which was to diminish the appeal of socialism to the worker, and to bind him to the state.[16] The legislation made allowances for those worker organizations which concerned themselves with the welfare of labour but which were not in any way associated with the socialist movement. 'The decisive question here was whether the ruling classes would succeed in making a politico–ideological breach in the working class via their trade union efforts and organizations thereby driving a wedge between the socialist party and the working class.'[17] This, at any rate, was the calculation of the Bismarckian state.

Yet these new craft unions which by 1881 had begun to be constituted, could not all be considered immune from the socialist bacillus. Former trade unionists established mutual aid funds and craft unions ostensibly for the welfare of their members and the efficiency of the trade. In Berlin, for example, there had reappeared by 1881 no less than fifteen craft unions. And in keeping with the new policy of leniency towards such bodies no special measures were taken by the police to prevent the expansion of this movement because it was hoped to guide it into anti-socialist paths.[18] Dieter Fricke reports that some social democratic craft union leaders at that time did compromise their principles and cooperated with the political police in order to save their organization and funds. In this way such functionaries were playing into the hands of the government's policy to detach the working class from the SPD. It is asserted by Fricke that the really militant functionaries were the ones who received their inspiration from the 'outlawed party'. But these were not numerous enough to capture the majority of the trade union leadership, and this explained the subsequent inability of the SPD to establish its primacy of authority in the German socialist labour movement.[19]

The facts of trade union life during the era of the Anti-Socialist Law would indicate a general reception of Marxist theory alongside Lassallean ideas, and under such circumstances it is unhistorical to expect that functionaries of the craft unions should have behaved as if they understood themselves to be the virtual agents of the SPD. The important fact is that there was a drive among workers to organize themselves and that very often the leaders were men who had been exposed in some degree to socialist theory.

By 1885 the number of craft unions had risen to 1,021 with a total membership of around 58,000. This had been due to the energetic leaders of local craft unions who had striven to establish affiliations of local craft unions on a national basis. Their function had been, apart from the occasional strike for better conditions, to establish mutual assistance funds. As early as 1884 the Berlin police had counted thirteen such centralized organizations.[20] Clearly the police throughout the Reich were keeping these developments under close surveillance in order to establish whether the craft unions were contravening the law. But Dieter Fricke reports that the Berlin police in the years 1882 to 1883 complained repeatedly that neither in Berlin nor elsewhere had it been possible to take action against those craft unions which had been re-established since 1878. In that time, only two (the cabinet makers [*Schreiner*] in Frankenthal-Pfalz and the shoe makers in Erfurt) had been banned under the Anti-Socialist Law, and then only temporarily.[21]

This phenomenon illustrates the confusion of the official government attitude towards trade unions. After the draconic measures of 1878, the election results of 1881 clearly indicated a need for a reorientation of policy. The rationale here was that a trade union movement which could be kept free from the socialist ideology would indeed act, socially and politically, as a conservative factor. Nevertheless, as has been seen, the chief protectors of the Reich Constitution (i.e. the political police) had observed that within a few years the unions were once again becoming hotbeds of socialist agitation. This caused the Berlin political police to recommend the passing of a law for the entire Reich; this would foster a healthy trade union movement whereby the natural economic function of trade unionism would be recognized but at the same time all dangerous social and political tendencies would be avoided. Nothing better reveals this dilemma than the anachronistic nature of the Bismarckian system. On the one hand, the Reich was becoming a modern industrial power while, on the other, it was commited to the preservation of a constitution derived from an absolutist, pre-industrial era. The above recommendation from the end of 1884 was never acted upon. Trade unionism had begun to spread to such a degree that it was no longer possible to treat it leniently. Thereafter the problem for the administration was to find more effective means to contain it.[22]

That the craft union movement was soon regarded as a source of undesirable agitation is evidenced by a detailed police report dated 30 January 1883 in which it was observed:

When the first of these new (craft) unions appeared, the Social Democrats behaved very coolly towards them; however, as they began in a surprising way to increase and to include numerous Social Democrats, the leaders of social democracy recognized very well the advantage which would be gained for their own party out of these tightly organized bodies if they succeeded in making them of service to themselves. For this reason it was given out that newly established unions everywhere should be supported and encouraged as strongly as possible. In Leipzig and Berlin resolutions were passed expressly for this purpose, the *Sozialdemokrat* depicted the trade union organizations as particularly suitable fields of agitation and emphasized that in them lay the future of social democracy.[23]

The Bismarckian state had then to devise some means of checking the effects of this growth if it could not legally restrict the growth itself. The effect, then, of police rigour towards organized labour was increased union militancy. In the years 1883 and 1884 not only the number of strikes rose but so did also the number of different trades involved, encompassing wider areas.[24] The response of the Bismarckian government to this disturbing development was characteristic. The Minister for the Interior, Robert von Puttkammer, perceiving that behind every larger strike the 'Hydra of violence and anarchy, the Hydra of revolution was lurking'[25] promulgated a decree on 11 April 1886 which demanded still stricter measures from the police and judicature against strikes and strikers in order to suppress the trade unions. Here the police were encouraged if called upon by factory owners to interpret strikes as excesses which occurred in the area between indictable offences and the permissable exercise of the right of coalition of workers, i.e. acts which did not necessarily fall under the heading of punishable offences. On such occasions the police were empowered to exercise their full authority. In particular, the police were to direct their attention to strikes thought to be influenced by Social Democrats. In this case it was argued, a strike had lost its economic purpose and assumed a revolutionary character. This justified the full application of the provisions of the Anti-Socialist Law.[26]

The Puttkammer strike decree signified the end of the era of leniency and ushered in one of virtual persecution against the trade unions. Although these measures were carried out with great rigour, they were still insufficient to wipe out the trade union movement.[27] The undisguised partiality of the authorities regarding trade unions once again had the opposite to the desired effect. As reported above, by 1885 they had outstripped their pre-1878 membership and were now to go on to become still more numerous and better organized.

As a detailed account of this movement lies beyond the scope of the present chapter, it will suffice to focus on a typical and highly significant example, namely the cabinet and furniture makers' union of Stuttgart under the leadership of Karl Kloss (1847–1908). This determined unionist had succeeded in 1880 in building up his union to the modest membership of 600,[28] and by conducting a successful strike in 1883 the Stuttgart cabinet makers provided the impulse for a coalition of all kindred local craft unions. Out of solidarity, then, for a proletarian victory over employers, there emerged a central organization of cabinet makers and related trades at a congress in Mainz, 17 December 1883.[29] Because of the outstanding organizational success which this move by Kloss initiated, it is possible to regard his achievement in centralizing the cabinet makers as the beginning of a new era in German trade union organization—the era of the centralized craft union.[30]

Taking Kloss in 1883 as an example—we know from his later career that his assessment of the real chances of trade union movement was essentially correct—it is possible to ascertain what union leaders in imperial Germany actually wanted to achieve. Certainly they were not utopian socialists but sober and practical men who were aware of the need for solidarity, discipline and organization.[31] Kloss described the economic conditions of the day as a struggle of all against all—a struggle which urged with compelling necessity the organization of labour into trade unions. Kloss' Marxian vocabulary indicates a more than nodding acquaintance with volume one of *Das Kapital*. Indeed, Kloss did not attempt to disguise the fact that his critical analysis of prevailing socio–economic conditions was based on Marxist theory. He spoke about the progressive concentration of capital in ever fewer hands which would be able to control not only the means of production and transport but also dictate public opinion through *Wort und Schrift* (the communications media of the day). Capital had long recognized that by means of the division of labour, production increased rapidly. Conditions had developed to the extent that individual craftsmen were forced to reproduce one type of article year in, year out. The time would come when a tradesman was forced just to produce a small part of the whole article. This observation caused Kloss to draw the conclusion that capital was striving for sole domination of production without concern for the personal or professional group interests (*Standesinteressen*) of others.[32] Capital did not wish to enter an alliance with labour; it would prefer to exploit a supine working class. But it was forced to come to terms with labour because labour was the source of all wealth. This fact enabled labour, through organization, then, to ward off the complete dictatorship of capital. Only in that way could labour ensure that which was its just right, the price for the possibility of existence.

Workers had to put aside any caste spirit and egoism because this hindered a concerted effort from all. Those who would not cooperate were like ostriches who felt the ground shaking beneath them and had their heads under their wings. Success could only come from 'organization of labour'. Any other means of holding back the achievement of capital's goals was like putting a sticking plaster on a cancer. Instead of organizing at the grass roots in order to be able to offer resistance at the top, many workers remained loyal to their medieval guild ideas and thereby played into the hands of capital. Others believed, in spite of the facts, in spite of the danger threatening the working class, that their salvation lay in seeking harmony between capital and labour—two elements which were diametrically opposed and which would never be reconciled.

Unfortunately the mass of workers remained indifferent.[33] And even among those who did join the organization there were many who could not see the idealistic side of the issue, who were blind to the great goal and who shied back from the sacrifice because the advantages were not immediately evident. Such people looked upon the craft union rather as a sickness insurance or another insurance institute; the value of the organization was only estimated in terms of money, not, however, according to its moral significance.[34]

All this Kloss put before his members to justify the need for higher contributions. The image he depicted of the supine worker was pathetic. And here one can gauge the indignation which impelled men like Kloss to action. Workers indeed felt the penury of their predicament but their modest expectations had become so much part of their nature that they were prepared more and more to submit to capital. In so doing they were jeopardizing their domestic happiness and endangering the mental and physical health of future generations by sending children into factories instead of letting them develop properly. In a word, such workers adapted their way of life to the conditions instead of opposing these to achieve a balance, to bring about a situation in which men had some control over their destiny; they submitted instead of reflecting how conditions should be changed to meet the needs of the population.

Here one sees the self-taught socialist translating the theory into the language of his fellow tradesmen. Kloss pointed out that although social conditions determined the attitude of the individual, these conditions did not determine the state of mind of humanity as a whole. It was rather humanity which should and must determine and regulate the conditions of life. For this reason it was necessary to recognize the facts, not just to accept them submissively, but to be able to remove the deficiencies and injustices from society. If the abolition of serfdom and slavery had been a great achievement in the development of civilization, both would have been delayed a lot longer if the mass of the oppressed had given up in mute resignation. And what applied to serfdom and slavery applied to the present situation of the working class. Kloss urged his cabinet makers to stand up like men and demand improvements, and so to demand further advances in the development of civilization.

Kloss had obviously reflected how best to begin the mobilization of the work force, and had reasoned correctly that first they must be informed of their condition in relation to the other sections of society. The means of instructing the workers was to be through the collection and publication of statistics. In the first place these aided in stirring up the lethargic masses by illustrating to them their true situation. Secondly, the statistics were intended to indicate to society the gulf which could so easily be bridged and one which was so frivolously ignored. Society had failed to appreciate that by allowing the welfare of the workers to decline the health of future generations of workers would be permanently damaged—and it was not only the working class who suffered thereby, but all of society. In practice, statistics illustrated that with technical progress more and more hands were becoming superfluous and that those who were fortunate enough to find work were forced to work such long hours that it was virtually a scandal for the times! People were forced to work overtime when in that time jobs could be given to thousands of unemployed colleagues.[35] This was a senseless over-burdening of the workers when at the time there were thousands without work exposed to want, misery and driven to crime. But even then the wages of those with work were insufficient to cover their daily needs. The only way to rectify these anomalies was to shorten the working day, and this Kloss argued would lead to higher wages. Statistics in fact showed that where shorter hours were worked the higher were the wages per hour; where longer hours were worked, there the wages were lowest per hour. Kloss also attacked Sunday work. So slight were the extra wages that they by no means sufficed to reward the worker for his sacrifices in terms of his health and deprivation of family life. The worker became alienated from his own family because the extra effort of his own labour was being devalued while the overtime he put in could be filled by his starving colleagues.[36]

In expatiating further on the value of statistics, Kloss claimed that they showed that wages were decidely inadequate. The proof lay in the comparison between incomes and expenses. Even by a very conservative estimate of the cost of basic food stuffs, apparel and footwear, the wages would barely cover these expenses. Moreover, in this comparison the other expenses of life such as medical and the ordinary family events of marriage, birth and death were not even considered, and still expenses exceeded income by hundreds of Marks.[37]

Kloss deduced then, that the working hours were too long, especially when overtime was taken into account. A journeyman in 1884 was, under these conditions, working seventy-one hours a week! A further lesson taught by statistics was the death rate among workers. Kloss took a conservative sample showing an extraordinary death rate among men in the 30–40 years age group. His employment of these facts, from the point of view of propaganda, was especially skilful:

What armies of uncared for widows and orphans, exposed to misery and hunger, and as a reward for work of the prematurely exhausted husband and father, charity! And why this misery? It is due to extreme over-exertion, inadequate food and lack of fresh air at home, all a result of the poor wages which do not cover the rent of healthy housing. Because the German wood-working industry is not productive enough to provide healthy working space or sufficient ventilation required by the technical regulations there is a lack of fresh air in the work shop. Those who in the face of these facts can still stand idly aside may do so, but do not let them come to us complaining about the want in their own family. Without effort there is no gain, without struggle no victory. Let us get up and organize! (*Auf zur Organisation!*)[38]

With this kind of appeal, the central union of cabinet makers went from strength to strength and pioneered the concept of centralization of local unions throughout Germany.[39] It proved, too, that it was possible for determined unionists to organize despite the general official hostility towards their movement. Ostensibly they had nothing to do with the banned SPD but the content of socialist ideology to be found in Kloss' appeal is more than obvious. Indeed, most of the unions were close to the SPD which although its own ideological position was fluid, continued to increase its electoral appeal. Likewise the workers were attracted to the so-called free trade unions (in contrast to the Hirsch–Duncker unions) because they were reputed to be ideologically aligned with the SPD.[40]

As the report of the city of Stuttgart administration to the Württemberg Ministry of the Interior about the craft unions during the Anti-Socialist Law indicates, they were indeed instruments of social democracy: 'In reality (so it was reported) these associations serve the leading figures, who are mostly decided Social Democrats, as seed beds for social democratic ideas, as means to agitatory ends to concentrate the mass of workers under the organization of determined leaders.'[41] This assessment of the function of such men as Kloss was perfectly correct. They carried the social democratic movement aloft at a time when it was supposed to lose its appeal to the working class.

The method by which they strove to do this shows a remarkable degree of patience and conviction. It was characterized simply by the recruitment of more and more workers into the craft unions and trying to get these centralized so as more efficiently to collect union contributions, collate statistics and coordinate strikes. All this presumed a high level of bureaucratic skill and effort. Clearly, the sacrifices required of the leaders were cheerfully made. Above all, however, the motives were plainly defensive, that is against the extreme abuses and deleterious effects of capitalism. The statutes of the various unions reveal their chief aim as being to pursue the interests of their members, excluding all political and religious questions, to attain the best possible working conditions in accordance with the law as laid down in the Industrial Code, section 152.[42]

The success of the centralization movement in the period 1878–1890 is reflected in the fact that the police records showed in 1886 that the trade unions had actually increased their membership far beyond what it was before the anti-socialist legislation. A conservative estimate counted 35 centralized unions with 2,351 branches and 91,207 members. There were also at least fifteen trade union newspapers most of which were social democratic in tone.[43] By 1890 there were 59 centralized unions, 3,305 branches with 237,039 members. They had 45 newspapers with a circulation of 148,689.[44] The reason for this upsurge may be attributed to the efforts of such leaders as Karl Kloss whose formation of the cabinet makers' union in 1883 gave the impulse for many others to organize. Josef Schmoele, writing in 1896, observed that with the founding of the cabinet makers' union a characteristic model of a social democratic oriented union emerged which found numerous imitators. In contrast to the printers' union and those affiliated with the Hirsch–Duncker unions, the distinguishing mark of the social democratic ones was their apparently common belief in the irreconcilability of capital and labour. These unions operated on the assumption that a real improvement in the lot of the proletariat could only come after radical change in the power relationship between the two, whereas all small gains as a result of a successful strike were only to be counted as minor steps on the way towards the ultimate goal.[45]

These observations were generally accurate. The notion of the irreconcilability of capital and labour appears to have been the common denominator of the free trade unions. The in-built hostility certainly gained expression during the 1880s, witnessed by the fact that the centralization movement of the craft unions was followed by a strike movement which became more intense as the decade drew to a close. If the centralization of craft unions was the chief characteristic of the first half of the 1880s, the second half was notable for the militancy of labour in the most extensive strikes in the old Reich's history—exactly what Bismarck's famous social-service legislation was designed to prevent. Indeed, the reorganized unions, particularly the centralized ones, created the precondition for a 'wages movement'. Organization was the prerequisite for a successful strike. And from the police point of view, the new union organizations of the mid 1880s were chiefly strike-making agencies which had transformed the earlier, fragmented and isolated local strike movements into a directed system which affected wider areas of the country.[46]

As observed above, this intensified activity provoked the Bismarckian state to react with the police terror of the Puttkammer strike decree. This effort to emasculate or tame the unions succeeded only in initiating an era of more frequent and extensive strikes culminating in 1889 in a series of strikes which encompassed sections of the proletariat not previously affected. For example, in May of that year spontaneous strikes in separate mines in the Ruhr had spread within a few days to become one of the largest and most significant ever to occur in Germany.[47] Approximately 100,000 Ruhr miners who had been virtually isolated from social democratic influence suddenly rose up against their masters. This resulted in the military being called in to suppress a movement for an eight-hour shift and improved wages. Although men were shot—five killed and nine wounded— the strike persisted because a strike committee was soon formed. Then, in surprisingly short time, the strike spread beyond the Ruhr to other mining regions of the Reich. Soon a total of 150,000 miners were 'out'. For the socialists this was a most encouraging sign because the Ruhr workers had been considered by the authorities as 'the best subjects, patriotic, religious and obedient. . .'[48] Indeed, Friedrich Engels had written to Bebel that here was an example where a previously indifferent and largely inaccessible group had been shaken out of its lethargy by a struggle for its immediate interests and driven by the exploitation of the employers and the oppression of the state into the arms of social democracy. Subjects from whose ranks the best soldiers of the Crown had been recruited now had enlisted in the front line of the proletarian struggle against capitalism and militarism.[49]

This exuberant assessment of the famous Ruhr strike by Engels had certainly over-estimated its recruiting value for social democracy since the Roman Catholic working-class population of that region had a built-in resistance to socialist ideas.[50] Nevertheless, the largest strike in the nineteenth-century Germany left its mark. The drive for workers to organize could no longer be held back. The entire purpose of Bismarck's Anti-Socialist Law and social-service legislation had been to create conditions in Germany which would have made strikes superfluous. This had manifestly failed. The fact that after eleven years of Anti-Socialist Law a massive strike such as that of the miners could occur pointed to the bankruptcy of such a policy. Until 1889 the largest single strike had encompassed only 16,000 workers.[51] So the impact of the 1889 strike was therefore great on the government on the one hand and on the political awareness of the proletariat on the other. It showed that the labour movement could become a mass movement, a disturbing realization for the ruling classes as it was encouraging for the Social Democratic Party.[52]

The turning point in the Ruhr strike came quite unexpectedly when three miners were deputized to seek an audience with the Kaiser. The delegates arrived in Berlin on 14 May 1889.[53] Indeed, the miners had been getting the worst of the strike because German industry was virtually unaffected being able to procure coal from outside the country. The miners were therefore anxious to negotiate, but the three delegates who were sent to Berlin had no official mandate from the mass of the strikers. It was purely a local isolated initiative. Nevertheless the delegation to the Kaiser was paternally received. The monarch then used his good offices to bring the mine owners to a compromise. A nine-hour shift was introduced as well as a wage increase and the waiving of the obligation to work overtime.[54] The strike was terminated, however, only at the beginning of June 1889; it had lasted a good month.

Superficially, it had seemed as though a moderately satisfactory solution had been reached, but the mine owners had only made concessions as a matter of tactical expediency;[55] they continued to victimize strike leaders by circulating blacklists which led to the dismissal of many workers whose only support was their new union's unemployment insurance, and this was soon exhausted.[56] Then the ensuing winter brought another series of isolated wild strikes, the direct result of increased coal prices. In retaliation for these new strikes the mine owners established their own strike insurance. So the basic significance of the greatest German strike up to the end of the 'strike year' 1889 was increased prices for coal and a certain closing of ranks on the part of the mine owners.

The higher coal prices ultimately penalized the poorest consumers. Moreover, the coal syndicate decided to limit production to keep prices up. In addition, the government bureaucracy in charge of mining regulations had never really understood the miners' point of view. As Max Koch reports, the communications between the public servants, the mayors of the towns affected and their police indicated that these local officials possessed not the slightest appreciation of what was motivating the miners, nor would they ever acquire it. Their education, social position and particularly the professional code of the Prussian bureaucrats had erected an unsuperable barrier between them and the men who worked at the pit face. Strikers for them were simply people who had broken their work contract with the owners and were, in addition, guilty of disobedience.[57] It is this official attitude which caused more disaffection among the miners than the actual wages issue.

No official investigating commission was able to grasp the effect of the poor conditions on the workers. The miners saw in the deterioration of their working conditions a deprivation of rights to which they had been subjected to an increasing degree and which they had impotently to accept. It must be emphasized again and again that it was not the wages question which played the decisive role but the relationship to the owners that expressed itself for the miners chiefly in the treatment they received at the hands of the mines' department officials, and in the question of the length of the working day.[58]

The gulf separating the mind of the German worker from that of his economic and political masters was indeed great. This explains the above reaction of the owners to the strike—a closing of ranks and an uncompromising insistence on the 'master-in-ones-own-house' attitude. Indeed, the underlying aim of the Anti-Socialist Law was to establish this view of industrial society which saw the master disposing over his servants as capriciously as he liked. The experience of the craft unions after 1879 and the intensified strike wave after 1886 could not have served as a better object lesson to the German working class that they were living under the yoke of an uncompromising capitalist dominated society.

The Puttkammer strike decrees, referred to above, had illustrated further whose side the state truly supported. The entire period of the Anti-Socialist Law only served to demonstrate the fact all enlightened socialist leaders had long since recognized, namely that the Prusso–German state was determined by one means or another to stamp out socialist-inspired trade unionism. More and more trade union leaders came to appreciate this and drew the conclusion that the existing state—despite the sympathy shown occasionally by the Kaiser for the workers—was irreconcilably hostile to them and their aspirations. Having made this observation it is not surprising that not only social democracy increased its electoral appeal over the period 1878–1890 but also that the unions experienced a veritable rebirth. The following table illustrates this:[59]

	1877	1886	1888	1889	1890
Centralized unions	36	35	40	41	59
Branches	1,266	2,351	2,007	2,226	3,305
Members	49,055	81,207	89,706	121,647	237,039
Trade union newspapers	16	–	31	34	45
Newspaper circulation	37,025	–	70,555	90,492	148,689
Funds in Marks	–	456,415	398,484	482,600	812,609

Reflected here is the so-called reciprocal action between the conditions of labour and the injection of socialist ideology into the union movement. All outstanding leaders were men who had become politically aware through their confrontation with the ideology as has been seen in the case of Karl Kloss. Their newly won convictions gave them the necessary rationale to explain to their fellow workers the nature of their common plight, and what is more important, what to do about it. Under the Anti-Socialist Law they did their utmost to construct *defensive* or *protective* organizations as far as the law allowed. More than that was unthinkable since the percentage of the work force which was actually organized was still very small indeed. Until a larger membership could be recruited only a defensive stance on the part of the aroused section of the working class was possible. By 1890 statistics revealed that the union movement in Germany consisted in the main of skilled tradesmen who were again to a large extent 'proletarianized journeymen'.[60]

It was in the specialized trades that the highest degree of organization could be achieved. Numerically by 1890 the largest unions were those such as the metal workers, brick-layers, tobacco workers and miners as this table illustrates:[61]

TRADES	MEMBERSHIP		CRAFT UNIONS
Metal workers	37,522	in	234
Brick layers	30,800	in	180
Tobacco workers	18,447	in	225
Miners	16,902	in	162
Carpenters	13,070	in	172
Printers	12,610	in	557
Tailors	10,806	in	166
Cabinet makers	10,403	in	127
TOTAL	150,560		1,823

So even the strongest membership figures for 1890 indicate the objective weakness of the movement in a country which employed in industry, workshops, and mines approximately 8,000,000 persons in a population of 49,500,000.[62]

Organizationally not much more could have been achieved under the Anti-Socialist Law which had been extended three times, in 1884, 1886 and 1888. In 1889 the question of making the provisions of the law even more stringent was placed before the Reichstag. The Chancellor, Bismarck, had wished to alter the bill to give it permanent force because in its original form it remained in effect for only two-and-half years and had to be renewed at these intervals. In 1889, Bismarck had proposed to embody the law as a permanent statute in the penal code of the Reich. In addition, the amendment envisaged giving the government the power to expel, not only as previously from districts proclaimed to be under a minor state of siege, but from the Reich as a whole, subjects whose association with social democracy could be interpreted as inimical to the public welfare. It was this feature of the bill which provoked heated and prolonged debate in the Reichstag. As W. H. Dawson observed, had the Chancellor allowed himself to be persuaded to drop the expatriation clause he might have secured the necessary majority to retain the bill in its original form, but he remained adamant and did not even appear in the Reichstag to participate in the debates.[63]

The contest in the Reichstag over the amendment to the Anti-Socialist Law is an eloquent commentary on the style of Bismarckian government. The chief argument for the draconic measure was that in future special powers would be needed against the Socialists since a diminution in their numbers could not be expected. The government would therefore still need the power completely to expatriate agitators as a deterrent to their return especially if those provisions were relaxed which hitherto empowered police to ban from their locality any suspected socialist agitators.[64]

The proposed amendment encountered opposition from parties of all complexions, but for different reasons. The National Liberals had wanted to adopt a more independent line towards the school-masterly Chancellor to impress the electorate. Part of this involved urging a more liberal policy of worker protection (*Arbeiterschutz*), so they were desirous of relaxing the more rigorous provisions of the law. The Conservative Party, on the other hand, generally endorsed the intention to tighten up the Anti-Socialist Law still further. The German Conservatives (*Deutschkonservativen*) adamantly opposed any slackening of the regulations designed to suppress social democracy, and were particularly hostile to the attitude of the National Liberals. Likewise, the Free Conservatives wanted the Anti-Socialist Law to become a permanent feature of the German domestic political landscape.

Of the other major parties, the Roman Catholic Centre Party had its own mind as to how to deal with the 'social problem' and made it clear that it would reject Bismarck's amendment. Likewise the Radical Party (*Freisinn*) objected to the principle of establishing laws which violated civic freedoms—in this case by suppressing political opposition by police action.

Not unexpectedly all the confusion particularly in those parties of the so-called Cartel (informal coalition) which had previously supported Bismarck unleashed great rejoicing in the ranks of social democracy.[65] And by the time the bill got through the second reading the expatriation clause had been eliminated; it was finally rejected on 25 January 1890 by 169 votes against 98.[66]

This was indeed the result of a curious constellation of parties. For the first time the Conservatives voted in the same bloc as the Social Democrats and the Radicals to throw out the repressive legislation, but for contradictory motives. The Radicals threw it out because it was too rigorous; the Conservatives because it was not rigorous enough. The Centre Party threw it out, too, because they believed in more subtle methods of coping with labour politics. The National Liberals would have retained the law had the expatriation clause been excluded. Now they stood there without any law, all because the Conservatives wanted to support the Bismarckian concept of a rigorous solution to the 'social question'.

The era of the Anti-Socialist Law was in January 1890 practically at an end; formally the prolongation of 1888 had to run until 30 September 1890. Basically this bizarre situation had arisen because of a misapprehension on the part of the Conservatives. They had chosen to reject the bill in its emasculated form in the belief that Bismarck would not have accepted it. That this was an error was only revealed later; Bismarck would indeed have been satisfied with the bill even without the police powers to exile some subjects. Certainly the Conservatives had no intention of favouring the Social Democrats by rejecting the amended bill.

They had falsely imagined that a new and more severe bill could have been introduced later.[67] The Cartel upon which Bismarck had so long relied was now in ruins, and the way was open for a new approach to the 'social question'.[68]

Immediately following Bismarck's defeat of 25 January 1890, the young Kaiser, partly in a bid to outmanoeuvre Bismarck and partly out of a genuine patriarchal concern to promote social cohesiveness, proclaimed his famous February Decrees (4 February 1890), much to the Chancellor's displeasure as will be seen. These decrees openly recognized the right of workers to self-help, and the Kaiser made the point that since earlier measures had failed to promote industrial peace it was necessary to adopt another approach. In order to regulate the issues which arose in the factory and workshop, workers should from now on have the opportunity of sending their representatives to negotiate with employers and the government departments.

The February Decrees, although vaguely formulated struck an encouraging note for the working class in general and the trade unions in particular. If they could form officially recognized representations of workers in factories to negotiate with management, then a great barrier to improving conditions would have been removed. Yet nothing could have been further from the Kaiser's mind than to encourage social democracy among the workers. The idea that workers might form councils to treat with management was certainly not intended to be an invitation to unionists to become workshop spokesmen.

Social democracy remained as before a movement to be eradicated. Instead of the direct ban of the Anti-Socialist Law era, the 1890s were to see, after an initial period of apparent conciliation, a series of more indirect measures of oppression introduced. As will be observed, these met with a fate similar to the final amendment to the Anti-Socialist Law, but the social and parliamentary struggle they engendered bore witness to the fact that the uncompromisingly authoritarian Bismarckian spirit was alive and well long after the Iron Chancellor had been forced to resign. Nevertheless, in that initial period of official relaxation and apparent monarchical good will towards all sorts and conditions of men, both the Social Democratic Party and the trade union movements entered an optimistic new phase of development, which as recent research has confirmed, constituted the major political challenge to the Reich. Only in answering the question how the Reich confronted this challenge does the domestic and diplomatic history of modern Germany become intelligible.

CHAPTER FIVE
The Wilhelmine Reich as Class State
1890–1914

It would be an error to believe that with the lapse of the Anti-Socialist Law in 1890 official as well as capitalist suspicion towards organized labour had evaporated. Bismarck's assessment of social democracy as a poison to be eliminated from the body politic remained. Certainly, the Iron Chancellor's departure from political life by no means signified a change of heart on the part of officialdom. Indeed, as social democracy and trade unionism spread, it became an even more imperative task for successive German governments to contain and eradicate it. This objective was the central domestic problem of the Wilhelmine Empire. Any explanations of the nature of that state, its rigidly authoritarian structure, its partisan police and judicature, its veneration of military values and its consequent illiberalism and finally its acceptance of war in 1914 as a solution to its imagined domestic and foreign policy problems cannot be grasped if the internal challenge of social democracy and trade unionism to that structure is ignored.

Awareness of this does not only help explain the German role in the outbreak of the First World War, it contributes further to accounting for the hostility to organized labour *after* the war, during the ill-fated Weimar Republic, the constitution of which, as shall be seen, had been very largely designed to ensure labour its just position in the state and the economy. From the start of the republic the forces of the right inwardly, and later openly, had resented the Weimar Constitution, precisely because of its recognition of organized labour, and this led to their misguided espousal of National Socialism.

There is a definite continuity in German history which can be observed by tracing through the position of organized labour within the state. The present chapter is concerned to examine why the state perceived social democracy and trade unionism as a threat and to indicate those pieces of legislation during the Wilhelmine Era 1890 to 1914 which demonstrate how hostile that state was to recognizing and accommodating organized labour in a way conducive to social harmony and equitability.

The image projected by social democracy in both its political and industrial wings was that of a dangerous revolutionary element that was out to destroy the nation, which in the eyes of most educated Germans was the most civilized, educated and culturally superior nation the world had yet seen. Indeed, it had not only produced the best scientists, musicians, artists, historians, philosophers, theologians and industrialists, it was in addition pioneer, under Bismarck, of the most progressive social legislation in the world. The German state was designed, therefore, to look after its subjects, especially its working class subjects from the cradle to the grave. In the light of this it was a matter of virtual incomprehensibility to the middle and upper classes why large groups of workers could be so churlish as not to appreciate their fatherland—and moreover to demonstrate this by electing repeatedly a party whose avowed intention was to destroy it. And, apart from voting for the SPD in increasing numbers, workers, particularly after 1890, were becoming organized in trade unions led by known Social Democrats. So both the state and industry saw themselves as under attack from social democracy—and this attitude towards the SPD and unions did not change appreciably until the outbreak of war in 1914. A reconciliation between the working class and the Wilhelmine state could not be brought about even though there were perceptive men on both sides who devoted themselves to this end.[1] Despite their efforts, social harmony was never to be achieved—much to the disadvantage of the German people, and ultimately to that of Europe and the world at large. What then was so apparently irreconcilable in the social democratic movement?

The first serious expression of irreconcilability between the Bismarckian empire and social democracy had occurred during the Franco–Prussian war as a result of which that empire was actually founded. Because leading Social Democrats had openly condemned that particular war as one fought for the selfish dynastic purposes of the Hohenzollern military monarchy, a war of conquest against the French people, they were imprisoned for treasonable utterances.[2] Whereas the vast majority of German people rejoiced at Bismarck's triumph, there was a querulous and disloyal, obviously anti-national party at work to spread dissension and subversion. This was obvious because the party officially had approved of the Marxist-led International Working Men's Association since 1869, and that in itself indicated loyalty to a revolutionary goal.[3]

Yet, if that were not a cause enough for suspicion, the party leaders, Bebel and Liebknecht, in particular had been extravagant in their praise for the uprising of the Paris workers against their reactionary government from 18 March to 28 May 1871. So spectacular was the uprising that it had taken 130,000 troops a whole week to suppress the Communards. The casualties were numerous though estimates vary from between 17,000 to 36,000. But the point is that all this was caused by an uprising of organized workers against the established order, and Bebel as Socialist leader in the Reichstag was brash enough to observe that the Commune was only a small outpost skirmish compared to what the future proletariat would achieve in Germany. As a result, good patriotic Germans were always suspicious of Social Democrats as subversives.[4]

The attempt by Bismarck between 1878 and 1890 to eliminate the movement, first by outlawing it and then by seeking to weaken the appeal of socialism by means of social-service legislation, was a manifest failure. Instead of disappearing the party gained more electoral support, and as a result of the exile in Switzerland, it became apparently even more radical. In the first place, at the Wyden Conference in 1880, the party decided, since it was declared illegal, to change its principle of striving for power by all legal means to striving for power by *all* means. This was misunderstood by critics of the right to be a confession of faith in anarchism whereas all it really meant was that in trying to keep the movement and organization viable, circumstances would frequently demand minor infringements of German laws. It was not intended to be a signal for anarchistic activity, neither was there any. Significantly, for the right, however, there was a declaration of sympathy for the emancipatory struggles of Russian nihilists without, of course, any thought of applying their tactics to the German situation.[5]

What did result from the twelve year ban on the party was the increased tendency for members to adopt a more uncompromisingly doctrinaire position since it was clear that the Establishment regarded them in any case as beyond the pale. Whereas prior to 1878 the Socialist Party official doctrine was in a fluid state, by 1890/91 intellectual attitudes had noticeably crystallized. This is evident in the adoption in 1891 at Erfurt of an avowedly Marxist based programme which discarded many of the merely reformist tendencies of the old Gotha Programme of 1875. The ideological leadership purported to believe that Marxism was *the* scientific form of socialism. Indeed, Engels himself had given his approval to the new revolutionary programme, the central feature of which was the intensification of the class struggle between capital and labour.

The fact that then as later, the party in practice continued to act as a mere radical parliamentary reform party—there was no actual plotting of revolution—has been the subject of much scholarly investigation.[6] Why did they adopt a revolutionary programme and continue a parliamentary practice? It certainly stamped the party with a particularly dangerous image as far as the non-labour forces were concerned. To answer this question as succinctly as possible, the most plausible explanation is that the formerly 'outlawed party' had to adopt a programme which set it apart from the most radical of the bourgeois parties. Otherwise it would not have any essential differences with that party, and the working-class electors would not have had any compelling reason to prefer SPD over the more radical of the liberal parties. As a leading German political scientist has expressed it, the Marxist theory was for German social democracy as well as for the other parties of the Second International the most important means of distinguishing their own movement ideologically from the bourgeoisie.[7]

Clearly, there was a great gulf fixed between the self-perception of the SPD as a party with both a revolutionary theory and a parliamentary practice on the one hand, and the parties of the centre and right on the other, to whom the socialists continued to appear as dangerous subversives.[8] And to intensify this image, the party in 1903 had officially condemned the revisionist theories of Eduard Bernstein precisely because it was essential to retain the facade of a purely Marxist party determined to await the inevitable revolution, since it was this facade that was the great and effective rallying point for the mass of polarized and alienated workers. In this regard, the ideology was both a strength and a weakness: a strength in that it gave the party an identity and hence vast electoral support; a weakness in that it struck fear into the hearts of the bourgeois population and thus prevented the working class from being positively integrated into the nation.

Finally, before leaving this question of the image projected by social democracy in the Wilhelmine Era, there is the unique contribution made by the writings of Friedrich Engels (1820–95) which for a long time affected the thinking of Social Democrats and simultaneously increased the suspicion of the bourgeoisie, and occasionally, their ridicule (Eugen Richter).

First of all, there was the widely discussed calculation of Engels, made around 1890, that the victory of socialism in Germany was, if the capitalist economy continued to develop as it had been, virtually a mathematical certainty.[9] Secondly, he argued that in view of the advances in weapon technology, an armed insurrection would only then have a chance of success if the majority of the army were on the side of the revolutionaries. In 1892 he wrote: 'The era of barricade and street battles is over for ever; if the troops are employed, resistance would be madness.' Thirdly, Engels taught that the most effective weapon of the proletariat was the franchise, a constitutional right already accorded to the German workers. If it were employed correctly it would lead of necessity to revolution. Fourthly and finally, Engels' strategy warned that German social democracy must not suffer a defeat. That is to say, the party must conduct itself in such a way so as not to provoke the Wilhelmine state against it. At all costs the party had to maintain its viability and increase, however gradually, its membership basis.

That these propositions had been received and understood by the party was evidenced by the fact that at the Erfurt Party Congress when the Marxist programme was adopted, party leader Bebel proclaimed that there were only few present who would not see in their lifetime the actual realization of socialism. Engels had calculated that at the prevailing growth rate of electoral support—he made a table of all elections between 1871 and 1890—the party would have by 1898 sufficient votes to enable it to assume power. Even allowing for inevitable fluctuations in growth, Engels reasoned that he had sufficient data on which to predict 'that social democracy in Germany would triumph within the foreseeable future.' Of this he was unshakeably convinced. After the lapse of the Anti-Socialist Law there was nothing that could hinder the progress of the labour movement to ultimate victory—unless it unwisely provoked a revolution or was forced into defending itself by hostile action of the state—or what was more likely, a war erupted between Germany on the one hand and the allies, France and Russia on the other. Above all, the socialist movement needed an undisturbed period in which to develop itself.[10]

From this analysis of the priorities of the movement, one would expect a critical outside observer to conclude that the SPD posed no threat whatsoever, since it was clear that it was not going to risk extinction by antagonizing the guardians of the established order. Nevertheless, the image of the SPD as a subversive political group persisted and grew. Perhaps even the concept of gradually increasing electoral support to win more seats in the Reichstag was more than sufficient to generate fear in the bourgeoisie and aristocracy. More than this, however, they feared the trade union potential for creating industrial unrest as had been recently demonstrated in the strike wave of the second half of the 1880s.

So while there was undoubted continued hostility towards the political wing of labour after 1890, it is more accurate to observe that the greater resentment was directed towards the industrial wing. Clearly, a strike movement had more impact on bourgeois society than volumes of revolutionary rhetoric—although the rhetoric was clearly regarded as the cause of union militancy. The old notion that 'behind every strike lurked the Hydra of revolution' persisted. It was coalitions of class-conscious workers that were the sinews of revolution in the mind of the bourgeoisie. So it was of supreme importance to cripple those sinews so as to prevent industrial disruption. And, since the Anti-Socialist Law itself had been unable to prevent that, new and more indirect methods had to be employed.

A new era of veiled oppression of the labour movement had then been inaugurated by the Kaiser himself in 1890. Bismarck's patently unsubtle methods of trying to destroy the appeal of socialism, first by outlawing it and then by offering the working class the inducements of his social-service legislation had given rise to the thought in the Kaiser's mind that he could solve the labour question by more perceptive means. It was this difference in approach that led ultimately to a secret power struggle between the young Kaiser and his old Chancellor. The great miners' strike of 1889 in which the Kaiser had intervened as mediator had caused him to reflect on ways and means of integrating the work force more satisfactorily into the Prusso–German monarchical system. After collecting expert advice, William II drew up a social political memorandum which he presented to the Prussian Crown Council on 24 January 1890. There was nothing in this programme that represented any break in principle with Bismarck's earlier concepts; it was simply a new application of these. All the Kaiser desired was the introduction of a greater degree of worker protection such as a prohibition of Sunday work and further restrictions of female and child labour. Beyond this he proposed an international conference on the problem of the protection of the factory worker.[11]

It was part of the Kaiser's plan then to make a public proclamation of these intentions, and it was this that brought him into conflict with the Chancellor. Bismarck was of the opinion that such a step would be an open encouragement to social democracy which was at the time gaining in popularity. But, since Bismarck could not veto his sovereign's intention he chose another way in which to frustrate the plan. By editing the list of the Kaiser's proposals, Bismarck made them appear to offer much more than was really intended, for example legal worker representation in factories and a normal working day.

According to K. E. Born, Bismarck's purpose was to arouse exaggerated hopes in the working class, which the Kaiser had no real intention of fulfilling. Further, it was expected that the Kaiser would be startled by the implications of the offers and would then back away from them. However, William II, obviously not seeing any mischief in Bismarck's edited version of his proposals actually signed the declaration which was then published as the February Decrees on 4 February 1890. The Kaiser was under the impression that the criticism of his plans originated from sources other than Bismarck, who was in reality the secret orchestrator of it. So actual disagreement between the Kaiser and the Chancellor on the social question was not the cause of Bismarck's dismissal; rather it was the issue by means of which the Kaiser sought to demonstrate his royal prerogatives over the Chancellor who, of course, had under William I become used to determining policy virtually unaided.

Pursuing his accustomed line, then, Bismarck on 25 February 1890 announced to the Kaiser his new policies that he knew would encounter hostility in the Reichstag, particularly because they included a new and more draconic version of the Anti-Socialist Law. Bismarck's idea was to dissolve the Reichstag altogether and rewrite the constitution so as to strengthen monarchical powers. The possibility of this, however, only temporarily appealed to the Kaiser who then on 4 March withdrew his support from Bismarck's plans of a 'coup d'etat from above'. The monarch's reason for this was his unwillingness to face a serious domestic conflict so early in his reign—in particular a conflict which could only be won with the help of the man from whom he as Emperor wished to become independent. It remained now for the Kaiser to find a suitable pretext upon which to conjure up a conflict with Bismarck. This was not long in coming; it was a complaint by the Kaiser that he was not being sufficiently well apprised of details of foreign policy by the Chancellor. With this Bismarck was given the opportunity to submit a request to be relieved of his duties. The Iron Chancellor's historic period in office ended on 19 March

1890.[12] Bismarck's dismissal in the context of the February Decrees and the intended prolongation of the Anti-Socialist Law is historically significant. In retrospect, it can be seen that his determination to reintroduce the Anti-Socialist Law was so great that he was contemplating a most radical revision of the constitution to do so.

The Kaiser, understandably, did not want to encourage the growth of social democracy, but on the other hand he was equally determined to be his own chancellor, and that meant letting Bismarck go. The personal struggle of the two men should not, therefore, be understood as being based on differences in principle as to how to deal with the problem of social democracy. As already stressed, the same attitude of fear and hostility towards the movement prevailed in official as well as bourgeois circles. The loss of the Anti-Socialist Law was then really the price that William II paid for removing Bismarck. It remained now to shape future legislation affecting the work force in such a way so as to frustrate the growth of social democracy and trade unionism. This was done, however, in a rather *ad hoc* fashion; no fully thought through conception was applied.

The imperial government in 1890 was particularly concerned to get a programme of worker protection legislation through the Reichstag, not least because of the Kaiser's initiative, by amending the existing Industrial Code. While there may have been a component of humanitarianism in the proposals, some were clearly designed to cripple the trade union movement. These amendments were to be in fact the legislative expression of the February Decrees. The details were devised by the Prussian Ministry of Commerce and then presented to the Reichstag on 8 May 1890.[13] As meaningful social legislation, the 1890/91 amendments to the Industrial Code represented an advance upon Bismarck's earlier measures which were all concerned with worker *insurance*. For the first time the state now assumed responsibility for worker *protection*.[14] While they were regarded in bourgeois circles as very progressive, a survey of the more important provisions indicates how objectively inadequate they were.

For workers in such places as mines, quarries, factories, building sites and workshops, all work on Sundays and public holidays was prohibited. For shop assistants work on such days was not to exceed five hours. Further, for the protection of workers' life and health it was made obligatory for factories to ensure proper lighting, adequate ventilation and to remove dangerous gases, vapours, dust and rubbish from the place of work. Machines were to be properly shielded to eliminate the possibility of accidents.

It was made illegal for children under thirteen to work in any of the above mentioned enterprises, and wherever children between thirteen and fourteen did work it was limited to six hours; for minors under sixteen to ten hours maximum daily. The daily rate for female labour over 16 was limited to 11 hours. Women and minors could not work at night nor were women allowed to work underground. Beyond this, the Bundesrat (Federal Council) was empowered to prohibit work for minors where employment might endanger health or morality, and the same body could impose a limit on the hours worked for all workers in factories where long hours could endanger health.

As K. E. Born reports, all these provisions were accepted by the Reichstag with only slight modifications.[15] He observes, however, that they did not introduce anything particularly new. Many industrialized regions had via local authorities already prohibited Sunday work, while the minimum age for minors to be allowed to work had only been raised by one year since the 1878 amendment to the Industrial Code. Neither was the general prohibition of female labour in mines such an innovation since regulations to enforce it already existed. Further, the empowering of the Bundesrat to ban females and minors in designated factories had existed since 1878. The only really new item was the power of the Bundesrat to determine the so-called normal working day for adult male workers on jobs particularly injurious to health. What this indicates is that the government had introduced really nothing innovatory but rather was seeking to extend the idea of worker protection by requiring industry gradually to accept the changes. Indeed, these details showed that the new industrial regulations imposed no special burdens on management at all in their application.

To some extent, however, other regulations did take account of the great strikes of the previous year. For example, the hours of starting and ceasing work including the times for rest pauses, the time and manner of wage payments; the period of notice, the conditions under which dismissal without notice might occur or alternatively when a worker might terminate employment were laid down. Finally, any penalties that offended morality or the sense of honour of workers were prohibited. What is of note here is that the labour regulations had to be approved by the local police authorities to see that they conformed with the new amendments. Formerly they had been imposed by management upon a submissive work force which had no redress if management altered the conditions. Now the conditions were binding on both management and labour, the latter being regarded under the amendments as a contracting partner. This represented a significant step forward, at least legally, since factory conditions could no longer be unilaterally determined by the owners. The state now had the right of inspection to see whether conditions corresponded with the minimal requirements set by the Industrial Code. Further, before the conditions of a particular factory were laid down, the workers were entitled to make known their requirements. This, however, did not allow the workers the right of codetermination or participation with management in fixing conditions. Owners were only obliged to hear the workers. It was left to management alone to decide whether to implement workers' wishes. The only obligation on management was to communicate the conditions to the local police department, not however, any changes required by the workers. All the police needed to know was whether the workers had been able to express their views.

If this idea had been to assign to the state the role of arbitrator between management and labour, it did not work because all the police did was to ascertain whether the work conditions corresponded formally with the letter of the law; they had no knowledge of how conditions really affected the workers in practice. The owner remained virtually the unchallenged 'master in his own house'.[16] There was certainly no intention on the part of the government to allow workers the right to negotiate with their employers.

If the foregoing amendments in the Industrial Code, passed by the Reichstag, brought little progress in humanizing labour–management relations, the real intention of the government was revealed in a series of amendments designed to place even further restrictions on the workers' right of association. The government's aim was to prevent the right of association that had existed since 1869 (paragraph 152 of the Industrial Code) from excessive use in strikes. The existing restrictions (that gained expression in the very next paragraph 153) consisted of penalties of up to three months imprisonment for persons seeking to coerce workers into joining trade unions or hindering them from withdrawing. Now in 1890, it was intended that these penalties be considerably increased.

Clearly, the experience of the great wave of strikes had driven both management and the government into devising new means of preventing concerted industrial action by labour. The principle behind which the government sought to justify this was that within the body politic there could only be one source of coercion—namely the state. Any other agencies which sought to exert coercion on subjects was acting outside its rights. And it was the state's duty to protect the minority of individuals against the coercion of the mass. Hence it was more than reasonable to maintain legislation that ensured both the position of the state as sole source of coercive power and the right of the individual not to be associated against his will with mass action such as a strike. It is in the light of this kind of thinking easy to see why German entrepreneurs were so conservative, and why after the great strike wave of 1889 they wished to see the penal clauses of the Industrial Code expanded.

In two crucial respects the existence of organized labour was to be made difficult if not virtually impossible by the projected amendments. First, there was a penalty foreseen for journeymen and labourers who left work prior to the regulation time. This entitled the employer to regard such cessation of work as a breach of contract for which he could demand a sum equal to the customary daily wage for up to six weeks of the period of the breach of contract! The provision accorded the same right to workers to demand a similar compensation from employers who discharged them prior to the agreed time. In justifying this measure, the government noted that numerous strikes involved actual breach of contract; and in this the employer was inadequately protected by the law. The purpose of this amendment, then, was quite clearly to discourage strike action by making it easier for employers to claim restitution of damage from striking workers. The existing provisions of a moderate fine had proved an inadequate deterrent to strikes. It was therefore deemed desirable to amend the law in order to establish a right to a predetermined penalty, because the calculation of the precise amount of damage sustained by an enterprise as a result of strike action was legally too cumbersome. Further, it was argued that the public sense of justice demanded a simple and rapid reparation. This would in effect satisfy the sense of justice of the injured party rather than guarantee full restitution of damages.

This remarkable piece of casuistry encountered, however, a certain amount of opposition in the Reichstag, not simply from Social Democrats. It was rejected in the first reading, but a committee, subsequently formed, on which no Social Democrat was appointed and which included only one from the *Freisinnige Parei*, then reformulated without altering the principle, allowing employers to withhold wages as security for compensation.[17] This section was augmented by an additional clause stating:

> If a journeyman or assistant has quitted work illegally, the employer may claim compensation for the day of the breach of contract and for each following day of the contract time or legal working time, during one week at most, to the amount of the local customary daily wage . . . This claim need not rest upon proof of loss.[18]

The fact that the same penalty was made applicable to employers who discharged workers illegally did not in the eyes of Social Democrats alter the overtly anti-labour character of the amendment.[19] As August Bebel pointed out at the time, here an exception was made against the worker. In contrast to public servants who received an annual salary, the worker was only paid *after* his work was performed. Now, in addition, a full week's wages was to be retained by employers as a bond against illegal stoppages. This was to Social Democrats concrete proof of the class prejudice of the German bourgeoisie. Certainly there was little sign of sympathy for the concept expressed by the Kaiser on 6 February 1889 that it was essential to convince the German workers that they would be in all respects treated as the other citizens of the state.[20] The Prusso–German state, was of course, prepared to recognize the working class as a group enjoying the same privileges as others, provided that workers remained passively submissive, and that meant having no truck with social democracy or trade unionism.

The second component of the proposed amendment to the Industrial Code that aimed to cripple trade unionism was paragraph 153. It read:

Whoever undertakes through use of physical coercion, threats or defamations,

1. to hinder employees or employers from participation in agreements [to improve the conditions of their trade or business] or from withdrawing from the same,

2. to influence workers to stop work or to hinder them from continuing or starting work will be punished with imprisonment for not less than one month. In cases of repeated offences the imprisonment is not less than one year. The same penalties apply to those who publicly incite workers to illegal stoppages or demand from employees the illegal dismissal of workers.[21]

It was frankly admitted by the government to the Reichstag that it was the strikes in recent times which were behind this amendment. Here were examples illustrating widespread breach of contract among workers. It was asserted, too, that these instances were caused by threats to workers by those who had incited the strikes. So widespread had this become that the existing paragraph 153 of the Industrial Code had proved to be an inadequate deterrent since the penalty provided was too mild, and as well, the penalty only applied if workers went on strike as a result of agitation. Now the penalty would apply to agitators even if no strike resulted from their efforts. This had now become justified, so argued the government, in view of the rash of strike movements at the time.[22]

It was clear that the government continued to regard strike action as a criminal offence. The government failed, however, to convince the Reichstag that more draconic measures than those already available were actually justified, and the amendment was rejected by a considerable majority, 142 to 78.[23] This, of course, did not mean that the bourgeois parties had suddenly become pro-labour but rather that they were confident that the existing penalties to contain strike action were adequate. In addition, there were those in the Centre and more radically democratic parties who felt that a more severe law would only serve to polarize German society to a worse degree than it already was.[24]

Had the amendment been accepted by the Reichstag it would have effectively destroyed at a blow any chance for a revival of the trade union movement. Any strike action would have become virtually a criminal offence by those both agitating and participating—and penalized accordingly. Understandably, the post-1890 trade union leaders delayed their plans to reorganize the movement on more centralistic lines until the outcome of the debate on the Industrial Code—especially paragraph 153—had become clear.[25] Indeed, the few years immediately after the fall of the Anti-Socialist Law in 1890 were rather uncertain ones for the trade union movement, while the SPD was by contrast full of confidence about the course of future developments. Despite these uncertainties, the trade union movement managed in time to establish itself as a separate focal point for the socialist labour movement in Germany, both to the discomfiture of the SPD, which claimed the primacy of labour leadership, and to the dismay of the state which feared the growing strength of both forms of organized labour.

The struggle of the union movement to establish itself in the 1890s is a subject for a later chapter. Here the focus is on the class fears of the Wilhelmine state as expressed in its anti-labour legislation. Since the key government amendments to the Industrial Code for the purpose of containing unionism had failed, and no party constellation could be contrived to reintroduce the

Anti-Socialist Law, other means of containing labour had to be sought. The next such move came in 1894 with the so-called *Umsturzvorlage* or 'law concerning changes and augmentations to the penal code, the military penal code and the law concerning the press.'[26] This was devised by the government as the logical continuation of the lapsed Anti-Socialist Law under another name. It would have given wide powers to the police to interpret both social democratic propaganda and trade union agitation as criminal offences against the state, society and the economy. The key clause foresaw:

> Whoever publicly stirs up the various classes of the population to acts of violence in a way endangering the public peace will be penalized with a fine of up to six hundred marks or with imprisonment for up to two years.

> The same penalty applies to anyone, who in a manner endangering the peace, publicly attacks religion, the monarchy, marriage or property by abusive statements.[27]

The fear of a violent overthrow of the existing order by the spread of social democracy had become intensified especially by the continued electoral success of the SPD which by 1893 had already 44 seats in the Reichstag. The need for a new method of suppressing organized labour was perceived to be very urgent. Ironically, for the bill to succeed the government needed the support of the Roman Catholic Centre Party with its 96 seats, and for this reason included the sections on religion and marriage. Precisely these features guaranteed the failure of the bill. Further, many leading intellectuals who might otherwise have been expected to oppose social democracy, and who saw themselves represented in the Reichstag by the liberal parties (and even a part of the Free Conservatives) perceived in the amendment certain dangers to intellectual freedom. These parties therefore lined up with the Social Democrats to defeat the bill to outlaw 'subversion'.[28]

Naturally this partial bourgeois alignment with social democracy did not by any means indicate a gradual acceptance of social democracy. It was simply that the anti-labour forces were as yet disunited. There still prevailed a certain confusion in liberal and educated circles about the nature of the Wilhelmine state. By the mid-1890s the Kaiser himself had become quite clear that all republican elements had to be eliminated, if necessary by draconic legislative means. The era of soft inducements to the working class to abandon social democracy was over. Class struggle, the idea of the pluralistic society and liberal institutions were all anathema to the official Prusso–German mind, and the main spearhead of such forces was politically and industrially organized labour. How to smash this remained the central domestic issue of pre-1914 Germany.

With the failure of the *Umsturzvorlage* in May 1895 new repressive measures directed against social democracy had to be devised. There was a genuine fear shared in government as well as military circles that the treasonable ideas and indeed the practice of socialism and trade unionism constituted an immediate danger to the state. The military were particularly concerned that the army be preserved from revolutionary doctrines in the ranks, and the idea of dissolving the Reich constitution and refounding the empire on a new and more conservative basis was again seriously canvassed. However, William II had lost his nerve for such a struggle and preferred to continue to try out more devious legislative ploys.[29]

Well aware that a reintroduction of the Anti-Socialist Law for the whole Reich would have no chance in the Reichstag, the Kaiser was inspired in 1897 to try a similar piece of legislation in Prussia alone. As Karl Erich Born relates, this so-called 'minor Anti-Socialist Law' would have empowered the police to dissolve all associations and meetings which in their assessment constituted a threat to peace and security. It was expected that by means of such a law all Social Democratic Party and trade union branches and meetings could be closed down. Yet the elasticity of the concept, 'endangering public peace and security of the state' enabled it to be applied to bourgeois associations as well. For this reason, only the two conservative Prussian parties voted for it, and it was narrowly defeated 209 to 205.[30]

In spite of this, the Prussian as well as the Reich governments were determined to persevere with repressive policies. The concept of winning over the working class by enlightened welfare legislation had been completely abandoned. Instead, an open confrontation with organized labour was preferred. Indeed, the new (1897) Reich Minister for the Interior, Count Posadowsky, took the view that first of all organized labour would have to bow to the existing order before the state would make any reforms in social policy.[31] By the end of the 1890s then, the Prusso–German leadership could conceive of no better domestic policy than one designed to stamp out organized labour. Count Posadowsky, as the minister responsible, set himself the goal of devising legislation that would appeal in particular to the various liberal parties as well as the Centre. Experience had shown that since 1891 these groups were not prepared to give the government what amounted to virtually unrestricted police powers over the right of assembly and association. But, even while Posadowsky was evolving a more subtle way to contain organized labour, the Kaiser himself suddenly intervened by proclaiming on 6 September 1898 in a speech to Westphalian farmers at Bad Oeynhausen that he would protect them from economic difficulties. This would be done by ensuring that those who desired to work could do so unmolested. A law to effect this would be introduced into the Reichstag within the year. Indeed, it was. It was perhaps the most disastrous example of the Kaiser's interference in domestic policy throughout his colourful and tragic reign. What became known as the *Zuchthausvorlage* or penitentiary bill unleashed a parliamentary struggle that contributed to the irreversible polarization of German society. Posadowsky is reported to have been most disturbed by the Kaiser's pronouncement because it torpedoed his concept of winning over the more liberally minded parties by subtle means.[32]

The Kaiser had, in effect, wished to increase police powers to deal more rigorously with strike agitators, in particular strike pickets. This had been the aim of the 1890/91 projected amendment to paragraph 153 of the Industrial Code that had been rejected. Now the monarch wanted the same thing under the guise of a law to protect industrial working conditions. The new law was expressly intended to replace the existing paragraph 153.

Its opening paragraph stated:

> Whoever undertakes by means of physical coercion threat, libel
> or defamation to induce employers or employees to participate
> in associations or agreements for the purpose of influencing
> working or wage conditions or likewise hinders [employers or
> employees] from participation in such associations or agree-
> ments will be punished with imprisonment for up to one year.
>
> In mitigating circumstances a fine of up to 1,000 marks may be
> imposed.[33]

In justifying this move it was asserted that since 1891 the excesses
occasioned by strikes had become so widespread that the legislature had the duty to ensure both the freedom of the work contract
and the individual rights of employer and employee to conclude
such contracts free from harassment. It was therefore necessary
in the interests of law and order to combat this terror with adequate legal means. This would not, it was argued, affect the existing right of association that allowed the right to strike as well as to
lock out. It was, however, considered impossible for an orderly
state to allow the use of 'objectionable and reprehensible' means
by protagonists—meaning of course the trade unions—to force
their opponents to submit to their demands. By 'reprehensible'
was understood all means designed to limit the individual's freedom of choice.[34]

The government was clearly out to curb the power of union
leaders. By vague implications these were accused of intimidating
workers into striking, often in quite pointless situations. From this
it was deduced that the *right* to associate had become, in the
hands of socialist inspired agitators, a *compulsion* to associate
which resulted in harassment being applied by strikers against
those really willing to work.[35] Therefore, under the pretext of
upholding the right of individuals *not* to be associated with strike
action, the Prusso–German state set out once more to stifle the
union movement.

The Reichstag debate over the new bill was extremely bitter.

August Bebel sarcastically described the *Zuchthausvorlage*, as 'a draft legislation for the agitation and advantage of social democracy' because of the indignation it had stirred up among wider sections of the working class.[36] Certainly, the government achieved the exact opposite from what was intended. By threatening such dire penalties to trade union functionaries, the very essence of the right of association was being attacked, and the union organization responded with a massive propaganda campaign against the bill. The result was that the bill was defeated in the second reading because the 56 Social Democrats on this occasion had the support of 102 Centre Party plus the various liberal groupings. This was significant since the Centre Party in particular was at that time in the process of forming its own Christian trade union movement and feared the bill would frustrate its efforts.[37]

What this futile exercise showed chiefly was the gulf in the differing concepts of the state that still existed between the democratic left and the government supporters. The latter were demanding in fact a completely subservient and quiescent attitude from labour. Any sign of working-class backbone in the form of militant trade unionism was immediately suspected as revolutionary. This was, of course, a tragic misreading of the genuine aspirations of organized labour, the thrust of which was to achieve recognition and integration within the existing state—the revolutionary rhetoric of many leaders notwithstanding. The advent of the twentieth century did not, however, bring with it any real improvement in conservative thinking about labour. The familiar pattern of seeking to dam up trade union expansion was continued, especially when the 1903 elections saw the Social Democrats increase their mandates in the Reichstag to 81, thus becoming the second biggest party in the land. Added to this threat of numbers was the publicity given to the 1903 SPD congress at Dresden which reaffirmed the official party line as Marxist revolutionary against the ideological challenge mounted by Bernstein and the revisionist trend.[38]

In the meantime, as the statistics show, trade union membership was also steadily expanding. The idea now of introducing legislation to curb its growth must have appeared quite illusory. It was out of the question, given the relative party strengths, that the Reichstag would endorse such a move. Nevertheless, the government felt constrained yet again to try. There was much discussion as to how the 'poisoning of the people' by social democracy could be countered. The Minister for the Interior, the same Count Posadowsky, in a further effort to be subtle about it, presented the Reichstag with a so-called Professional Associations Bill in November 1906.[39] His rationale was to give the unions a certain degree of legal recognition so that they might better be controlled. It was the well-established Prussian tactic of giving with one hand and taking away with the other. Posadowsky's strategy was to strengthen the less militant Christian trade unions against the social democratic movement. Thereby, he reasoned, the workers could become organized in unions that did not have revolution as their goal. There were, however, several major provisions to granting unions legal recognition. The first was that agricultural labourers could not be organized, and the second was that unions could be liable to pay restitution of losses sustained by a firm as a result of a strike. Further, strikes which affected national security or essential services would result in the unions concerned losing their legal identity and suffering the confiscation of their assets. Clearly, under these terms, any large scale strike might be officially declared to be endangering national security, and the socialist union leader, Carl Legien, a Reichstag deputy, emphatically drew attention to this point. The new bill was simply a further example of the government's anti-socialist tactics.

Another provision which aroused Legien's hostility was that requiring unions to make available to police their membership lists, a device to enable employers to discover which of their workers was union organized.[40] Against all these disabilities then, the advantage of having legal recognition for unions was cancelled out. As a result, not only the SPD opposed the bill but also the more radical democrats and the Centre who were most concerned for the rights of agricultural labour. The National Liberals were divided on the issue, since they believed that the growing unanimity between the SPD and union leadership would lead to increased labour militancy. There was indeed great confusion concerning the nature of the labour movement among government and bourgeois circles generally. In the case of this bill in 1906 to accord trade unions legal identity and simultaneously to surround them with serious restrictions the issue which sealed its fate in the Reichstag was the ban on organizing agricultural labourers. The Centre Party which then controlled 100 seats made its support contingent on the removal of this ban. Other smaller parties, too, would have supported the bill in that case.

Indeed, as Karl Erich Born reports,[41] the Reichstag debate on this bill showed that those parties committed to social reform really wanted to allow the unions freedom of movement and equality before the law. These did not demand, as the government did, that they first make a confession of faith in the existing state, which for the socialist trade unions was asking the impossible. The Prusso–German power elite wanted to allow a labour movement, but it must be loyal to a system which existed to protect the vested interests of privileged groups. This, of course, was like asking protestants to support the Papacy. The social democratic union leadership was pledged to destroy the system of social and economic privilege in Germany so it was totally unrealistic on the government's part to expect them to become suddenly quiescent and politically neutral. In the light of the widespread legalistic oppression exerted against the socialist unions in particular, the government had hardly been pursuing a course likely to persuade the union leaders to change their mind about the Prusso–German state.[42]

The maladroit way in which successive German ministries since 1890 sought to cope with the threat of organized labour to the state was an indication of the power-elite's inability to devise a social policy suitable to the changing social and economic structure of the Reich. Nowhere is the permanent constitutional crisis of Wilhelmine Germany better illustrated than in its schizophrenic attitude towards the trade unions and their right of association. On the one hand, as the Industrial Code stated, every German was free to coalesce with others for the purpose of improving the conditions of trade, commerce and labour. But as has been seen this right was immediately curtailed by paragraph 153 of the Industrial Code. And the invocation of its provisions by courts had been almost exclusively applied to organized labour while organized capital remained unmolested. Indeed, the penalties applied to unionists under this provision were invariably for acts that were not indictable under the criminal code.[43] This undeniable feature of class justice was not appreciably improved by the introduction of a national law of association in 1908 (*Das Reichsvereinsgesetz*) which was supposed to herald a new era of industrial relations in Germany.[44]

The ostensible intention of this new measure was to apply a uniform law of association to the entire Reich thus replacing the existing different state laws of varying degrees of liberality. To rectify the wide-ranging anomalies of this situation had been the goal of all parties from the National Liberals to the Centre.[45] The Social Democrats had, of course, always wanted a completely untrammelled right of association. Although they were not to get it on this occasion, the law that was passed did form the basis for future liberalization. There were a number of aspects of it which particularly offended the socialist unions who had debated in vain in the Reichstag against these restrictions. First of all these included the obligation for all political associations to obtain a police permit before holding a meeting, and unions continued to be regarded as such.

Secondly, the requirement that the language of negotiation in all associations was to be German, was of particular disadvantage to the unions because it meant they could not organize the large numbers of Polish and Italian workers within the Reich. These, it was alleged, were frequently brought in as strike breakers by German employers.[46] Finally, the new law did not allow either the organization of persons under the age of eighteen.[47]

Here again was a case of giving with one hand and taking away with the other. All subjects of the Reich were free to enjoy the right of association but those that could be classified as political had to acquire police permission to assemble as well as to submit to police surveillance of their meetings. These could be dissolved if the permit could not be produced or a non-German language employed in the meeting. Such provisions were clearly designed to restrict the influence of the socialist unions in particular. Only under the pressure of war (in 1916) would the government deign to abolish these.

It has been stressed at length that the major domestic political problem of the Reich was that of coming to terms with organized labour. But the Wilhelmine state was exceedingly shy about making reforms in the social–political sphere out of anxiety about the spread of social democracy and its challenge to the sole authority of the state.[48] Paradoxically, the growth of social democracy, then, had forced the power elite into a pugnaciously defensive position that blinded it to the essentially reformist and genuinely patriotic sentiments of the vast majority of socialist organized labour, including their leaders. For the latter, however, the harshly exploitative nature of the Prusso–German state confirmed it as the willing instrument of capital interests and the sworn enemy of socialist organized labour. So great was the polarization between the government and socialist trade unionism that by 1913/14 labour leaders were seriously expecting the power elite to attempt a radical constitutional change thereby enabling the labour movement to be declared illegal. Only the advent of war in August 1914 liberated the SPD and the socialist trade unions from this 'gnawing uncertainty'.[49]

CHAPTER SIX
The Trade Union Struggle— Centralization to Neutralization 1890–1900

As indicated in the previous chapter, the fall of the Anti-Socialist Law in 1890 signalled the start of a new phase of organizational development for both wings of labour, although the removal of the infamous legislation had not really altered the police-state condition under which trade unionists sought to re-establish a centralized leadership. Despite this, however, it is in this period that the German socialist unions managed to regroup under the leadership of Carl Legien and establish themselves as the viable industrial wing of the labour movement. In order to achieve this they had to overcome both the chicanery of the state as well as a deeply rooted scepticism within both party and union ranks.

One of the most awkward phenomena in modern German social–political history for communist historiography to explain is the emergence of a centrally led national trade union movement between 1890 and 1900. East German authors such as Wolfgang Schröder recognize as positive the movement of unions to coalesce into something resembling a unified national organization but they are quick to criticize the union leadership, especially the future chairman, Carl Legien, as opportunistic. This is because the unions refused to acknowledge the continued tutelage of the SPD and insisted on determining their own policies.[1] This chapter deals essentially with the process by which this was achieved, and illustrates to a large extent the inherent autonomy of trade unionism within the industrial society.[2]

The year 1890 was one of decisions of far-ranging consequences for the German trade union movement. At that time a number of unions in Hamburg had sought to implement the 1889 decision of the newly convened Second International on the May Day demonstration. As a result of their stoppages the employers instituted a lock-out. This was a provocation that the Hamburg trade union commission (set up in 1887) had refused to ignore. In order to overcome the impotence of fragmentation, a meeting of all trade union organizations was called for the purpose of establishing an effective defence 'against the attacks of arrogant entrepreneurs'.[3]

The outcome of this step was a conference in Berlin on 16 November 1890 that devoted itself chiefly to the question of setting up a national trade union umbrella organization and selecting a commission to convene a general trade union congress. With regard to the organization question two forms were considered, the 'central' and the 'local', and the former preferred. This is the one that leant heavily on the frustrated model of Theodor York, whereas the 'localists' championed the idea of unions in one centre being integrated more closely with the party organization. While the centralists emphasized the primacy of the economic struggle, the localists stressed the political struggle. The ensuing debate over these principles concerned, in effect, the essential nature of the labour movement. Whereas the localists conceived of it as chiefly a political movement, the centralists saw more clearly that the changed economic structure of Germany required (as it had done in England) the existence of a strong and ultimately autonomous industrial wing to protect labour against capital. The task of popularizing these ideas as well as meeting the objections of critics was assumed by Carl Legien, the newly elected chairman of the provisional General Commission, as the embryonic central body was now called. This Legien did in the Commission's official organ, *Das Correspondenzblatt*. His article series on the organizational question constitutes a landmark in the intellectual history of German trade unionism, and was conceived essentially as a repudiation of the propaganda of the localists on the one hand and that of the Hirsch–Duncker union on the other, who as indicated had been inspired by the liberal movement and would not acknowledge the class struggle.[4]

Legien's concepts and vocabulary identify him as an agitator who had critically applied Marx to the predicament in which he saw labour in Germany to be. Since the laws of association prevented unions being politically aligned, the only course of action was to form the largest economic coalitions of workers possible. And as the unions had formed the preparatory school and base for the political movement, especially during the period of the Anti-Socialist Law, it was appropriate, now that that law had lapsed, for both the political and industrial wings of labour to organize separately.

Further, since capital in Germany still possessed an immeasurable amount of power and was in a position to out-manoeuvre organized labour in economic conflicts, it was essential that workers recognized that they could only overcome their weakness by organization. This would gain expression only if the greatest possible number of workers were organized in their trade if their various craft associations were bound together in a viable central body that disposed over adequate funds. Power lay, in short, in the size of the organization.[5]

Legien was disappointed with the less than enthusiastic support he got for his ideas from within the Social Democratic Party. At its first conference after the lapse of the Anti-Socialist Law (held in Halle, 12–18 October 1890) the trade union issue was dealt with obliquely under the heading of 'Strikes and Boycotts'. Here, the union spokesman, Karl Kloss, urged the party to get behind the efforts to centralize the unions. The party conference responded by passing a loosely worded resolution that federalization of the union movement should proceed *where possible*, a formulation that conveniently allowed for the continued existence of the localist union movement.[6] Clearly, in 1890 the party was not at all of one mind with regard to the future of trade unions.

Legien had noted and regretted this, and was thus moved to initiate the propaganda for his organizational concepts. The localists who really formed the industrial wing of the so-called 'young ones' or radical left of the SPD persisted in their isolationism.[7] For Legien, centralization and federation of unions was a natural development, indeed a necessity that had to emerge, given the structure of the economy as it had become. The local unions had only been in a position to exert an influence on wage and working conditions as long as production and consumption of a commodity was confined to one locality. But, once this production and market expanded beyond one locality into the next, there resulted the unavoidable necessity for unionists to link up with their neighbouring colleagues in order not to disadvantage them in their income by allowing the market to be flooded with their products. Legien posed the question of how much more necessary it was for unionists to coordinate their activities through federation when commodities were being produced not only for the next town but in fact for the whole world. In this situation worker solidarity could not rest on mere declarations of sympathy. The same situation arose with the question of the supply of labour. When it was possible for journeymen to get work easily wherever they went, the local union could maintain a reasonable wage level. Nevertheless, as conditions had developed, the railway and the steamship could transport thousands of workers into a city resulting in the displacement of local workers. For both these reasons, then, Legien regarded centralization and federation of unions an essential precondition for achieving a living standard commensurate with human dignity. A further point which Legien stressed was that only a centralized union organization would dispose over the human and financial resources to set up branches in the many regions where workers were as yet unable to organize themselves.[8]

As an additional justification for his concept Legien cited the fact that industrialists were forming up into centralized bodies in order to oppose organized labour, and these had to be confronted on a unified basis. This could only be done via organization; mere political indoctrination as the localists advocated did not help. And here Legien refuted the argument that only the localists contributed to raising the class consciousness of the workers. It was really the centralized craft unions which carried the ideals of labour movement into areas that were cut off from all political enlightenment! This had been done particularly well under the Anti-Socialist Law when the craft unions successfully avoided giving the appearance of political activity. Nevertheless, they still raised the class consciousness of the workers. Legien then argued persuasively that this could be most effectively continued if the craft unions were centralized and federated. If this could be achieved, the struggle against capital for a shortening of the working day and week would be more efficient, and successes in that respect would attract more and more workers into the movement.

The argument from localists and theorists that a concentration on purely trade union action at the expense of political indoctrination would lead to a diminution of class-consciousness was repudiated by Legien as a futile one. He and his friends were firmly convinced that the growth of support for the socialist party was directly linked with the spread of trade unionism. The party could then only welcome the more efficient organization of the industrial wing.[9]

In order to hasten the acceptance of a trade union federation in Germany, the General Commission drafted a carefully thought-out organizational plan which was published on 25 April 1891. Its expressed aim had been to achieve a uniform and systematic procedure for trade union action under the prevailing German law, in particular in strikes and lock-outs, and to guarantee effective mutual support.[10] To bring this about, each craft association would centralize to form one administrative focal point for that trade to be known as the *Zentralverband* (central association). The individual craft associations representing the various trades would then seek to improve the economic interests of members as allowed by paragraph 152 of the Industrial Code. In practical terms this meant regulating conditions of work and the remedying of abuses in places of work, the propagation of education among members, the establishment of hostels and labour exchanges, the compilation of statistics relating to the trade, the provision of financial support in strike actions decided in accordance with the statutes of the union, and finally, to provide financial aid for members travelling or involved in legal entanglements resulting from infringements of paragraph 153 of the Industrial Code and related sections of the Criminal Code.

The central association of related craft unions (construction workers, wood-workers, metal-workers etc.) should then link together to form the actual *Union* by setting up a common executive (*Vorstand*) consisting of the chairman of the centralized member craft organizations. This was a clear revival of York's concept of 'mixed unions'. The functions assigned to this projected *Union* were five-fold. Firstly, they were to plan and finance the. agitation for the affiliated craft associations. Secondly, they were to produce a newspaper to ventilate matters of concern to the member groups. Thirdly, with regard to strike action found necessary by affiliated associations and which could not be effectively carried out, the union was to be empowered to supply the necessary funds. These would be provided by the other member associations in proportion to their membership. Fourthly, the *Union* was to promote the compilation of the statistics of the individual organizations and to publish the findings. Fifthly and finally, the union was to centralize as far as possible the administration of the affiliated hostels, labour exchanges and branch offices in individual towns.

Over the projected *Unions* was the umbrella organization of the General Commission itself. This body would link the various *Unions* to each other, as well as be responsible for matters of common concern to all trade unions, and it would be elected by a biennial trade union congress. The specific tasks of the General Commission that were envisaged by the draft plan included the direction of agitation within regions and industries where no unionization had yet taken place, the production of a newspaper to publish items of general concern, to provide a breakdown of all statistics compiled by the affiliated *Unions*, especially of strikes, and finally in urgent instances, with the approval of the *Unions*, to direct funds from a specially established source for strike action.

It was expected that the above organization could be financed by a weekly levy of at least 15 pfennigs on all members of affiliated craft associations. Of this, ten per cent of their total income would go to their own *Union* which would in turn contribute twenty per cent of their income to maintain the General Commission. Centralized craft organizations which were not affiliated in a *Union* were required to contribute two per cent of their income to the General Commission.

With this organizational plan Legien hoped to equip the trade union movement in Germany for the expected massive economic struggles with capital. He had wanted simply to build on existing foundations to make the trade union movement more effective. There had been many instances of ill-planned strikes resulting in defeat as well as frequent duplication of organizational effort in the same area by trade unions of related crafts. With this plan such inefficiency, it was hoped, would be overcome.[11]

Of central significance to Legien's plan was the concept of political neutrality. No excuse was to be given to the authorities to dissolve trade unions for infringing the laws of association by becoming involved in party politics. This concept took some time to become established, as will be seen. What is important, however, in 1891 is Legien's understanding that trade union political neutrality did not imply political inertia on the part of the working class. On the contrary, the exclusively economic struggle of the trade unions was seen as a vital process in the overall struggle for the emancipation of the proletariat.[12] The end goal was, of course, the elimination of wage-labour to achieve the full reward of labour. That this would only ultimately be achieved by political means did not release the unions from the obligation to pursue their economic struggle within the framework of capitalism since this was the essential precondition for the future success of the political struggle.

As Legien observed, the degree of persecution of the trade union movement by both capital and government was positive proof that the unions were right to centralize and federate to become stronger. Oppression was levelled only at those forces which were seen to be dangerous to the capitalist order. This insight was clearly understood by the General Commission and formed the rationale for the tightening-up of trade union organization.[13]

The derivation of Legien's strategy from that of Theodor York some fifteen years earlier is thus quite clear. But, as indicated, there were those in both party and union ranks who were as yet unable to recognize the 'logic of facts'.[14] This emerged when Legien was preparing the ground for the national congress that the General Commission was obliged to convene after the Reichstag had completed its amendments to the Industrial Code.[15] This, as has been seen, took place after a series of debates lasting from

17 May 1890 until 6 May 1891. In then trying to gauge the feeling of the various unions towards a national congress before the end of 1891 Legien canvassed their chairmen. As a result he reached the conclusion that an early congress would not be popular. Firstly, many unionists had not yet grasped the implications of a higher union organization, and secondly, the funds of many unions had been depleted. This latter point was of serious practical consideration, as Legien observed, in a time of economic decline.

Of the 59 union bodies in existence at the time, forty responded to Legien's questionnaire. Twenty-three wished to postpone the congress while the remaining seventeen wanted to go ahead immediately. A time early in 1892 was to be determined. This was clearly in Legien's own interest. His propaganda on the organization question had not yet won universal approval. He was acutely aware of the opposition of the localists but there was still scepticism about the future role of the General Commission even in the ranks of the centralized unions. In order, then, to avoid the possibility of an abortive congress, Legien conceived the idea of a preliminary conference of union chairmen to adopt an organization statute (later to be ratified by a congress) and to act as a steering committee for the projected congress.[16]

In this way Legien hoped to gain the majority approval for the tactics to date of the General Commission. Already on 25 April 1891 Legien had published his draft statute of organization and he now proposed to win a declaration of assent to it from existing union bodies. For this purpose he called a conference at Halberstadt for 7–8 September 1891. Forty-two delegates representing thirty-nine unions including thirty-eight chairmen of centralized unions attended. It was here that the General Commission encountered the concrete expression of the widespread scepticism regarding its existence. The published report of the deliberations reveals that Legien's strategy was by no means fully understood by many union leaders. Nevertheless, it was accepted in all essentials by 25 to 4 votes.[17]

Therewith the first significant hurdle was overcome in the process of creating a national union body. There was still, however, the gauntlet of the projected trade union congress. This was finally called for 14–18 March 1892, also in Halberstadt. The ideas expressed in the congress deliberations provide the best possible insight into the conceptions of the articulate German worker of the time. The congress also illustrated to what extent Carl Legien was already at the very beginning of his career the clearest thinking and most far-sighted of all union leaders in Germany. In his opening address as chairman, Legien emphasized that the trade union organizations alone would not solve the social question but that they could contribute essentially to the workers' struggle for emancipation. Like pioneers, the trade unions had to level the ground for the achievement of a higher intellectual understanding of the working class, and by winning better wages and conditions to preserve the workers from immiseration and stagnation. By doing this the union movement would enable the working class to fulfil the historical task that had fallen to it.[18] This same clarity and force of rhetoric was to characterize Legien's later speeches at this crucial congress.

Having been forearmed with the approval of the chairman of the centralized unions for his organizational plan, Legien confidently introduced the debate on it in full awareness that it had still many bitter critics. He affirmed that there were two decisive points to consider in selecting the most appropriate form of organization. Here he was at pains to refute the cases of both the localists and those who championed the so-called industrial union.[19] Two points existed here: how large was the number of organized as opposed to unorganized workers, and what were the legal hindrances to all efforts at organization? The fact that the overwhelming majority of the workers was still outside the organization, compelled one to select a form in which the stirring up and recruiting of workers was most efficient. On the second point, Legien emphasized that the right of association in Germany allowed workers to form up in any way they chose *provided that politics was kept strictly out of the unions*; although here Legien distinguished between party politics on the one hand and interest-group politics on the other, which if the unions were allowed full freedom of movement, they should be allowed to pursue. Essentially, however, it was the struggle within the economic sphere that was the true task of the unions.

Legien made these points in order to illustrate the impracticability of both the localist and the industrial union positions. Experience had shown that the best way to get workers organized was through their own craft organization. This was because there existed still a great deal of craft consciousness and caste spirit among tradesmen.[20] Further, argued Legien, in view of the fact that the Anti-Socialist Law had destroyed all previous efforts at centralization, there was a prime need to reconstruct on the remnants of organization and to emphasize agitation as a means of overcoming the indifference of the masses.

The reception of these ideas at the Halberstadt Congress was not overly enthusiastic, despite Legien's graphic illustration of how disastrous was the recently staged strike action of the printers' union.[21] However, neither could the champions of the alternative forms of organization (localists or industrial unions) gain anything like majority support. The outcome of this decisive congress was a compromise which, although it severely watered down the General Commission's plan, left it in a basically recognizable form. After a great deal of unedifying debate, the congress adopted a resolution merely *recommending* the centralization of related craft associations by means of so-called cartel agreements, although it recognized the centralized craft association as the basis of trade union organization.

Beyond this the General Commission was retained and empowered with most of the functions that Legien had envisaged, except that no special strike fund was created for it to administer, nor did it receive the financial support it originally expected. Nevertheless, the resolution was the basic confirmation of Legien's efforts. There now existed for the first time in Germany a national trade union organ that was to extend its influence far beyond the limits of the imagination of its founders.[22]

As indicated, the Halberstadt Congress of March 1892 created the second focal point for organized labour, the essential precondition for the emergence of an opposite pole to the SPD executive. Not unexpectedly there were critical voices raised, but it was the central organ of the SPD, *Vorwärts*, that caused the General Commission most annoyance. They countered by writing that a section of the party seemed to believe that bourgeois society would soon be collapsing, apparently having been influenced in this belief by Engels' article on 'Socialism in Germany' in *Die Neue Zeit* (No. 19 1891/92) which *Vorwärts* appeared to endorse. The tenor of feeling among socialist theorists was that in view of the imminent collapse of capitalism, all effort in building up the industrial wing of labour at the expense of the political was futile. This the General Commission found most difficult to understand. Their polemicist in the *Correspondenzblatt* (most probably Legien himself) did not go so far as to criticize Engels' famous prediction, but he did not conceal his exasperation with the theorists who could not see that even if the collapse of bourgeois society was imminent, there was nothing to lose and everything to gain by building up efficient trade unions as fast as possible. If there was to be progress in the entire movement it was folly for the unions simply to cease functioning and wait on future developments, making no effort to achieve in the present what was possible in order to be able to build upon it later. In short, it was argued that if the unions stood still, time would pass them by without their having remotely fulfilled their purpose. It was, however, recognized that if the SPD concentrated its efforts solely on achieving reforms in the present, it would lose its revolutionary character. But such practical aims were the task of the trade unions, and these, as had been pointed out many times, provided the essential basis for the entire labour movement. The General Commission then reproached the SPD critics for lack of logic. They had in the party conferences (Halle 1890 and Erfurt 1891) recommended that the trade unions create a centralized form of organization, and now as this had taken place the organization was being subjected to harsh criticism.[23]

Whenever SPD sceptics ventured to doubt the efficacy of the fledgling trade union movement, the General Commission was quick to defend itself. One of the chief arguments among SPD journalists was that the failure of the Halberstadt Congress to create a stronger central organization was proof that such a body was superfluous.[24] This line of reasoning brought a hostile rebuff from Legien to the theorists. It was very easy, he wrote, to prove theoretically that trade unions could be dispensed with, but only a theorist could put forward such arguments. Whoever had daily to take the knocks from the employers thought differently. The oppressed worker threw all the theory overboard and sought through the unions to ward off the knocks in future. By bringing home to the worker the fact that he could do something against the maltreatment meted out by the employers, a union meeting stirred up support for the labour movement even more effectively than a party meeting which concerned itself with theoretical matters.

Because the SPD press was at best lukewarm about the trade union organizational structure Legien grew more and more forthright: 'Half measures have a damaging effect', he wrote 'Either the unions are considered necessary and are given support or they are considered superfluous, opposed and regarded with hostility. We must be able to demand this much from our party comrades that they clearly declare their point of view and give their reasons . . . The unions were not formed as a result of theoretical discussion but emerged out of practical necessity.'[25] Further, he argued, the bourgeois society had struck very deep roots which could not be expected to disappear in the near future.[25] Indeed, at the SPD conference in Berlin, 14–21 November 1892 Legien (who was delegate for Hamburg) declared that it was necessary for the party to gain clarity on the union issue for three reasons. There was the notion abroad that since the lapse of the Anti-Socialist Law, unions which had carried the movement during that period of ban were now superfluous. Further, the numerous lost strikes in recent years had also demonstrated their ineffectuality in the face of the concentration of capital. And finally, there was the fact that the party was expanding its membership so dramatically as to include small entrepreneurs who were obviously opposed to unionism! Legien, however, urged upon the SPD the necessity for party members to join the unions so as to give them their support. *All theory was grey*, he proclaimed and insisted upon the importance of practical work. He feared that if the SPD did not express its solidarity more unequivocally with the trade union movement than it did at the Halle Conference of 1890 then the life thread of the movement would be cut.[26]

What Legien really wanted was that the SPD would more directly represent the union cause in the Reichstag, but there was little inclination among the party executive to act as a trade union party. The mistrust already aroused between the two wings of labour was further intensified by Legien's commentary on the significance of the International Workers' Congress held in Zürich, August 1893. This meeting which proclaimed the need for stepping up of trade union activity on a national basis was fuel to Legien's fire. He took the opportunity via the pages of the *Correspondenzblatt* of instructing 'those in Germany who always placed the party above the unions' that wherever they were neglected, as in the USA, the party suffered accordingly. In Germany, it was the union-organized workers who were the regular troops (*Kerntruppen*) of the party, and for this the unions expected that more emphasis in the party press should be placed on attracting the indifferent masses to the unions, especially as the German delegation to Zürich had supported the resolution on trade union action.[27] The party press, according to Legien, needed to exert more influence in favour of the unions.

The theorists, however, were not inclined to respond to this appeal because they regarded the weakness of the unions in 1893 as being due to the general economic slump, and no amount of propaganda would help them until the economy improved.[28] Legien, for his part, took the view that particularly in times of depression, the unions were very necessary institutions and that the SPD could do a lot for them by urging party members to join the union of their particular trade, a step which had indeed already been recommended at the Halle Conference.

By taking up cudgels in this aggressive way for the union cause against the opinion of the party press, Legien finally incurred the displeasure of the party executive, but at least achieved the placing of the union issue on the agenda of the Cologne Conference of the SPD in November 1893. Indeed, the party executive represented by Ignaz Auer had privately reproached Legien by letter for his all too exuberant claims for the union movement. But this only fired Legien to put the union case before the party conference with what was regarded by the older members as youthful arrogance. He repeated his belief that unions were the preparatory school for the political movement and elaborated this by saying that in order to recruit those workers who had no idea of the economic and political struggle against capital one could not begin by using complex political theories. The best method was that of the unions which was offering the workers material advantages while at the same time illustrating the absence of harmony between capital and labour. In this way workers who were indifferent were won over, so the unions were an excellent means of agitation for the political movement.

Beyond this the unions were a better school than the party in training the character. The worker was encouraged to make sacrifices cheerfully for his comrades, whereas all the party required was that members went to the polls once every five years, or at the most, to go to a monthly branch meeting and pay a small contribution. In contrast, the unions demanded constant and increasing material sacrifices from their members. In a strike, for example, the unionist wagered his entire livelihood. This sort of training could only be offered by the unions and for this reason they were the best institutions for preparing the working class for the greater struggle of the future—and, as Legien pointed out, for the final decisive struggle people would be needed who were prepared to risk everything. But, while claiming all this, Legien conceded that the unions only functioned as a palliative within the present society and that he did not overestimate their significance. Nevertheless, they deserved to be encouraged and not ridiculed. The facts were, however, that the SPD press had been particularly hostile to unionism, and Legien confronted the conference with a series of damning examples of anti-union journalism. The central themes of this was that unions were ineffective in bringing about a change in the relationship between capital and labour and that it was only the struggle for political power which would do this; the economic struggle only led to splits in the ranks of the workers without bringing them enduring advantages.[29]

As chairman of the General Commission in which body trade union activity was supposed to be concentrated, Legien considered it his duty to repudiate the charges of the party journalists as well as those of party leaders. Against their beliefs he asserted his conviction that the General Commission would survive beside the party executive. Ignaz Auer of the latter body had written in this matter to Legien pointing out the 'correct' relationship between unions and party. Auer used the analogy of artillery in the army, i.e. a weapon to be employed at the discretion of the leadership. He considered that the General Commission was trying to separate the unions from the party and set up a rival organization but these high flown plans would never be realized. The German labour movement was not like the American under the leadership of a man such as Samuel Gompers. Auer warned that the General Commission was striving after too much independence.[30] Indeed, other critics at the conference claimed that Legien had nothing less in mind than to make the General Commission into a parliamentary committee of the union movement which desired to negotiate with party leaders on the basis of equality.[31] Against all this Legien maintained that the further development of the union organization could in no way damage the party, nor could the unions ever get into a position of variance to that of the party since the leadership of the unions was always in the hands of those who were politically active.[32]

The tenor of the 1893 confrontation between Legien and the SPD executive was clearly determined by the fact that a younger man (Legien was only 31) had stood up for an idea which, as far as the leadership was concerned, was in the process of rapidly becoming irrelevant. If what Friedrich Engels had predicted were true, then the intensification of trade union activity in 1893 was indeed a wasted effort. The counter-attack on Legien, especially from August Bebel who virtually threatened him with a party trial if he did not behave himself,[33] made it appear as one member (Albert Paul) stated that the SPD debate on the unions had become the guillotine of the trade union movement.[34] In addition to Bebel's comments, those of Clara Zetkin were strong evidence that the conceptions of Marx and Engels about the increasing accumulation of capital were well entrenched at least in the upper echelons of the party. This process was constantly diminishing the area in which unions could hope to have a lasting success. Permanent achievements could only come from the political wing of the labour movement.[35]

Legien's wish that the SPD come out with an unequivocal statement of support for the unions was not granted. Instead, his suggestion that party leaders join their respective unions was ridiculed. All that the conference would do was to repeat the general 1890 declaration of support for the unions, a fact which was tantamount to an official reproach to Legien when considered against the background of the resolution of the international congress which had recently taken place in Zürich.[36]

The treatment of the unions by the SPD as a subordinate, ancillary organization with virtually no future in the labour movement must be seen in retrospect as the first step in a process of liberation of the unions from party tutelage—a process provoked by the party's lack of interest and understanding of the self-determining nature (*Eigengesetzlichkeit*) of unionism.[37] As Hans-Josef Steinberg has pointed out, although the official Marxist ideology of the Erfurt Programme was understood fully by only a few SPD members there was, however, a widespread vulgar Marxism which communicated ideas of and beliefs in a 'scientifically founded' natural development in the direction of a so-called *Kladderadatsch*, i.e. some form of social upheaval. This concept remained nebulous and undefined but it was part of the ideological equipment operating amongst wide groups within the SPD at the time.[38]

While, on the one hand, this general belief militated against Legien's conceptions of the need for union struggle, on the other the very vagueness and utopian nature of the eventual crash confirmed Legien's statement of 1892: that all theory was grey, with the result that there was sufficient divided opinion in the labour movement to allow the common sense of practical trade union activity to proceed along its own way. Legien argued, too, that whenever the *Kladderadatsch* came there had to be people available sufficiently trained by the unions who could assume the task of administering a 'socialized state', and this obviously made sense to many. The need to band together into unions was seen by Legien as a natural response of the workers to the intolerable conditions of capitalist society, and in channelling this natural drive into socialist-oriented unions he believed he was furthering the interests of the party more than the localists who feared that the forging of a 'second hammer' in the labour movement—the setting up of a quasi-federal body—would lead to discord between party and unions. This belief among party members was revealed to Legien by the 'most rabid representative' of the localist union concept during the Cologne Party Conference who confided to Legien that the root cause of the dispute was not that unions failed to do any lasting good for their members, but that they could grow too strong beside the party organization.[39]

The year 1893 saw an all-time low in union membership, but this did not deter the General Commission from seeking to devise plans to make the movement more effective.[40] Legien now set out to mobilize the centralized unions in a plan which, had it been realized, would indeed have turned the General Commission into a parliamentary committee. This project, initiated so soon after the hostile party conference, indicates that Legien was not in the least intimidated by the strength of party feeling against him. He had, after all, been reproached with *Grössenwahnsinn* (megalomania) by Richard Fischer.[41] One of the functions of the General Commission was to convene a trade union congress if a majority of the centralized unions were in favour. In September 1894, then, the General Commission circulated confidentially a possible agenda for approval by the affiliated unions. It was pointed out that a congress which merely dealt with the General Commission's report and the thorny organizational question would not achieve much. One should tackle such key issues as the legislation governing the right of association as well as existing factory legislation—accident prevention, workshop inspection, workers' rights etc.[42] These were, of course, matters which the SPD should have been dealing with, but Legien observed that the party had little time to go into such social–political issues and that these could be best dealt with in depth by the unions.

In entering this sphere, of course, the General Commission was aware that it would provoke criticism from both within and without the labour movement. Yet the evidence suggests that Legien was trying in his own way to force the issue over the prohibition on unions discussing political questions. He believed that the law was only a rubber stamp of prevailing conditions or a confirmation of existing social relationships. It was time to force new changes. If the unions on a nationwide basis energetically claimed the right to agitate for social political reforms (*Sozialpolitik*) then the Reichstag would have to accord them that right by amending the law.[43] This belief about the nature of law was a constant feature of Legien's thinking, but in 1894 there were too few unionists prepared like Legien to challenge the authorities, and so the majority of the chairmen of the centralized unions refused to agree to a congress with an agenda which could bring legal complications in its wake. But, in addition to this lack of support, one union publicly denounced the 'dark plans' of the General Commission and declared its intention of terminating its contributions to that central body.[44] It was argued that the plans to have a conference on social political issues showed that the General Commission had insufficient work to occupy its time and that it should be disbanded. Moreover, the SPD organ, *Vorwärts*, also queried the motives behind the 'dark plans'. In an issue of 27 January 1895 it was coolly pointed out that a trade union congress which dealt with social political legislation could lead to 'misunderstandings'. There would then be two bodies created which would give directives to the SPD (i.e. the trade union congress and the party conference) and there was certainly no need for this.

It is evident that at this time the party saw itself as enjoying the unchallenged primacy in the labour movement. *Vorwärts* stated unequivocally that the party had created in its annual conference the organ which determined the principles as well as the tactical manoeuvres of the movement. If the unions had acquiesced in the proposals from the General Commission, *Vorwärts* was convinced that before they were implemented the approval of the party leaders would have to be sought.[45] The champions of the small localist union movement went even so far as to state that if Legien's plan succeeded then both the party executive and conference would be rendered ineffectual (*kaltgestellt*).[46]

This assessment by the localists undoubtedly imputed to the General Commission intentions it never had, although their prediction that a rival body would emerge to challenge the primacy of the party proved quite correct. However, in 1894 the General Commission was merely seeking to employ the centralized unions as a lever in the social–political struggle. But to envisage this at the time was to challenge the authority of the SPD which became understandably suspicious, and indeed, as was the case with the glovemakers, some unions disagreed strongly with Legien's tactics. As a result, a trade union congress could not be organized until May 1896 in Berlin. The agenda which the General Commission prepared was restricted to less dramatic issues such as unemployment relief and the question of union organized labour directories. The most controversial issue was the General Commission's desire to set up a reserve strike fund for itself to administer, a move which would have considerably increased its power. In the event it was an ironically optimistic hope in view of the fact that there were five motions submitted to the congress actually to dissolve the General Commission. In addition, there were resolutions to diminish its powers, although some unions such as the wood workers wanted to increase its competence.[47] So the 1896 congress was to see a confrontation of forces which would determine the fate of the General Commission.

Two opposing schools of thought in the German union movement sought to establish their concept of the future form of the union organization. The majority of the powerful metal workers were hostile to the federalist tendencies of the General Commission and claimed it was an expensive and superfluous body. They wanted to abolish it so that they could be left to expand the concept of an industrial union without having formal links with other groups. The wood workers, on the other hand, who had a long tradition of centralization, desired to see an even greater concentration of forces in line with the General Commission's own policy. In this, the creation of a separate strike reserve fund for the General Commission was a key issue. It would have greatly increased the Commission's ability to carry out its agitation policy in under-organized areas.[48] Indeed, there had been over the four years of its existence numerous applications from unions to the Commission for strike support in the form of loans. Yet all these had to be rejected since it had neither the funds nor the powers to raise them.[49]

The outcome of the 1896 conference was then a compromise. The General Commission was reconfirmed as an institution by the healthy majority of 78 to 43 and Legien returned as chairman with 97 votes. But the competencies of the Commission were only increased in one respect: it was accorded the right to convene a

congress at least every three years and whenever half of the affiliated unions desired it.[50] No central strike fund was provided. In
view of the amount of hostility in some quarters the mere fact
that the Commission was retained as the central coordinating
body of the trade union congress must be considered a victory for
Legien's concept of the future of the organization. The only dis-
appointing aspect from his point of view was the continued opposition to the establishment of a strike reserve fund. Instead, it
was left to the union cartels in areas where strikes occurred to be
responsible for collecting funds on an *ad hoc* basis.[51] To this
extent the Commission was still emasculated when it came to
coordinating and directing the strategy of the wage struggle of the
entire union movement. Nevertheless, with the gaining of the
endorsement of the 1896 congress the General Commission had
become a permanent fixture of the trade union movement.
Already, the two main lines of its policy had been adumbrated.
The first was to establish itself as the unopposed central coordinating body—there were still the energetic champions of the
localist position to overcome—and to become the recognized
mouthpiece of the industrial wing of the labour movement. The
second aim was to act as a lever for gaining improved social and
factory legislation, but above all it was for liberalized rights of
association because, as Legien saw it, this was the prerequisite for
extracting social–political concessions from the state.[52]

Legien's appearance at the SPD conference, October 1896 in
Gotha, after his moral victory in Berlin in May of that year, was no
longer that of a novice on the defensive but of a maturing labour
leader, clear in his own mind about what he was after and how to
get it. This new-won confidence is in part explained by the
dramatic and persistent economic boom of 1895 which naturally
also served to benefit the unions whose numbers and finances
picked up correspondingly.[53] Further, by 1895 the extension of
union activities in the spheres of travel subsidies, unemployment
insurance, sickness and invalid benefits as well as the usual strike
support had risen significantly. All this indicated that those arguments that such benefits would delay the decision in the class
struggle found little echo among union members.[54] 'Grey theory'
was no substitute for material social improvements.

The winning of social improvements was for Legien the first function of the union movement and he was fearless in proclaiming the right of unions to engage in *Sozialpolitik* as distinct from party politics—a distinction which the state was reluctant to make. The entire issue concerning unions and *Sozialpolitik* had two critical facets. In one direction the laws governing union activity ruled out the unions from discussing any kind of political issue, and in the other direction, the SPD looked upon itself as the sole political mouthpiece of labour. Legien was of the conviction that if sufficient numbers could be persuaded to join unions and to agitate for welfare-type legislation, that is to technically break the law, then, as the history of the British unions indicated, the law would be eventually changed to the benefit of the workers. However, the numbers organized in the mid-1890s were not a large enough base for the agitation Legien envisaged. It was necessary to mobilize the SPD to represent the union case more energetically in parliament.

The opportunity to do this was provided by the Gotha Conference of the SPD in 1896 when the issue of worker protection was placed on the agenda, but with a noticeable lack of enthusiasm on the side of the party leadership. Parvus, however, had been making energetic propaganda on behalf of the unions during 1896, urging that the SPD place more emphasis on the proletarian class struggle by supporting the unions.[55] The discussion at the conference developed into one concerning whether unions might involve themselves in *Sozialpolitik*. Max Quarck, one of the most prominent SPD personalities, ventured to disagree with chairman Bebel by stating that welfare questions, far from robbing the unions of their effectiveness, gave them new tasks in criticizing the existing legislation. It was wrong that only the party should concern itself with these issues when other organs could do it better. Quarck was therefore in favour of the unions pursuing *Sozialpolitik*—even though this was strictly outside the law. Indeed, they were already doing this in centres such as Frankfurt. Public meetings on the theme of social policy had been held, indirectly sponsored by the trade union cartels. How these meetings managed to side-step policy interference was not recounted by Quarck.[56]

All this was exactly what Legien had been advocating. When he spoke in the debate he stressed the distinction between *Sozialpolitik* and party politics. Naturally, unions were not expected to involve themselves in the latter, but they were by their very nature bound to pursue *Sozialpolitik* as it came under the heading of economic struggle. And then Legien made a statement which was the basis of his thesis that the free trade unions should not be considered a mere tool of the SPD. 'In the economic struggle all forces need to be concentrated without enquiring into the political creed of the individual.'[57] He went on to state that *Sozialpolitik* was not the sole preserve of the SPD. One could pursue *Sozialpolitik* without being a member of the SPD. Indeed, all parties did so in so far as it suited them. The unions were forbidden to do so according to the letter of the law as it stood in 1896, but Legien promised that as soon as the ban on the affiliation of political associations in Germany was lifted, the unions would do so with or without the approval of the SPD.

This type of straight talking by Legien must have had some impact on the party conference since it did vote for pushing social legislation, particularly for the eight-hour day and for 8 p.m. shop closing. Of course this was merely agreeing to conduct agitation on behalf of the unions within the legislature.[58] There was little chance of ever getting such measures through. The unions, for their part, intensified agitation for these goals in public in open defiance of the law and without reference to the SPD. The dual process of union emancipation from party tutelage and of the trade unionization of the labour movement had moved a step further. Legien's concept of employing the union movement as an independent instrument for transforming bourgeois society was crystallizing. More agitation, meetings and protest action would not of themselves achieve such things as the eight-hour day. It was numerical, and hence financial, strength of the growing union movement which would tell in the long run. 'The organization is everything!' (*Die Organisation ist alles!*), Legien instructed the SPD at the Gotha Conference of 1896.[59]

In this defiant outburst of confidence there is clearly the implication that talking and theorizing was a waste of valuable time and effort. Indeed, the subsequent history of free trade unions indicates that this was true. All hopes were placed on building up a massive trade union bureaucracy behind which stood an army of organized workers. But before this could be realized, there would have to be a liberalization of the laws governing the right of association and assembly, a fact which Legien squarely recognized. The government for its part regarded the socialist unions with profound mistrust and, as has been seen, had made two unsuccessful attempts since 1890 to introduce legislation to curb union and socialist activity. In line with this policy the government once again announced its intention in 1898 to bring down legislation which would effectively kill the union movement. This was the previously discussed *Zuchthausvorlage* which would have empowered the courts to sentence strikers or strike agitators to prison for up to twelve months. The announcement was the signal for Legien to begin an extensive propaganda campaign against the bill and for a liberalization of the right of association. For Legien, this right was the keystone of his concept of class struggle since it was the basis of the union movement.

The significance of his propaganda campaign is that it demonstrated the political will of the majority of the militant working class. The General Commission on its own initiative had taken up cudgels for a political issue which touched it most closely. The bill was thrown out on 20 November 1899. Only the Conservatives and a section of the National Liberals were for it. However, since all other parties for their own reasons were united in opposition to it from the beginning, Legien's propaganda was only one contributory factor in the defeat of the bill. Nevertheless, the unions had focused public attention on the injustice of the existing laws of association and it was not surprising that three weeks after the rejection of the *Zuchthausvorlage*, the government changed course and agreed to remove the ban on political associations affiliating. This was not done, however, in response to union agitation but rather to keep the Centre Party and the National Liberals on the side of the government for other crucial legislation (in this case, bill concerning naval and canal construction). The Centre Party wished to foster a Christian trade union movement in opposition to the socialists and of course demanded a relaxation of the ban on affiliation for this purpose.[60]

The Roman Catholic Centre Party had been encouraging a Christian trade union movement since 1895 and after the defeat of the *Zuchthausvorlage* this new form of unionism was actually welcomed by the government as a suitable alternative to the socialist movement which was, in their view, republican and revolutionary. So a policy was adopted, similar in philosophy to Bismarck's social policy, of trying to wean the three million socialist voters away from the SPD and the free trade unions. With these developments, the General Commission saw an added reason to proclaim its neutrality or formal independence from the SPD. The Christian trade union movement, which was officially founded in 1899, could present an alternative to German workers who had religious or monarchist sentiments. So in 1899 the 'neutrality question' once more loomed large in SPD–trade union relations. It was not a new issue in the socialist movement because, as has been seen, Theodor York had as early as the 1870s insisted that trade union neutrality was essential so that they could recruit all workers regardless of their religious or political inclinations, and at Halle in 1890 Karl Kloss had observed that the unions would best flourish if kept neutral! Legien was always aware of this, and in 1899 at the trade union congress in Frankfurt he strenuously repudiated the idea that unions were SPD organizations.[61]

The neutrality issue had been relegated to the background after 1890 when Legien and his colleagues were anxious to have SPD support in reviving the union movement. In any case, the laws of association imposed an official neutrality upon the unions but there was no doubt in anyone's mind that the so-called free trade unions belonged in the socialist camp. However, by the end of the decade, the hitherto accepted association with the SPD no longer suited trade union policy. The General Commission had developed its own determined views on the role of the unions in the class struggle and by 1896 had seen the need to escape the tutelage of the party once and for all. The social policy issue and then the founding of the Christian trade unions by Adam Stegerwald provided both the impetus and the rationale for emphasizing the independence of the free trade unions.[62] The foundation of a competing organization on a denominational basis constituted a deadly challenge to the free trade unions who claimed to be the sole representatives of the workers' interests. The name 'free' was intended to denote that membership was independent of religious or political affiliations.[63]

The 'neutralization movement' at the turn of the century caused at first a degree of disquiet in SPD circles, chiefly because it was believed that it could damage the political emancipation struggle of the working class.[64] However, Legien, von Elm, Leipart and other leading unionists emphasized that the free trade unions had always been neutral in the sense that they had no official party affiliation but insisted that this neutrality did not mean that they could not enter the field of *Sozialpolitik* which affected all workers regardless of their personal political leanings. The General Commission saw no contradiction between their assertion of strict party neutrality and the pursuance of the class struggle in the Marxist sense. Here can be seen an interesting re-emphasis of Marx's concept of unionism in the class struggle as he was alleged to have expressed it in 1869. Nevertheless, the Commission had to reinforce this concept at the turn of the century because the party leaders were reluctant at first to accept the principle. They continued to believe that, because the unions had once appealed for party support in 1893, the motor of the union movement was the SPD. The admission that unions followed their own laws of development was not readily made by the party leadership.[65] Eduard Bernstein summed up the attitude of the party executive in 1900 when he wrote:

> For the early socialists the trade unions were for a long time only a necessary evil. A necessary evil in two senses: It proved impossible to dispense with this form of the movement permanently. Considerable sections of the working class could not be won away from the trade union movement and many workers could only be moved by the hope of social betterment into joining a working class organization. For good or ill unions had to be tolerated. But in the majority of cases this toleration was fairly grudging.[66]

Indeed, there was much confused thinking in party circles until the plain facts of trade union strength made them reassess the role of unions. There then appeared a series of statements from critics of the unions which indicated that the policy of the General Commission had gradually won acceptance by party spokesmen. It was recognized in view of the new situation that the unions must exert their strength as a growing pressure group to force the extension of social legislation in their interests.[67] Even Bebel had conceded at the Hanover Party Conference of 1899 that it was in the chief interests of the unions to dissociate themselves from political parties. How otherwise could they hope to win Roman Catholic workers? The union movement was not social democratic but rather a proletarian class movement.[68]

Legien was so far emancipated from the idea of union subordination to the party that he was able to state in July 1900 in the *Sozialistische Monatshefte* that the unions should no longer be considered the recruiting school for the SPD; they were more. They were the means by which the workers were made aware of their situation, trained to solidarity and the readiness to make sacrifices in the struggle for their common interests. Workers who acquired these characteristics would be the best fighters in the struggle to liberate the working class. There was, therefore, no need to fear that the labour movement would stagnate if the free trade unions remained politically neutral.[69]

The emergence of the Christian trade unions as well as the General Commission's independent propaganda action against the *Zuchthausvorlage*, together with the unexpectedly large increase in union membership, all combined to bring about a revision by the SPD of their understanding of the role of trade unions. In 1900 August Bebel made a genuine attempt to place this phenomenon within the general framework of Marxist theory and came to the conclusion that the political neutrality of the unions was not inconsistent with it. Indeed, Bebel went so far as to envisage the cooperation of all three trade union organizations in the sphere of social policy agitation.[70] All party-political and religious polemics should be put aside so as to bring about effective cooperation. And because the chief area of union activity was in the sphere of *Sozialpolitik* the unions need not be linked with any particular political party:

I advocate, therefore, that party politics and religious debates

be kept out of the unions but I advocate that they pursue
worker politics and class-struggle politics all the more and all
the more energetically . . . It is therefore the duty of the trade
unions to pursue politics within the framework of their tasks.[71]

The General Commission could only but confirm these views.
The fact of union neutrality did not alter the class-struggle function of the unions. Both party and union chairmen believed in the
power of socialist ideas in themselves to convert, however gradually, the union organized worker. Bebel was, of course, still convinced of the limits of trade union effectiveness, but nevertheless,
this change of attitude towards the policy emanating from the
General Commission must be seen as another clear victory for
Legien's style of labour politics. In ten years of steady and determined work, Legien had actually liberated the unions from SPD
tutelage. The developments during the next decade would show
that it was the party which had to fear the tutelage of the General
Commission.

CHAPTER SEVEN

The Trade Union Struggle: Equal Status and Recognition, 1900–1914

As all attempts at periodization are only working approximations, depending upon what theme one is bent on following through, the first fourteen years of this century form a convenient unit because during that time a series of issues came to a head which had their origins in the previous decade, and this process significantly promoted the emancipation of the union movement in Germany. Few contemporaries had been able to recognize what had been taking place since 1890 in the German labour movement. Hindsight has now confirmed what 'Parvus' (Alexander Helphand) observed in 1900, namely that the greatest achievement of the German workers since the lapse of the Anti-Socialist Law (1890) had been the emergence of the trade unions. And he went further to state that in the political developments of the past decade there had been nothing that could even be remotely compared with that for its significance in the proletarian struggle.[1] As Heinz Langerhans has observed, if others saw the process of trade union emancipation they could not or would not recognize its significance. The attitude of the SPD executive in 1900 to the 'neutralization' process was essentially the same as towards the earlier 'centralization'. This had been virtually to refuse to draw the brutal conclusion that the unions had become *de facto* an independent force. The party leaders, Bebel and Kautsky, still insisting on the primacy of the party, adroitly side-stepped the issue and instead tried to preserve the appearance of complete unanimity between the political and industrial wings.[2]

For Bernstein and the revisionists, who considered the SPD in any case as merely a radical reform party, there was no particular danger for labour unity in the trade unions' struggle for independence. The leftist radicals in the SPD, however, did not share this equanimity of the revisionists. They, led by Rosa Luxemburg, demanded the subordination of the unions to the party leadership. It was their view that the trade union struggle should be led by the party in order to coordinate the day-to-day struggle with the final goal of the entire movement, thus preserving an overall unity. Up to 1900 Luxemburg had considered the German trade unions vastly superior to the English, precisely because she had believed them to be subordinated to the party. Now that they had won their neutrality, she saw the danger of fragmentation and a wrong-headed concentration of energy on everyday issues.

Indeed, for the left in the SPD the industrial wing was simply a necessary form of worker self-defence against the more blatant outrages of capital, but without any prospects at all on its own of ever eliminating the commodity character of human labour. Trade union activity in all its aspects never got beyond the labour of Sysiphus. So, as Langerhans has summed it up, the 'emancipation' of the union movement in Germany was officially ignored by the party executive, recognized and welcomed by the revisionists, but observed with growing disquiet by the leftists who opposed it both in their theory and practice.[3] The period 1900 to 1914, then, was one of unresolved tensions within the entire social democratic movement. Those between the trade union movement, on the one hand, and the party executive together with the radicals, on the other were manifested around the key issues of the continuing intra-union struggle with the localists, the May Day strike, and most dramatically of all, in the famous mass strike debate.

Even though the champions of the localist trade union concept had had to recognize defeat at the Halberstadt Congress of March 1892, they had not been compelled by SPD pressure to dissolve themselves and accept the principles of centralization. They continued to see themselves in the first place as agents of political rather than economic change. However, until 1896/97 the localists had remained more or less in touch with the General Commission, but then decided to establish a new association altogether. At that time the ban on political organizations from maintaining organizational contact had been lifted so the opportunity for a complete break with the General Commission was seized.[4]

Under the name of *Freie Vereinigung deutscher Gewerkschaften*, the new body sought to compete with the General Commission. It did not, however, attract great numbers. In 1898 the sum total of localists was only 15,792 against 491,955 affiliated with the General Commission.[5] In spite of this relatively small number, the localists were able to sow much discord between the centralists' movement and the SPD. This can be attributed to the decidedly anarcho–syndicalist ideology of the localists' leader, Dr. Raphael Friedeberg, who was later to play an active role in stirring up the mass strike debate. Under Friedeberg's leadership, the localists pursued an openly revolutionary goal, seeking to impress the entire SPD with their own stamp. They repudiated all revisionist and state-socialist ideas as well as liberal reforms with state aid, and sharply condemned the dearth of revolutionary energy within the SPD executive; but above all they were hostile to the apparently state-friendly stance of the General Commission. In other words the localists were uncompromising revolutionaries, and for this reason repudiated strongly the growing tendency among other unions to enter into wage agreements as a weakening of the class struggle.[6]

It appeared as though the aim of the localists was the merging of the political and industrial wings of labour into one fighting unit. In view of the strength of the General Commission, this would have been hopeless had it not been for the sympathy enjoyed by the localist conception with such SPD leaders as Karl Kautsky and Ignaz Auer. The latter never really accepted the notion of trade union neutrality and independence. A situation had to emerge which forced the SPD leadership to make an unequivocal choice between the two concepts of unionism.

Such a situation arose in Hamburg after the turn of the century. A small localist group of stone-masons had technically acted as strike-breakers in that they refused to recognize the wage agreement achieved between the centralized stone-masons' union and the Hamburg building industry. Instead a small group of 103 stone-masons preferred to enter into piece-work agreements that clearly undermined the existing agreed wage. By way of disciplining this group the General Commission demanded their expulsion from the SPD. This demand was then upheld by the three SPD branches in the city of Hamburg (18 June 1901) who in turn applied to the party executive to expel those stone-masons who were members from the party. There were fifty in all. The SPD then set up a tribunal under the chairmanship of Ignaz Auer which unanimously rejected (15 July 1901) the application by the local branches to have these men expelled.[7]

The indignation of the General Commission knew no bounds. That the SPD could sanction strike-breakers was beyond their comprehension. As a consequence an acrimonious press campaign raged between those unions loyal to the General Commission on the one hand, and those who for a variety of reasons supported the SPD decision not to discipline the piece-work stone-masons, on the other. The SPD executive remained unimpressed, even when the three Hamburg local branches appealed against the tribunal's decision.[8] The view was taken that the affair was a purely trade union one that did not concern the party, especially as it was found that the Hamburg piece-work stone-masons acted out of 'honourable motives'. Against this, the General Commission demanded that the SPD uphold the principle that workers who disadvantage the trade union of their particular craft simultaneously violated the principles of the party. The only avenue now open to the General Commission was the next SPD conference (22–28 September 1901 in Lübeck). For the trade union leadership the matter was by no means of purely union concern, but one which affected the entire labour movement, especially the party. The facts were that the piece-work stone-masons had established not only a rival union but also threatened to destroy the gains made by the recognized union of the majority of stone-masons. Such a matter concerned the party acutely since the minority rival group included many party members.[9]

The General Commission insisted on discipline and solidarity, and thereby won the support of sufficient influential party men to have two resolutions adopted that clarified the issue and simultaneously advanced the cause of trade union emancipation and independence. Both resolutions are milestones in the history of party-union relations. The first one was a means of relieving the party executive from having in the present case and in the future to take sides in disputes involving party members who in their role as trade unionists violated the principle of trade union solidarity.

The second resolution to gain the conference support had been formulated, characteristically by the revisionist, Eduard Bernstein. It stated:

> The struggle of the working class in the political and economic sphere demands the uniform concentration of all forces in the organizations involved. The basic condition for this struggle is the exercise of strict discipline in the action and the respect for the resolutions of the majority by the minority according to the principles of democracy.
>
> Whoever disadvantages the party or his trade union in a dispute conducted by them through actions or separatist efforts leading to contrary actions violates the established vital principles of the labour movement. For this reason the local branches of the party are empowered to expel such members as long as they persist in these actions.[10]

This resolution guaranteed a new right to the General Commission, a cause of some satisfaction to the chairman. It amounted to the power to ban from the SPD all elements of the labour movement that came into conflict with the major trade union body. In this case, the party executive had had to bend to the will of the General Commission in a matter of principle, and that at a party conference. The SPD could not avoid recognizing the General Commission as the *de facto* representative of social democracy in the industrial sphere, but was powerless to secure the right to intervene in union affairs, as the unions could not be affiliated with any political party.

The case of the localist Hamburg piece-work stone-masons had revealed a bizarre situation. The SPD executive had, via its tribunal, decided to overrule an expulsion order of three local branches against some fifty members. Yet, because the trade union leadership saw in this a threat to the solidarity of the industrial wing of labour, they were able by virtue of their support in the party conference to force the executive into revising their original position.[11] The implications for the future of the rival localist movement were obvious, but, because certain radicals in the party sympathized with the localists, the party was bent on effecting a reconciliation between the localists and the General Commission.[12] This factor delayed a final unequivocal settlement of the localist issue for some time. However, by 1906 within the context of the mass strike debate the General Commission was able to demand, as a precondition for cooperation with the party executive, that the latter sever all connections with the localist movement.

The key issue was that the localists persisted in an anarcho–syndicalist style of agitation which had always been contrary to the policy of the General Commission who measured progress towards socialism in the numerical size of the trade union organizations. And because by 1906 the General Commission had become so invulnerable, it was possible by 1907 for it to demand that the SPD require the dissolution of the localist organization.[13] This was effected, and at the Nuremberg Conference of the SPD in 1908 the SPD actually welcomed the conversion of a section of the localists to the central union organization, at the same time making it clear that the unrepentant ones had adopted a position hostile to the SPD.[14]

In this way, the General Commission's demand at the 1906 Mannheim Conference of the SPD for the expulsion of anarcho–syndicalist trade unions had been at last implemented. The localist threat to the centralized unions and to the policy of a peaceful advance towards socialism had been eliminated and simultaneously also the basis of the revolutionary romanticism of a section of the SPD. From now on, German socialists were to behave and speak even more soberly and pragmatically than before. The parallel disputes over the May Day demonstration and the mass strike will show even more clearly that the pragmatic policy of the General Commission gradually displaced the theoretical component in the policy of the SPD to become the dominant feature of German social democracy.

The May Day Dispute

In their efforts to implement the resolution of the Second International of 1889 regarding a worldwide demonstration for the eight-hour day on 1 May, the German unions, especially in Hamburg, had encountered the overwhelming power of capital. Their puny efforts had resulted in widespread lock-outs, and it was this that had led, as has been seen, to the centralization movement among German unions. It was early recognized that where union organization was inadequate there was no chance of carrying out a May Day strike without the risk of owner reprisals in the form of lock-outs. This made the General Commission after 1890 extremely sceptical about provoking factory owners. It was a problem with far-ranging consequences for party–union relations, because the party at its 1890 conference in Halle resolved to recognize 1 May as a regular holiday in accordance with the resolution of the International on the question, but with certain reservations. It was recognized that if there were obstacles actually to stopping work on 1 May, the marches and demonstrations in the open air were to take place on the first Sunday in May.

Although this technically provided a loophole for both party and unions to organize the May Day demonstration to suit local conditions, the party was at pains to give the appearance of implementing the spirit of the International's May Day resolution. The unfavourable economic situation had, however, always hindered this. For this reason, the SPD conference in 1893 at Cologne recommended that only those workers and unions ought to strike on 1 May who could do so without damaging the interests of the workers.[15] In this way the SPD did not oblige the unions to strike but only expressed its recommendation on the way to demonstrate. The demonstrations were also to be organized according to the judgment of the unions concerned, without reference to the general party directives. But despite this flexibility, the unions for the most part refused to become involved. The reason given was that the demonstrations were occasions for political propaganda and should therefore be the responsibility of the SPD itself.[16]

As a result of this, the May Day demonstration in Germany became an embarrassment to the SPD as the leading party in the International. The latter's subsequent congresses (Brussels 1891, Zürich 1893 and London 1896) continued to urge the matter, and in response the SPD at its 1896 conference in Gotha formulated the following resolution:

> The party conference obliges workers and workers' organizations, besides taking part in other rallies also to strive for a general stoppage on 1 May, and wherever there is a possibility, to cease work on 1 May.[17]

Here for the first time, the SPD stipulated that the responsibility of the demonstrations (in whatever form) rested with the unions. The latter were by no means edified by the prospect. As long as union funds were not threatened they had raised no objection to the May Day demonstration. There had, nevertheless, been occasions when individual unions demonstrating on 1 May had provoked lock-outs that had proved extremely costly to the unions concerned. The resultant discussion in union ranks was that a May Day demonstration *in the form of a strike* could not be carried out,[18] and there the matter rested until the 1904 congress of the International at Amsterdam. On this occasion a resolution was passed *obliging* all proletarian organizations to strike on 1 May whereas previous resolutions had only *urged* the stoppage.[19] There was still, however, the loophole that the strike should only be carried out if no disadvantage to workers would result. Nevertheless, by this stage the SPD had begun to feel particularly bound by the international resolution and began to exert itself to convince the unions of the importance of the principle involved. The General Commission was, of course, aware of the Amsterdam resolution and of the SPD's wish to see it taken seriously by the unions. The latter had, however, at the 1902 congress in Stuttgart passed a resolution to the effect that while SPD resolutions were authoritative in the sense of upholding a standard to be striven for, they were not binding.[20]

Here again was an issue where the SPD tried to assert its primacy over the union movement in vain. At the 1904 SPD conference in Bremen, the General Commission was scolded by the party executive for its refusal to submit to party directives. In 1904 the SPD was particularly sensitive to the May Day issue because the formulation of the May Day resolution at Amsterdam had been made with the collaboration of German delegates who were trade unionists.[21] But now the General Commission dissociated itself from this decision and Legien as chairman rejected out of hand the idea of any great demonstration that would consume union funds. In addition, because a participation of unions in May Day strikes in accordance with the Amsterdam resolution would threaten those wage agreements already achieved, the General Commission proclaimed that the strict execution of a May Day strike was irreconcilable with the interests of the trade union movement.[22]

With this, the SPD reproached the General Commission for having adopted an attitude similar to that of the British trade unions, and in so doing threatening to cripple the German labour movement by splitting it into two wings![23] Clearly the party leadership that had only recently condemned revisionism was still in 1904 (despite the earlier neutrality debate) maintaining the fiction of a uniform labour movement in Germany, a fiction that implied a primacy of the political over the industrial wing. The reproaches against the General Commission from within the SPD had, however, no effect. On the contrary, the General Commission seized the opportunity in 1905 to debate the issue at the trade union congress in Cologne. Its attitude was summed up by Commission member Robert Schmidt when he said, 'The larger the trade unions become, the more responsible becomes our attitude towards the workers. We may not waste any resources but rather deliberate whether they can be usefully applied.[24]

Another leader, August Bringmann, enquired,

> What use has been the May Day demonstration in the past? . . .
> In my experience the May Day demonstration has affected the
> unions like a foreign body in the human organism. Of course
> we have not previously taken an attitude against it; we have felt
> obliged to adopt a benevolent attitude towards the resolution
> of international congresses and the Social Democratic Party.[25]

However, at this stage of development, Bringmann demanded
from the trade union congress a repudiation of the above resolutions. The congress was clearly in no mood for submission but was
reluctant to provoke an open break with the SPD over this issue.
So for this reason no repudiation was moved. Instead, the congress supported a motion to require the further discussion of the
issue at a future international congress.[26] Thus the confrontation
with the SPD was tactfully postponed. This the party had
observed, and at the next SPD conference (1905 in Jena) the
anti-party attitudes of the Cologne trade union congress were
criticized. It was said that the union had lost a great deal of the
socialist spirit.[27] Naturally the spokesman of the General Commission (Richard Schmidt) disputed this reproach. If indeed trade
unionists queried whether there was any point in making great
material sacrifices for a questionable demonstration, this was not
to be regarded as an abandoning of the class struggle.[28]

So the positions of the party and the unions on the May Day
strike became irreconcilable. For the General Commission any
unnecessary provocation of capital in Wilhelmine Germany was
utter foolishness. There would be widespread lock-outs resulting
in a weakening of the union organization. Therefore the best way
to demonstrate for the eight-hour day was by holding evening
rallies and marches after working hours, at least until the unions
had consolidated their strength. When that point was reached,
and a successful stoppage could be staged, the General Commission would have no objection to the May Day strike. For the time
being one only set one's sights on what was possible, and that
meant simply evening rallies. It was not a matter of principle as

the party seemed to hold but rather one of tactics, in the same way as the SPD had debated its participation in past elections or its attitude to parliamentarianism.[29]

Sentiments of this nature originating from leading unionists in the party reaped the criticism of party stalwarts that the revolutionary conviction of the unionists depended upon the size of their money bags.[30] Union pragmatism thus encountered the as yet immovable wall of revolutionary fervour in SPD ranks, and the party at Jena in 1905, ignoring the mass of union reservations about the May Day strike proceeded to pass a resolution in which the old formulas of duties and demands were repeated and indeed unanimously accepted.[31] In the following year at the crucial Mannheim Conference of the SPD the May Day issue was overshadowed by the mass strike debate, the outcome of which *de facto* concluded the May Day discussion, as shall be seen.

Ironically, the position of the General Commission was brought home very clearly to the SPD when in 1906 some 2,000 Berlin electricity workers had been locked out as a consequence of this strike on May Day. These workers then turned not to the General Commission but to the SPD itself for financial support. The SPD executive then advised unions not to strike on May Day if it could lead to a lock-out! Then, at the 1907 SPD conference at Essen, negotiations were initiated between party and unions on how to share the cost of supporting locked-out workers. Agreements on a *modus operandi* were finally achieved after serious doubts had been expressed from within the party ranks. One SPD delegate had prophetically commented on the course of the debate: 'The motion to regulate the question of financial support by instituting a sharing of it between the party and the unions is nothing more or less than the secret strangulation of the May Day demonstration.'[32]

Naturally, the party executive had not wanted such an outcome but in the face of the overwhelming financial strength of the General Commission, the SPD was powerless. The final form of agreement between the party and the unions stipulated that the staging of future May Day demonstrations would be left to the local branches of each organization to make their own arrangements. If a lock-out then resulted both local organizations of

SPD and unions would have to produce funds in amounts proportional to their respective membership. They had no claim on the central funds of the SPD or the General Commission.[33]

This final regulation of the May Day issue negotiated at the Essen conference of the SPD in 1907 was without doubt another victory for the General Commission. Nothing was in effect changed. The policy of the General Commission prevailed without the letter of any international agreements having been violated. The SPD could not, however, press for a more radical approach to the issue. The result was that the May Day demonstration strike for the eight-hour day as a symbol of the international class struggle had become a dead letter. The General Commission under Carl Legien had imposed its concept of the class struggle on the entire German labour movement. This tendency emerges even more strongly in the parallel debate over the mass strike question.

The Mass Strike Debate

The trade unions had been named the bearers of the May Day demonstration by the SPD but, as has been shown, declined the honour in practice. Very much the same kind of situation arose over the mass strike issue that ran virtually concurrently with the May Day question, whereby it must be observed that the SPD had in 1896 nominated the unions as the organs to execute the May Day strike. In the case of the mass strike question the unions had to fight for the right—mainly of course with the aim of preventing the staging of a mass strike. The entire debate proved to be an exercise in confirming the emancipation of the trade union movement from party tutelage.

As with the May Day demonstration, the general and mass strike question had been subjects of lively discussion within the Second International since its foundation in 1889. From the beginning, however, the German delegation to the International had treated the general and mass strike questions with a distinct reserve. For example Wilhelm Liebknecht had in 1889 rejected a

French motion to call for such strikes to demonstrate for the eight-hour day on 1 May. He, as a leader of the German delegation, argued with Engels' ideas, namely that a general strike, to be successful, presumed such a strong and uniform organization of the working class that simply could not be achieved within bourgeois society. And he added, that if the workers had built up such organizations, they would be already masters of the world, in which case a general stoppage of work would be great foolishness.[34] The French motion was then rejected with an overwhelming majority.

In the course of time, however, the idea of widespread strikes had gained in popularity, and the 1893 congress of the International at Zürich accepted a cautious formulation by Karl Kautsky of the German delegation as a basis for discussion: 'The mass strike can become under certain conditions an effective weapon not only in the economic but also in the political struggle. It is, however, a weapon the successful application of which presumes a powerful trade union and political organization of the working class.'[35]

In this way the discussion within the International on this issue was directed away from anarchistic tactics towards attainable political goals by judicious use of the strike weapon. Caution became the keynote of the debate. By the 1896 London congress of the International, Carl Legien affirmed that the mass strike could not be executed unless sufficient strongly organized unions were there to carry it out.[36] The strength of organization appeared to Legien, as one would expect, as the chief precondition for any strike, including the political. It was a typical trade unionist's attitude that was clearly repudiated by the SPD radicals.

At the 1903 party conference in Dresden, Dr. Raphael Friedeberg, the well-known advocate of the general strike moved that this issue be fully discussed at the next SPD conference.[37] However, although Friedeberg's motion was rejected the reasons which he adduced for it are important to note, particularly because he received the support of such notables as Kautsky, Stadthagen, Klara Zetkin and Rosa Luxemburg.[38] Friedeberg was of the opinion that the SPD was losing ground among the working class because, as he put it,

> the mood of the proletariat and their conception of the class struggle have changed . . . Proletarian mass action served the labour movement best because thereby the ideals of the class struggle were placed more in the foreground. And political goals could be achieved through such action.[39]

This formulation provoked an immediate reaction from Carl Legien who argued that if the general strike was simply a means to stir up class-consciousness, he would have to reject it because the German labour movement already had the trade unions. Indeed, the idea of a general (or mass) strike was veritably dangerous because workers might conclude that it was pointless to keep up their union membership if all their long-term goals were to be reached by a general strike, in short the collapse of capitalist society. Legien preferred to sustain the old method of expanding organization because discussion of the general strike (he did not differentiate between general and mass strike) was virtually the same as discussing the revolution to which, as Legien believed, the bourgeoisie would resort to crush the working class once the latter appeared a real threat.

This rationale for not discussing the mass strike at all was championed fearlessly by Legien with the support of the General Commission. It was the bourgeoisie that would unleash the revolution, not the proletariat, because the former would seek to deprive the working class of the rights they had won. In that event, the working class would have no alternative but to defend themselves. This idea of revolution was, of course, not shared by the SPD radicals, but time was to show that Legien's conception was the more characteristic of Social Democrats generally.

After the 1904 International Socialist Congress at Amsterdam had urged the use of the mass strike, Karl Liebknecht had moved at the next SPD conference in September 1904 at Bremen to have the matter placed on the agenda for the following year.[39] However, Liebknecht dissociated himself from the anarchist concept of general strike as represented by Raphael Friedeberg, and described general strike as 'general nonsense' which only discredited the positive idea of mass strike.[40] But these subtle distinctions in the mind of SPD intellectuals were lost on the General Commission, for as soon as it became known that the SPD would debate the question at its 1905 conference, it was resolved to get in first and make the trade union view clear beforehand. This was done at the trade union congress held in Cologne 22–27 May 1905. By now the unionists were clear about the distinction between the concepts of an anarchistic general strike and the so-called political mass strike. Yet they still condemned the latter as being inappropriate for the defence or attainment of political reforms in the Reich, even though it had been successfully used in other countries.[41]

The chief union speaker on this occasion, Theodor Bömelburg, noted admonishingly:

> After all that has been said one could observe that one can certainly discuss the political mass strike but one must reflect very seriously whether one implements it. In the German trade union movement we have to see that the discussion about it stops, and that the solution be left to the future, for the appropriate moment. We all know how much trouble it has been to get the unions to their present level.[42]

Bömelburg's ideas on the mass strike were identical to those being expressed in union circles about the May Day strike. Both meant incurring unnecessary risks to union organization. And Bömelburg rebuked the various SPD leaders by observing that they were doing no good service to the labour movement with all their talk of mass strike, particularly since these party people had no idea of practical work.[43] In the light of these views, then, it was not surprising that Bömelburg's resolution was formulated in unadorned and unequivocal terms. It also represented the views of the General Commission. While it stressed the readiness of the unions to defend existing basic rights it stated:

> the tactics for any future struggles of this nature [mass strikes]

must be dictated, as in all other cases, by the prevailing conditions. The congress therefore considers all attempts to prescribe a particular tactic by propagating the political mass strike as reprehensible; it recommends to organized labour energetically to oppose such attempts.

The congress holds the general strike as it is championed by anarchists and such people lacking any experience in the field of the economic struggle to be unworthy of discussion; it warns the working class against allowing itself from being deflected from the day to day work of strengthening worker organizations by listening to and spreading such ideas.[44]

This resolution was accepted with only seven votes against.[45] And in doing this the General Commission claimed for itself the right of veto over the future calling of a general strike. It wanted to determine whether and when this weapon should be employed, as well as to regulate the intensity of the class struggle in its own interests, claiming to be able better to judge the conditions of the working class than the SPD executive and the various theoreticians.

The party executive was, however, still anxious to discuss the mass strike question, although it is doubtful whether they would have really taken a different view from the General Commission had it not been for the constant urging of the International and various dramatic strikes both within and without Germany. An added factor at this time was the need to demonstrate that the party executive was the ultimate authority in the German labour movement, and not the General Commission.[46] The apparently high-handed decision of the latter body constituted a virtual challenge to the SPD executive and could not be ignored. The party press had begun a lively propaganda for the idea of mass strike, and leading personalities such as Kautsky and Bernstein pressed for an open discussion of the matter. Bebel himself, who a year previously had written against the mass strike was now prepared to challenge the trade unions' declared position at the next party conference (1905) in Jena. The evidence is that Bebel wished to confront the unions himself in order to assert the primacy of leadership in the overall labour movement.[47]

The atmosphere at Jena was tense, Legien as spokesman for the unions had to withstand many severe attacks. Bebel for his part did not openly demand union submission to the party but was quite clear that the Cologne resolution of the unions on the mass strike could be dangerous for the future of socialism, and warned against those voices in the labour movement which regarded the trade unions as the actual bearers of the class struggle. The key question whether the unions ought to submit to a SPD resolution was skirted by Bebel. He was content to underline the proposition that the party was the highest authority in political questions and that trade unionists as citizens should have a livelier interest in the political condition of the state and not only concern themselves with the economic factors in society. Clearly Bebel was implying as strongly as he dared that the unions must acknowledge the primacy of party leadership.

It must be kept in mind that Bebel himself did not cultivate any illusions about the practicability of general strikes. His strenuous efforts to ventilate the issue in open debate must be seen primarily as an attempt to assert the authority of the SPD. He even went so far as to reiterate the condemnation of the anarchist concept of general strike but championed the idea of mass strikes in order to defend existing rights if they were threatened by a reactionary government. Bebel emphasized: 'We will not provoke, we defend ourselves. The political mass strike is not merely a theoretical but also an eminently practical question concerning a means of struggle that eventually should and must be employed.'[48] However, Bebel was astute enough not to envisage use of the mass strike without thorough organization and agitation, coupled with political and economic propaganda so that the masses would be sufficiently enlightened and financially viable to withstand it.[49]

Against this purely defensive use of the weapon the unions could have had little objection. Legien also agreed that in extreme cases the working class be defended with all means available. Nevertheless, he insisted that the words 'mass strike' be struck from the resolution since it smacked too much of anarchism. Further, he could see no justification, despite the often oppressive policies within the Reich, for employing this strike weapon. The risk involved was too great. And here Legien revealed his profound reservations about the matter. His ideas emerged from a rational and sober analysis of Wilhelmine society and his understanding of the temper of German labour:

> If the general strike, or whatever you call it, comes, that sig-
> nifies for me the beginning of the revolution. Once the masses
> are on the street there will be no calling them back. It will be a
> case of bend or break. The party is seeking new means of
> struggle because the idea of violent resistance has been wrongly
> given up. I have never shared the view that revolutions in the
> old sense are no longer possible today. I am convinced that
> when our power has grown to such an extent that we are
> dangerous to the bourgeoisie, *they will risk it. They will force us
> in front of the bayonets*. But when this point of time is reached
> the bayonets will fail, that is the means of power over which the
> bourgeoisie disposes. Have not the greater part of our people
> been soldiers? Don't they know how to use rifles? I say there-
> fore: if it comes to mass action, then we will be standing in fact
> before the revolution. Then there will be no chance of backing
> off. . . In certain respects I consider the propagation of the idea
> of the political mass strike to be dangerous. If you do not draw
> the necessary conclusion that the mass strike is the beginning of
> the revolution then you are demanding something of the work-
> ing class that I under no circumstances would. If the working
> class are not to resist if they are knocked about, then do not
> demand that they go into the streets, because as soon as the
> masses are on the streets they will be knocked about, and I do
> not expect them to take it without retaliation. We must train
> the workers that they have sufficient self-awareness and self-
> respect so as not to accept rough handling and that as soon as
> they are attacked they will retaliate.[50]

While the essence of Legien's speech was an appeal not to provoke the bourgeoisie—something which as has been seen, even
party chairman, Bebel, agreed with—the SPD conference

accepted a motion for the widest possible implementation of the mass strike weapon in given situations, by 287 votes to 14.[51] An open break between the General Commission and the SPD executive on the basis of the Cologne and Jena resolutions now appeared unavoidable. The union leaders remained adamant that they would not tolerate any mass strike propaganda. Reacting to the Jena resolution of the SPD the *Correspondenzblatt* made it emphatically clear that there could be no question of the SPD enforcing its resolutions on the unions. There could only be negotiation on the issue in given instances. Any propaganda that urged the preparation of a catastrophe—as the unions saw discussion of the mass strike—would be strenuously opposed.[52]

The effect of the Jena resolutions on certain sections of the SPD was, however, of a completely different order. A lively agitation for the mass strike was unleashed whereby the trade union attitude of extreme caution was severely criticized.[53] Here the parting of the ways between the two wings of labour can be clearly seen. For the unions, the SPD attitude smacked of revolutionary romanticism (*Revolutionsromantik*) while the party abused the unions for their apparent timidity. This debate was, of course, strongly influenced by the Russian revolution of 1905 which had had widespread repercussions, and which had been unleashed by a spontaneous series of mass strikes. But whereas radical spirits within the SPD (such as Rosa Luxemburg) enthused over the events in Russia, the unionists saw in them nothing worthy of imitation. At a conference of the affiliated union chairmen in February 1906 the implications of this divergence with the SPD were examined. They were pleased to note by then a certain diminution in the party's eagerness for revolution. This would enable a better climate of relations with the party executive, the party press and the party generally. It was noted by the union leaders that the entire polemics over the neutrality question, the May Day strike and the mass strike were really questions of tactics and not of principle.[54]

In spite of this note of reconciliation, the unions gave not an inch and refrained from drawing any conclusions of principle. On the contrary, they insisted that there could, under no circumstances, be any submission of the unions to the party. Indeed, it was stressed that the SPD must become accustomed to the idea that the unions were to be recognized as a power factor of equal rank with the party! And that meant full party recognition of union resolutions as well as the right of veto. The union leaders regretted the lack of understanding within party ranks for union problems.[55]

That the looming confrontation between party and unions over the mass strike did not develop to breaking point in 1906 is due to the behind-the-scenes efforts of Legien and Bebel to preserve a semblance of labour unity. Prior to the party conference of that year, the General Commission met with the SPD executive to discuss the criticism in the party press of the union congress in Cologne the previous year. The party was at pains to commit the unions to the mass strike in principle. But the General Commission refused to revise its 1905 stand, nor would it recognize any future party resolutions. To this Bebel responded that the party, too, was really concerned to avoid a political mass strike because conditions in the Reich did not promise a successful outcome. The party leader added, however, that should such a strike become unavoidable, the unions should not seek to hinder the party in its execution. Indeed, the official leadership of the strike should remain with the party.

Bebel then sought to mollify Legien by conceding that the party would abandon any propaganda for the mass strike, but if it should break out spontaneously, then the union leaders would remain neutral; the party would assume responsibility for supporting the strikers. Legien agreed.[56] In this way the Cologne resolution remained intact, and Bebel who saw the weakness of his position had had virtually to admit that a political strike against the will of the unions was a practical impossibility. In this an apparent compromise had been reached, indeed a secret pact between the two representative bodies. This was intended to be the end of the matter had it not been for the mischief created by the still active localists who embarrassed Bebel by reporting these agreements in the localists' organ *Einigkeit*. The party leader was accused of reversing his position. It was argued, that, 'the German workers at Jena were either already deceived, or the power of the General Commission based on the Cologne trade union congress resolution concerning the mass strike is so great that party decisions can be retrospectively rendered illusory and the German workers duped'.[57]

A public clarification became therefore unavoidable. The next party conference (September 1906 at Mannheim) became a turning point in party–union relations. Legien and Bebel emerged as the chief protagonists, and while they tried to keep the debate unemotional, they could not entirely ban the polemics. As indicated the atmosphere had been strongly influenced by recent events in Russia and within the Reich itself. Bebel retreated little from his earlier stated position at Jena, but admitted that a large union organization was the precondition for any mass strike. And as proof Bebel pointed to the failure of the mass strike in Russia, a fact due to the inadequate level of unionism in that country. In Russia there existed no basic rights whatsoever, and the workers' struggle had been for the most elementary conditions of modern political life. By way of contrast, there was no justification for such a struggle in Germany. Only if the existing basic rights of the working class were threatened—the franchise and right of association—would the mass strike weapon have to be employed.[58] Bebel then expressed the view that if workers' rights were threatened by the state, even those workers not organized in unions or even SPD supporters would join in spontaneously. Bebel reasoned that a defensive mass strike would therefore be worth contemplating. On the other hand, the working class could not carry out an aggressive mass strike since it was too weakly organized. In order to avoid a blood bath one had to win the unions for the mass strike idea since they would be essential for carrying it out, though Bebel omitted to stipulate who would determine the timing of any future mass strike.[59]

The effect of Legien's views on the party leader was becoming more and more evident. There was scarcely any real difference between them. Indeed, Legien proclaimed, 'We are in agreement that in the given moment all means at our disposal will be applied. If it really comes to a mass strike then the unions will be in the forefront'.[60] But despite this, Legien let it be known that he would not agree to the education of the unions to mass strikes. Rather, the labour movement would flourish best on the basis of legality, refusing to offer violent resistance. Legien observed that the Prussian government was so hostile to organized labour, that a political mass strike against it would only end in bloodshed. In view of this, the political mass strike could only be conceived of defensively. There would be no provocation of the state. The idea of exerting pressure on the state for concessions was unrealistic in view of the latter's superior strength. Legien could envisage achieving results if, for example, the miners could stay out for ten to twelve weeks. But before such action was feasible there would have to be a sufficient number of workers organized.[61]

For Legien in 1906 the unions, with still only a fraction of the working class organized, were only getting started, and nothing reckless should be undertaken to damage this process. He therefore insisted that no discussion of general strike should be encouraged. Only in the event of a 'great provocation' would Legien support the mass strike. 'If it comes to the stage where we have to apply this weapon', he said, 'then the unions will be the organs to carry it out. And they will supply the largest number of leaders.'[62] By arguing in this way Legien successfully defended the Cologne resolution. He did this by supporting Bebel's interpretation on the one hand, while on the other refusing to do anything to 'prepare' the mass strike. The SPD was by now clear that it could do nothing about this and was compelled to enter into a face-saving agreement on it with the General Commission, wherein the claim to sole leadership in the labour movement by the SPD had to give way to a recognition of equal partnership with the unions. This was done by appearing to reconcile the irreconcilable. The key passages of the lengthy resolution stated:

The party conference confirms the Jena resolution on the political mass strike asserting that the resolution of the Cologne trade union congress does not contradict the Jena resolution, and considers all debate over the meaning of the Cologne resolution concluded. . . The trade unions are indispensable for the raising of the status of workers within bourgeois society. They are not of secondary importance to the Social Democratic Party which has to lead the struggle in the political sphere for the elevation of the working class and for its equality of privilege with the other classes of society. . . In order to achieve a uniform procedure in actions which affect the interests of party and unions equally, the executives of both organizations should seek to come to a common understanding.[63]

This resolution known as the Mannheim Agreement, the most hotly debated in the history of pre-1914 social democracy, characterizes a development that could scarcely have been predicted by the authors of the Erfurt Programme of 1891. A viable and subsequently powerful trade union organization had emerged, and Legien together with his lieutenants propelled this movement forward with unrelenting energy. Despite the severe criticism from sections of the SPD and the localists, they continued their practical work and perceived themselves as loyal socialists. And while the union leaders were sensitive to the often destructive attacks of theorists they felt instinctively that their activity must be in harmony with the theories of Marx and Engels, although no one—including Legien—had had either the time or training to elaborate a plausible theoretical framework for the style of trade unionism they practised. Of one thing they were convinced: the SPD politicians without a union background and who consequently did not understand their position, were less than helpful to the real cause of socialism.[64]

The mass strike debate illustrated this quite graphically. The party leaders such as Bebel, and even the revisionist, Bernstein, emphasized the essentially peaceful character of the political mass strike. It was chiefly to be applied in defending existing basic rights such as adult male suffrage which was the precondition for the survival of the SPD. Rosa Luxemburg as a leading theorist on the other hand looked upon it most favourably as the ignition factor for social revolution, and was devastating in her criticism of the unions for their timidity. Paradoxically, however, as Langerhans has observed, Legien's view that mass strike would unleash a revolution coincided with his chief detractor, Luxemburg. Both saw it as promoting violent upheaval, but Legien rejected it precisely for this reason.[65]

The SPD had as a party clearly not wanted to precipitate a

revolution, but in Mannheim it had to abandon its claims to sole leadership of the labour movement. This transformation in the position of the unions had begun at the 1893 SPD conference in Cologne, at which time the young Legien had been accused of megalomania. Even in 1899, Karl Kautsky, refusing to read the signs, could write that the 1893 Cologne debates had shown clearly how the strength of German social democracy was really derived from the SPD and that even the union leaders were aware of this.[66] In the Mannheim Agreement which Kautsky had helped to compose, any suggestion of union dependence on the party was eliminated. The unions had achieved the right of codetermination within the labour movement, a fact which was to influence significantly the future course of German political history.

CHAPTER EIGHT

Trade Unions and Internationalism — a Conflict of Priorities

The relationship of the German free trade unions to the Second International is an issue which cannot be side-stepped in a book of this kind. Indeed, it is more than of merely peripheral relevance, particularly in view of the fact that current research in East Germany has condemned the politics of the free trade unions as virtual class betrayal.[1] The main reason for this, as has been seen, is not only the latter's successful emancipation from the tutelage of the SPD, but also their capacity in important issues to impose their own policy over that of the SPD executive. This is particularly crucial in the period up to the First World War during which time the free trade unions, by increasingly pursuing policies of their own devising within the German labour movement, developed an almost schizophrenic attitude to the spirit of the Second International. It is therefore a crucial exercise to investigate the attitude of the free trade unions to internationalism, since this attitude sheds a revealing light on their relationship to their own nation.

In 1907, no less an observer of German social democracy than Robert Michels in his famous treatise on the relationship of this movement to international socialism pointed to the outstanding position of both the German party and trade union movement within the International.[2] He emphasized that the Second in contrast to the First International consisted of a plurality of national organizations which were not bound by any unifying programme. It was in fact a loose kind of association which possessed at the very most a moral authority over the member states. Two factors are, however, of particular significance. First, the German Social Democrats were, within this loose international association, both in the fields of theory as well as practice, the recognized leaders. Secondly, it must be borne in mind that the free trade unions as a component of German social democracy had from relatively insignificant beginnings won for themselves an increasingly independent role which exercized not only great influence on the party, but determined its very direction. This meant that by virtue of their expanding organization, the German free trade unions became the most important single organization within the entire International. When the Second International was founded in Paris in 1889, the Germans had been able to send, despite the Anti-Socialist Law, eighty-one delegates. Virtually all of these had been, or were still, active trade unionists. Among them was Carl Legien.[3] These men, however, had not come to Paris *tabula rasa* to receive an injection of the newly revived international spirit; they were already champions of their own German trade union tradition which, as has been seen, was well established by 1875.

The idea of an independent national trade union organization was one which, as earlier chapters confirm, could not be suppressed. It re-emerged with great vigour after the lapse of the Anti-Socialist Law. And one of the effects of the persecution of trade unionists under that law was to throw the craft unions onto their own initiative, to cut organizational ties with the SPD, but simultaneously to strengthen the ideological identification with that party. It is this ideological identification which was a phenomenon as important as it was confusing to the members. This is because the 'ignition function' of the ideology among the self-taught trade union organizers did not lead to them becoming rigorous theoreticians. For them social democracy represented not only a philosophy of history but also, and chiefly, an emancipation movement. And if the leaders of the SPD have been shown to have been in reality eclectics, so much more were the trade union leaders who placed greater emphasis in any case on practical questions. Nevertheless, the general confession of faith in socialism made also by the trade union leaders served from the very beginning to veil the character of the dualism between party and trade unions.

In considering the question of the relationship of German social democracy *as a whole* to the Second International, this 'veiled' dualism of party and unions must always be kept in mind. For this reason the SPD under Bebel's leadership was never uniformly oriented towards the International. To argue, as some do, on the basis of such statements as the following from *Der Sozialdemokrat* (8 April 1886) that Bebel's party was always internationally oriented is somewhat misleading: 'We are international because the capitalist exploitation of man by man is international, and the interests of the workers of all lands are the same. . .'[4] There continued to exist, despite this piece of persuasive rhetoric, very different interests within the various working men's organizations. This became increasingly evident at each successive congress of the International, especially in the attitudes of the German delegation. Precisely because the Germans were best organized, had the reputation of being ideologically better equipped and were, in addition, most successful in national elections, they became automatically the leading, and at the same time, most conservative group within the International. And if the party leaders had from the beginning behaved conservatively it can be no surprise that the trade union leaders took up a still more conservative—read national—position.

The relationship of the trade union leaders to the SPD executive has been covered earlier in this book, particularly the friction between the two, which resulted from their involvement in the International. When in 1904 Karl Kautsky attempted to locate the source of this friction he put it down to the inadequate exchange of ideas between the two wings of German labour. As a consequence there had been differences of opinion over tactics.[5] But this was an explanation resulting from an acute embarrassment. It implied that the trade unions would have acted in phase with the party had there been more frequent formal contact at the executive level. If that had been the case, it might have been expected that the union leaders would have bowed to their ideological mentors. But, as has been seen, the internal situation of German labour did not allow for such consultation; the trade unions had already achieved their independence. If there was no recognition of the primacy of the party on the national level there was even less chance of it when questions touching the International arose. The SPD had to accept this *de facto* independence of the unions and try to maintain a unified front to the outside world. This fact of German trade union independence was to have long range effects on the International.

But this is not to say that if the free trade unions had recognized the primacy of the party from the beginning (and submitted to it) then perhaps the unity of the Second International might have been preserved. There was, first of all, never any question of the trade unions recognizing the unconditional primacy of the party; and secondly, quite apart from the trade union issue, the SPD itself was never an ideological unity.[6] Even if there had been total reliance on the submissiveness of the unions to the party there would still have been the opposition within the party—not only from revisionist circles—to allowing an international body legislate for the national party.

There was, however, an additional complication in the party-versus-trade-union issue. At virtually every congress of the Second International, the extension of national trade union organizations was encouraged or at least assumed. It was recognized, just as Marx himself had done, that a flourishing trade union movement was the indispensable precondition for an active Social Democratic Party. August Bebel actually dealt with the trade union question in his address to the foundation congress of the Second International in 1889 in Paris. He reaffirmed the central importance of the trade unions as follows:

Originally it was a fairly widespread belief among us in Germany that the trade union movement, the associations of craftsmen with their emphases on the everyday questions of practical life was a hindrance to the development of socialism. However, we have become gradually clear regarding the error into which we had fallen. The impossibility of winning the masses at a blow for the total and ultimate goal of socialism, the impossibility of reaching this goal as it were directly, forced us of itself to pay more and more attention to practical measures that were suitable for arousing first in the workers their class consciouness. The results that have been achieved in this way are excellent.[7]

This open recognition of the indispensability of trade unions by the leader of German social democracy must have made a particular impression on the ten twenty-eight year old Carl Legien. His future activity is witness to his unshakeable conviction of the rightness of Bebel's observations. By the same token, the ideas of the other great German Social Democrat, Wilhelm Liebknecht, on that occasion (Paris, 1889) must have strengthened Legien's later position. In the debate over the May Day celebration and the general strike, Liebknecht proclaimed his view that such strikes were impossible because they presumed a strong and unified organization of labour which at the time nowhere existed and could not exist in bourgeois society.[8]

It was this concession to the necessity of expanded workers' organizations that runs like a red thread throughout the history of the Second International and which the German trade union leadership championed with the greatest determination. It is indeed completely understandable that Legien as chairman of the German national union body appealed to these resolutions of the International, particularly at that time (between 1892 and 1896) when he had to fight hard against those who challenged its very existence. For example, while under attack from the SPD executive member Ignaz Auer during 1893, Legien was able to justify his stand by quoting the recommendations of the Zürich Conference of the International, 6–12 August of that year.[9] On that occasion two resolutions of the highest significance for the trade union movement had been passed. The first arose from the need to intensify the struggle for the eight-hour day. To this end it was recommended that the unions as well as the workers' parties expand their respective organizations on a national as well as international level. It was resolved:

The trade union organization of workers has to conduct the extra-political free struggle with the entrepreneurs for the eight-hour day in order thereby to pave the way for the legal introduction of the eight-hour day for the entire working class.[10]

The second resolution was also a welcome affirmation of the

Legien concept insofar as it also recommended an extension of national trade union movements as the precondition for the strengthening of the international movement. It stated that the trade union movement was of basic significance for the political struggle of the workers. This enabled Legien afterwards to instruct the SPD that a neglect of the trade union movement would severely impede the progress of the party, and he cited the example of the pathetic achievements of American socialism which paid no attention to trade unions. In Germany, on the other hand, the trade union organized workers had always been the regular troops of the party.[11]

Clearly, these resolutions of the International were of great moral assistance to Legien at a time when the General Commission was under severe attack. As has been seen, he was not deterred, and energetically set about strengthening the national organization. The later congresses of the International brought similar affirmations of his position, the basic concept of which was that strong national bodies were the indispensable precondition for an active international organisation. And while the core of rationality in this concept is undeniable, the insistence on a priority of the needs of the national organization was bound to lead to a crippling in the spirit of the Second International. Member states were urged to build up the most viable trade union organizations possible in order to be able to defend and strive for the extension of basic rights, thereby growing to a point where they could offer each other practical help in times of industrial conflict. The difficulty here was that in time a range of disputes arose as to precisely how the already organized power of the working class could be employed for the attainment of various goals, namely how to demonstrate for the eight-hour day or how and when to stage international general strikes.

The Germans—both party and union men—had always taken a cautious and pessimistic attitude with regard to international worker militancy. They stressed that the organization of the working class had not yet developed strongly enough to guarantee success in any projected action. Just how the German Social Democrats had to be virtually compelled into discussing the question of the general strike is a phenomenon which can only be understood against the background of their internal party–union relations, already discussed. This entire process in which the unions revealed their essentially nationally based attitude to the International is a compelling illustration of how dependent the International was on the degree of organization achieved by the individual member states. Indeed, if the best organized group (i.e. the Germans) did not feel called upon to jeopardize their institutions through a confrontation with militarism and capitalism, it is scarcely surprising that the weaker members did not wish to take the risk in their own countries.[12] This, of course, was the key problem of the Second International. The German free trade unions had from the start both welcomed and cultivated international contact—admittedly with a high degree of sober realism—and were even able in 1902 from their own funds to set up and actually conduct the first international secretariat of the trade unions affiliated with the Second International. This makes the behaviour of the German union leadership particularly significant for the understanding of the essential nature of the movement. On the one hand it was characterized by an almost frigid caution and restraint, while on the other by an exemplary organizational and administrative efficiency.

All this focuses on the problem of how the free trade unions could affirm the principles of internationalism and yet in practice behave in so obviously a patriotic way, especially in view of the fact that they were so oppressed by their own government. A survey of their reactions to internationalism before 1914 confirms that the leaders were extremely sober and practical men, not easily swayed by illusions, no matter how noble in theory. Admittedly, one could ascribe their realism to a complete lack of imagination, but this would be less than just in view of the task which they had set themselves. This was nothing more or less than the inner transformation of the Wilhelmine state to a democracy wherein the proletariat would be guaranteed their rightful participation in the achievements of a higher culture.[13]

The way in which the leaders of the free trade unions estimated the Prusso–German military state determined to a large extent their behaviour towards the International. On the other hand, their idea of the masses played a decisive role in their strategy to transform this state by employing strictly legal methods. A judgment of Carl Legien from 1893 concerning the phenomenon of Wilhelminism is very instructive:

> As long as we are confronted with an opposition [the state] which regards cur-like submissiveness as the expression of patriotism and which allows itself to be guided by the will of a few, then the party will also have to demand a certain concentration of the will of all. In short, the workers' organizations will always have to bear the character of their particular country. Under a democratic constitution, the worker organization will be a more democratic one, while in absolutist state systems it will be the other way around; the organizations of the workers need an absolute central authority.[14]

The subsequent history of the trade union leadership had borne witness to the validity of this in the practice of the German situation. The General Commission under Legien became indeed a central authority and a law unto itself. In 1893 it was Legien's conviction that the workers would have to steel themselves for a protracted and disciplined struggle in order to reach a level which was commensurate with cultural standards prevailing at that time. The struggle would have to be waged against a state whose combination laws reminded him of Russian conditions, a state wherein no full right of association was yet guaranteed.[15] Such a situation demanded a tightly organized and disciplined working class which would in time, following the English example, wrest basic rights from the state. At that time, Legien observed, there were twenty–six different combination laws in the German states—'each more reactionary than the other'—and because of this Legien saw no other possibility than the continued expansion of the organization until the state had no other choice, as a result of the changed circumstances, than to reshape legislation accordingly. Any attempt by the working class to achieve this by force would lead to a blood bath. Legien maintained this attitude for his entire career.[16]

As late as the year 1893, Legien believed that any attempt by the German and Austrian trade unions to affiliate with an international organization would lead to their immediate dissolution by the administration.[17] For this reason he always remained sceptical with regard to the possibilities of a concerted international action by trade unions. Only particular *ad hoc* international arrangements and cartel agreements could be entered into.[18] For Legien there were but limited possibilities for international action. Indeed, in 1895 he was very pessimistic about an international trade union movement and accordingly took a stand against the French committee for the organization of the international general strike. This committee believed in 1895 that the possibility of a general strike on the international level was worthy of discussion and so they wished to convene an international congress to ventilate the problem.

At that time Legien was of the opinion that as far as a general agreement was needed—and that was all that could be achieved by an international trade union congress—it could take place at an international socialist workers' conference held in conjunction with it. Theoretical questions of far ranging significance ought in any case not be discussed or decided at international trade union conferences. The chief value of such gatherings lay in the personal contacts of the various delegates which gave expression to the feeling of community and international solidarity.[19]

For Legien an international trade union congress would only be of value if it were in the position to create a positive basis for a common action.[20] This, however, presumed a high degree of trade union organization which (as Legien observed in 1895) only the British trade unions possessed. In Germany, on the other hand, there was not even unanimity whether a German trade union congress would legally be allowed to discuss the affairs which touched organized labour most closely. Under these circumstances it was urgent that each national organization was strengthened before cooperation on an international level was advocated.[21]

These objections to premature international agreements are fully understandable in the light of the difficulties Legien encountered in realizing his ideas for a centralized trade union movement. Clearly, it would be necessary to bring ones own house in order before one assumed obligations which one could not guarantee to fulfil. In retrospect, it is interesting to observe that an international trade union secretariat was only formed shortly after the turn of the century, at a time when the General Commission had established itself as the unchallenged central body of the free trade unions. And just prior to this, Legien had had to declare his policy on an issue raised by the Dutch trade unions. They had mooted an international boycott against Great Britain because of the war she was waging against the Boer Republics in Southern Africa. Legien rather acidly criticized the intention of the Dutch trade unionists to help their kinsmen in this way. It was scarcely Legien's intention to endorse British policy against the Boers. Rather he wished to point out that a continental blockade by trade unions against Britain with the aim of crippling the entire British maritime commerce was illusory: success in the final analysis would depend upon whether the British seamen and transport workers would cooperate. What Legien commented here was typical for his sober way of thinking:

> The blockade of British maritime commerce is not supposed to be an end in itself or an act of revenge, but rather the means of influencing the British government to bring about a rapid peace. This goal would not be achieved because the British workers not understanding the intention of the whole exercise would believe it to be directed against the economic pre-eminence of British commerce and *against the future of their own livelihood*, and would respond to it with defensive measures which would make the continuance of the blockade impossible.[22]

Legien could thus see no real possibility of carrying out such an operation. Indeed, the attempt would miss its mark by virtue of its effect on the British shipping owners. The latter would urge the defence against such an international intervention as an issue of national honour and in that event could rely on the loyalty of the British workers who, as indicated, would frustrate the action. Now, if one transfers Legien's opinion about the British workers

to those of his own country we have illuminated a further aspect
of his motivation. At that time he expressed the following views
about his British class colleagues:

> The idea of the International is nowhere met with greater scep-
> ticism than just in British labour circles, and if the beginnings of
> international cooperation in the trade union sphere can be per-
> ceived, then the British worker is far more difficult to warm for
> international political actions since his enthusiasm for old Eng-
> land's greatness, power and independence stand in stark con-
> trast to this.[23]

It would certainly be difficult to find a better characterization of
the German workers' attitude to trade union internationalism.
Their readiness in allowing themselves to be dragooned into such
a political action at the instance of some international body was
just as absent as in other industrial countries. To what extent then
were the free trade unions prepared to commit themselves to
international agreements? Legien was most emphatic that the
trade unions must direct their best forces towards raising the
living standard and representing the interests of the working class
in their own country. However, inasmuch as the entire process of
production, marketing and transport together with the money,
goods and labour market were internationally linked, it was
clearly prudent that the trade unions should devote a section of
their energies to maintaining contact with foreign trade
unions—even if it was merely to defend oneself from deleterious
influences from outside.

The two most important areas requiring international cooperation were, according to Legien, the control of the labour market
and mutual help in the event of significant strikes. It was here that
the interests of various trades coincided with their opposite numbers in foreign countries. Out of their mutual needs resulted the
international contact. Even before the foundation of the International Secretariat in 1902 there were already thirty-two of the
free trade unions which had some arrangements with their counterparts in other countries.[24] The reason for this was that in times

of rapid travel no trade union could make progress without disseminating constant information to their members about conditions, especially the labour market, in the surrounding countries. This was because there was a more or less regular exchange of labour between Germany and her neighbours.[25]

At this point it ought to be recalled that one of the chief arguments for establishing a centralized trade union leadership in Germany was the need for reliable information about strike movements and boycotts at home and abroad so that the introduction of strike-breakers could be prevented. The importance of this is clear if one takes the case of the Hamburg dock labourers where a strike was to be called and the owners found themselves in a position to recruit labour from other countries with a minimum of delay.[26] The need to maintain a central office for both coordinating and disseminating this kind of data was as obvious as the complementary need to maintain contact with outside trade union organizations. The prime need to defend ones own organization so as to ensure its progress demanded the cultivation of relations with the foreign unions of a given trade. And Legien observed that the value of international agreements of this kind depended upon how strong the organization of each country was. Wherever they were still weak, then 'internationality' existed only on paper. For this reason there could be successful cooperation between the allied unions only on the basis of strongly developed national unions. The first precondition was, then, the extension and consolidation of one's own unions, which should be able to maintain themselves financially independent from their foreign brother organizations. A situation in which a strong union was frequently required to provide financial support for a weak brother union in another country was the surest killer of internationalism.[27]

The key points of Legien's reflections on the internationalism of trade unions can be summed up as follows. It was essential to possess exact information about the situation regarding foreign trade unions. This was the basis for the flourishing of international solidarity which, provided ones own national organization was not disadvantaged, could guarantee the success of the trade union struggle. In order to fulfil this task it would not only be necessary to set up central trade union bodies in each industrial nation but also to see that the trade union organizations were consolidated to the extent that they could actually carry out the tasks which their international affiliations might impose upon them.[28] And what is significant concerning Legien's observations is that he noted repeatedly that not all nations had yet reached this stage of development.

Clearly, until that was the case there could be no possibility of ambitious international action such as a general strike or a boycott. Of course, this reasoning has been reproached for being over-cautious, and merits the same kind of criticism which the French labour leader, Jean Jaurès levelled against Legien's party colleague, Karl Kautsky, in 1903. At that time Jaurès accused Kautsky, as chief ideologue of the international socialist movement, of regarding the socialist revolution as a child's clay money box which one must fill right up before it was opened:

One collected a million Socialist votes, then two, then three million. Ones heart pounded with expectation but it was still not enough. One ought to wait and collect more, four million, five, six million. That would be the decisive number. That would be the majority! Now one can open the money box and attempt to employ the socialist forces which it contained. But what misfortune if impatient or ambitious persons broke open the money box too soon.[29]

That the German free trade unions were filled with the same chary spirit has been sufficiently demonstrated. When they were faced with their most important decision, namely how to behave at the outbreak of war in 1914 they preferred, as Legien expressed it, to protect their own skin.[30] They were by no means plagued by a guilty conscience for having thereby committed class betrayal in view of the fact that their action in practice meant supporting the fatherland in the war. Indeed, the General Commission's decision to pursue a policy of civic truce vis à vis the imperial German government had prompted the more famous decision of the SPD parliamentary party of 3 August.[31] Far from being a *volte face*, it had been but the logical continuation of the General Commission's well–established priorities with regard to the international labour movement. Foremost among these was the maintenance of the viability of ones own national organization. And because the other national organizations were in general far weaker than the German, Legien and his colleagues saw no realistic prospect of success in undertaking a common international action such as would have been in accordance with the 'spirit of Basel' to try to stop the war.

The rapid sequence of events frustrated Legien's attempts to contact his foreign colleagues with a view to preparing some action against the war.[32] The strength of Prusso–German militarism and the weakness of trade union internationalism compelled the free trade unions to decide for the fatherland. And, of course, the decision was considerably eased by their analysis of the real causes of the war. It had arisen out of the contradictions of capitalism, whereby the triggering factor was the British policy to bring about the ultimate destruction of the growing industrial and commercial power of Germany.[33] An investigation of the wartime policy of the General Commission indicates the degree to which a sober assessment of national realities had triumphed over the sentiment of internationalism in the mind of the German trade union leaders.

CHAPTER NINE

In Defence of the Fatherland

Without exaggeration I may well say that our situation in the approximately twenty-five years since we have had a coordinated trade union movement in Germany has, with regard to previous times, changed little: enemies on all sides, slanderers on all sides . . . We are striving for the equality of the workers and we have in this area, as many a concluded struggle with the employers proves, made already a few advances. However, although our trade union movement has attained recognition in this area, it has not been possible to move those circles to guarantee equality who ought to have the greatest interest in recognizing it. The trade union movement is concerned that the working class does not completely degenerate, that it is intellectually and physically held aloft, truly not least in the interest of the general community whether it is called the parish, state or Reich . . . Our task remains, therefore, to wrest in unrelenting struggle against all our opponents the equality which is incomprehensively denied us.[1]

Of the 'unpatriotic socialists' of 1914, those of the German free trade unions were surely the most remarkable. At their last pre-war congress (Munich 22–27 June 1914) they had been girding their loins for a protracted confrontation with Wilhelminism as the issues debated on that occasion indicated. Paradoxically, however, when the Reich appeared to be encircled by an iron ring of powers bent on its elimination from the ranks of the great industrial and trading nations, a totally new note was struck by trade union stalwarts, though the phenomenon of worker patriotism was by no means limited to Germany. What is most significant in this instance is the conscious attempt by the trade union leadership to exploit the war to turn a so-called negative to a positive integration of the working class into the German state. In order to appreciate more fully the magnitude of this task it will be necessary first to note the real position of labour within the monarchical–military system as well as the immediate goals of the socialist unions as expressed in June 1914. We must then examine their assessment of the causes of the war and account for their response to it.

Franz Neumann, reflecting in 1932 on the progress of the trade union movement in Germany, observed four phases of evolution with respect to its relationship to the state. These were: the period of prohibition until 1890; the period of toleration up to the Great War; the period of recognition during the war leading to the period of incorporation into the state during the Weimar Republic.[2] On the eve of the war the toleration by the state of the trade unions was grudging in the extreme. As the quotation at the beginning of this chapter indicates, the trade unionists perceived themselves to be still in very much a defensive position vis à vis the state and the employers. The socialist labour leaders were especially embittered by the attitude of the state because, as is expressed again and again in their deliberations, they saw a healthy, efficient and educated working class as the true basis for the nation's greatness. For this reason the oppression that organized labour encountered was regarded by them as incomprehensible. And this oppression was as intense as it ever was in the fateful summer of 1914.

Pursuing their well-established strategy, the congress of that year focused on the central issues which constituted, in the trade union view, the major areas of contention with the Wilhelmine state. These were the long-standing issues of a neutral labour exchange, the protection of black-leg labour, the organization of foreign workers, the administration of the Reich law of association, the legal recognition of collective agreement, and social welfare legislation. So, as has been shown in Chapter Five, the struggle of the unions with the Wilhelmine state was essentially a struggle for full citizenship rights. It was, however, in the light of the self-understanding of the Wilhelmine power elite, an attempt to convert that elite to a more modern appreciation of the role of labour in a highly industrialized society and to register this in a correspondingly revised legal system. Again, it was a strategy conceived to transform the negative into a positive integration of the working class into the state. This strategy rested on the assumption of the long-suffering patience of the working masses and the belief that a rational state must in time recognize the need to accommodate the expanding and politically articulate force of organized labour.

However, as the recent research of such German scholars as Fritz Fischer, Imanuel Geiss and Dieter Groh (to name but a few) has clearly indicated, the so-called 'nation' or power elite had no intention of conceding to even the modest demands of liberal opinion let alone the more radically democratic ones of organized labour. Bismarckian paternalism in politics as well as the *Herr-im-Hause* attitude of industry not only persisted unabated in governing and industrial circles in 1914, but they were determined to stifle all expressions of democratic will, in particular that of social democracy. As Matthias Erzberger, spokesman of the Centre Party, stated in 1913, the chief domestic political task of the Reich was the elimination of the threat of social democracy.[3] So the idea that the latter movement could not be accommodated within the Reich was hardly an unspoken assumption: instead, it was a widely held attitude shared by most non-labour groups within the Reich. This explains the reluctance of the government to concede all the demands being made by the trade unions in the areas of social policy (especially the right of association) enumerated above.

Indeed, as the rekindled debate on German war aims has demonstrated, one of the key factors influencing the German decision to wage war against the Entente powers in 1914 was the so-called internal threat of social democracy. It was assumed in ruling circles that a war would not only aid in bridging the internal social divisions within the Reich but it would also strengthen the militaristic–monarchical system.[4] So, apart from the desire for expansion and annexations on the part of German imperialists and the associated concern of military leaders to break the power of the Entente to enable the Reich to breathe freely, there was the underlying determination to shore up the foundations of the Bismarckian–Wilhelmine constitution against the perceived attacks upon it by the forces of democracy. In a sense, this was a war-aim that was organically part of the overall programme of imperial German *Weltpolitik*—indeed one of the chief motivating forces of it.

Seen in this light, the actual effect of the war on the structure and character of German society is very dramatic indeed. The nation entered the conflict with the clear intention of damning the rising tide of democracy, but as will be shown, the majority of the forces of democracy in Germany determined to support the war in the expectation that it would bring them the democratic reforms for which they had so long and ardently campaigned. In this way, the dilemma posed by the decades of negative integration was to be solved by the war. Both polarized sections of German society hoped for positive integration of the other, but on their own terms. The nation expected the working class to be reconciled with the monarchy by abandoning allegiance to social democracy, while the latter, with the trade unions to the fore, imagined that their obvious indispensability to the nation would result in a series of modernizing democratic reforms.

If the aforementioned series of demands made at the 1914 trade union congress in Munich illustrate the extent of the polarization of the classes on the eve of the war, so also does the nature of the army's contingency plans to arrest known social democratic 'agitators' in order to prevent the possibility of revolution should a war break out. Under article 68 of the Reich Constitution which empowered the Kaiser to proclaim a state of war (*Kriegszustand*) if public security were threatened, the provisions of the 1851 Prussian Law of Siege were to apply. This virtually transferred all police powers to the commanding officers of the military districts into which the Reich was divided, and the officer corps was particularly well instructed in how to deal with internal disturbances.

In the immediate pre-war years, the army was clearly preparing itself for the possibility of social democratic inspired insurgency during elections, strikes and May Day celebrations.[5] In the event of a situation of war being declared, army authorities had directed that those persons who were expected to incite people to disturbances were to be arrested. The directives for such action were contained in regulations dating back to 1908 for the IV Army Corps. These were so exemplary that the Prussian war ministry recommended them in 1912 to be adopted by the remaining corps. The kinds of persons to be arrested included not only socialist agitators but also newspaper editors and even members of the Reichstag whose immunity from arrest would be intentionally disregarded. In addition, by 1911 over seventy newspapers and journals of which fifty were trade union organs had been listed for suppression. However, at the discretion of the local military commander other publications could be forbidden, and further, clubs or associations deemed hostile to the state were to be closed, if necessary by force. Meetings of any kind were supposed to be generally banned.

It must, though, be noted that the actual calling out of troops to suppress insurgents would only occur if the civilian authorities and police were judged unable to cope with the situation. All these contingency measures indicated that the gravest domestic political problem of the Reich was how to confront and eliminate the challenge to its order from social democracy. As Wilhelm Deist has observed, the concern among military authorities was due to their recognition of the fact that the army, as it was constituted, did not possess the means of coping with a political mass movement which had arisen out of the changing social and economic tendencies of the period. In other words, the Prusso–German military monarchy with its quasi-feudal social–political assumptions was experiencing great difficulty in adjusting to the social–political restructuring of Germany which was the inevitable concomitant of a modernizing industrial economy. This is evidenced by the fact that amended guidelines (25 July 1914) had been prepared for the contingency of a state of war. It is significant that these were introduced in the very days before the actual outbreak of hostilities.

The modified guidelines originated in the Prussian war ministry and evince an undeniably nervous concern lest a too rigorous application of the contingency measures might alienate large sections of the population.[7] Nevertheless, the determination of the military authorities to prevent any disturbances which might hinder the efficiency of the army at a time of national crisis was undiminished by these latest provisions. This is shown by the regulations which empowered the army authorities to abrogate sections of the Law of Association as passed in 1908. By invoking the Law of Siege, the army could effectively ban and dissolve all assemblies of citizens for the duration of the war that were deemed prejudicial to the conduct of the war.[8] This juxtaposition of cautious restraint beside a ruthless determination to stamp out deleterious (i.e. socialist) influence in the community bears witness to the dilemma confronting the Wilhelmine state. This stands out in high relief when it is considered that the majority of generals commanding officer corps as well as the bulk of the officer corps were totally convinced of the necessity for decisive and energetic action against the internal enemy in the event of a state of war being declared. There was a complete absence of any will to find a political solution to this situation; military expediency alone dominated the mind of the individual officer. And this inflexibility was born of a long tradition of professional consciousness, the expression of which was contained in the nature of the army instructions on how to deal with the social democratic threat. Indeed, the Prusso–German constitutional provision for proclaiming a state of war and siege had become for the army a weapon in the domestic political struggle.[9] In short, as far as the consciousness of the officer class was concerned, a state of war was to be the opportunity to bring about a reckoning with those elements irreconcilable with Wilhelminism.

As events subsequently illustrated, the fears of the nation which the contingency plans of the army clearly expressed, were without foundation. The trade unions which would have been the major democratic instruments of opposition to war were far from contemplating any protest strike action as the previous chapter has shown. Indeed, in retrospect, it could be observed that they had spent many years adroitly side-stepping the issue. Yet, in the year immediately before the war, as research has shown, the trade union leadership had to exert its great strength in order to discourage the SPD executive from any suggestion of committing

German social democracy to a general strike, should there be an outbreak of war.[10] The party leadership had for some time been clear that if the Reich was determined on war there was very little which the working class could do to prevent it. August Bebel, as party chairman until his death in 1913, had no illusions as to the ability of anti-imperialist forces in Germany effectively to restrain the Wilhelmine state from its expansionist intent. Any resistance inspired by Social Democrats would have been, so Bebel believed, ruthlessly put down by Hohenzollern militarism.[11] This view seems to have been shared by Bebel's successors because they, too, considered a general strike in the event of German mobilization to be impractical. It was impossible for them to commit the SPD to the famous Hardie–Vaillant amendment of the 1910 International Congress in Copenhagen which demanded such action. Since this amendment had not been adopted but simply passed on to the International Socialist Bureau for further discussion, it had been treated evasively by the German delegation. Ironically, it was to have been included under the general theme of imperialism on the agenda of the congress of the International planned for Vienna at the end of August 1914. But even if the war had not intervened to frustrate international socialism's efforts towards enforcing world peace, the evidence is that the Germans would have continued to adopt a non-committal stance on the general strike issue.[12]

The reasons for this evasiveness on the part of German social democracy are to be found to a large extent in the trade union attitude. The latter was made clear in no uncertain terms at the end of 1913 when the General Commission met together with the SPD executive to discuss the issue. Gustav Bauer, as Deputy Chairman of the General Commission, had openly expressed what Bebel had apparently secretly feared, namely that the Social Democrats could do nothing to prevent a war. This would especially be so if the proletariat were swept along in a wave of patriotic fervour. Such a situation was the inevitable result of the capitalist system which would always wage war when it suited its interests and would always be able to whip up the support of the masses by patriotic slogans to do so.

By arguing in this way, Bauer evidently saw war as the inescapable fate of states under capitalism. As far as the proletariat were concerned, it was up to them in their own country to determine whether a war would be of advantage to them, and to act accordingly. This was because, as Bauer observed, economic blocs would be fighting each other, and as long as the proletariat lived in closed economic blocs, they had a vested interest in seeing their own flourish. It would be quite erroneous to imagine that the proletariat could regard the struggle between two economic blocks as concerning only the rival capitalists of those blocs.[13] The pointed implication was that any discussion of staging a general strike to prevent an outbreak of war would be totally unrealistic. At a subsequent meeting of the General Commission and the SPD executive, (11 December 1913) convened especially to discuss the question of propaganda for the so-called mass strike, Legien took the opportunity to instruct the SPD once again that it was not in the interests of the German trade unions. He made it unmistakably clear that the SPD should not commit itself to any resolution made by the International whereby it stage a general strike in order to prevent war breaking out. Indeed, the General Commission and the unions, in Legien's view, ought to explore the possibility of making a front against the general strike propaganda coming from other countries. This would, of course, presume that the SPD executive took a stand against those vocal German advocates of the general strike.

Legien sought to strengthen his position asserting that the propaganda for general strike would deter people from joining the trade unions as it had already done in France. This robbed the unions of power for the event when it became necessary to call such a strike. Legien adduced again the familiar argument for steady organization and disciplined membership, as the surest means of assailing what he called the capitalist–feudal–clerical citadels. Those social democratic theorists who saw little value in the trade union movement had proved how remote they were from understanding the mentality of the masses. The theorists aroused among them no enthusiasm for becoming organized when they denigrated the achievements of the trade unions. And further, argued Legien, the demand of the general strike theorists that the problem be openly discussed at party and union congresses was naïve because it would reveal to the opposition the tactics of social democracy. The wisest course was to cease all discussion of general strike and only to employ drastic action to defend existing rights if and when they were threatened. Legien argued that it was clearly necessary to organize with that unpredictable time in mind, rather than to distract the masses from the indispensable everyday tasks by encouraging 'general strike illusions'. Indeed, all anarchistic propaganda that damaged organizational work should be condemned as anti-revolutionary. Its method of fighting played into the hands of reactionary forces and would result in the proletariat being clubbed down and their painstakingly constructed organizations destroyed. As Legien proclaimed:

Without the trade unions which have so often been put down by the advocates of exclusively political action (*Nurpolitiker*) as inferior, the illusory plan of the general strike propagandists cannot possibly be carried out. If the trade union leaders declare themselves against this tactic, then it cannot be started, even if the campaign against the trade union bureaucrats brings further successes. The mass of trade union members will thank their representatives if they energetically oppose the irresponsible planners.[14]

Legien's indignation with his critics on the left wing of the SPD was, of course, misplaced. The party leaders themselves had no intention, as has been seen, of calling a general strike. Nevertheless, they had felt compelled to give the impression to foreign Socialists that they were earnestly contemplating it, and also to keep the German government guessing over what the SPD would do in the event of a mobilization or actual war.[15] However, as Legien explained, even the discussion of the possibility of general strike was counterproductive for the trade union movement. At any event the SPD leadership had thought it wisest to take cognizance of the General Commission's attitude without formal comment. This in effect meant recognizing the Mannheim Agreement and accepting the *de facto* veto of the trade unions.[16]

As was seen in the previous chapter, it is not possible to reconstruct with complete accuracy the behaviour of the trade union leadership in July–August 1914. Writers such as Susanne Miller have gone so far as to assert that the attitude of the trade unions to the international crisis and the impending war had virtually pre-empted any decision by the SPD executive to adopt a policy of opposition or protest with regard to the actions of the Reich government.[17] This assumed that the party leaders might have acted differently in that situation had they not been dependent upon the unequivocal support of the unions for an effective strike action. The evidence is rather, as Groh has shown, that the SPD leaders, despite genuine reservations in certain cases, had agreed that in view of the wave of patriotism which engulfed the masses in all nations it would have been self-destructive to offer resistance to the government's policy of war. This is because a unilateral strike action in Germany would have rendered the country vulnerable to attack (particularly from the feared and hated Russians); and in addition, it would have provided the government with the longed-for pretext to destroy social democratic organization. In short, the SPD leadership had been sobered by the knowledge of its own weakness in the face of the brutal realities of the situation into making an endorsement of their militaristic government's policies. In this they were assisted because of the successful government tactic of depicting Russia as the aggressor. The obligation of the SPD to national defence had never been challenged in socialist ranks. Any reservations within the party about supporting the Hohenzollern state in a war were then dispelled by Russia's apparent aggression.[18]

In order to gain clarity, however, regarding the thesis that the famous SPD vote for war credits in the Reichstag on 4 August 1914 had been effectively forced by a prior trade union commitment to national defence, it will be necessary to examine the trade union assessment of the July–August crisis. Legien himself is on record as having registered great fear on 3 July 1914 that the assassination of Archduke Ferdinand of Austria at Sarajevo on 28 June would make a world conflagration unavoidable. He attributed this to irresponsible war-mongers within the Habsburg Empire.[19] The same assessment is evident in the leading article of the *Correspondenzblatt* on 1 August, by which time the Austrian war against Serbia must have appeared as incontrovertible proof of the former's aggression. In addressing itself to the prospect of war, the trade union organ warned that it would not only bring great suffering and sacrifice for the working class in terms of loss of life but it would lay waste the economy and produce mass unemployment in all industries with the exception of armaments. It would cut off foreign trade, cause food shortages and price rises. Such a situation must arise if Germany was fighting on three fronts and isolated from foreign trade. On top of this would come the gigantic cost of the war in maintaining the army and navy. Who was to bear it all? It would fall heaviest upon the working class. The author then expressed his sorrow for the fools who allowed themselves to be carried away by the outpourings of nationalist zealots. Among the workers there would be no place for this because they would have 'to drain the cup of suffering to the dregs.'[20] With this reproach to the chauvinists there followed a remarkably accurate analysis of the crisis. It was understood that Germany and Austria needed to maintain close contact given the alignment of powers. However, the *Correspondenzblatt* emphatically rejected the idea that Germany be harnessed in the service of promoting Austrian imperialism in the Balkans.

The assassination was, understandably, condemned, and the desire of the Austrian government to punish the offenders was recognized. But the Austrian haste over the question of the ultimatum was considered unjustified. The accused needed more than 48 hours to examine the charge, and furthermore the Austrian government bore a measure of guilt for stirring up the greater Serbian agitation. The economic bullying of Serbia by Austria had had to stir up the former's nationalistic passions. Indeed, in the entire Balkan conflict Austria had sought territorial expansion, and the assassination was being used as a convenient pretext to accomplish this. This situation compelled the German working class to demand that the Reich government restrain the Austrian ally to avoid an escalation of the crisis, in fact to exert pressure on Austria to end the war just begun with Serbia.[21]

The belief that the Reich could have exerted a restraining influence upon Austria–Hungary in the crisis was, in the light of recent research, extraordinarily accurate. However, once German involvement became a foregone conclusion there is no evidence that the union leadership wished to criticize the government for mismanagement of the crisis. This indicates that the government's tactic of making Russia appear the aggressor had worked particularly well with regard to the social democratic camp. Of course, this was the domestic–political object of the manoeuvre: part of Chancellor Bethmann Hollweg's calculation in the crisis had been to win over the Social Democrats to the concept of a war of national defence in order to obviate any danger of revolution on the home front which a war of aggression could have provoked. Because of this, it is less than just to accuse the German trade unions of blatant opportunism. Legien was at the time apparently convinced that the trade union leaders of the other, then enemy, countries would understand the difficult position of the Germans.[22] Since the crisis had obviously been created by the Austrians and brought to the point of no return by the Russians, the class duty of the German unions was to do everything in their power to alleviate the future suffering of the German working people.

As indicated in the previous chapter, the General Commission had met in Berlin on 31 July to deliberate what was to be done in the face of the 'situation of threatening war' that had just been proclaimed. It is debatable whether, as Legien asserted after the war, the purpose of this meeting was merely to decide what to do with trade union assets in case of their possible confiscation by the government rather than to offer the government a truce in exchange for their continued freedom. Certainly at some point between 31 July and 2 August 1914 the union leadership had come to an arrangement with the Ministry of the Interior, which resulted in the assurance that they would not be molested if the unions made no difficulties for the government.[23] Legien appears to have taken the initiative in this matter since he reported to the affiliated trade union chairmen on 2 August that he had made an offer of help to the Ministry of the Interior to assist in bringing in the harvest. He mentioned also that future negotiations with the ministry were planned in order to set up *ad hoc* committees to oversee work envisaged as a result of the war situation. The ministry had given assurances that the justified wishes of the workers involved regarding conditions would be considered.[24] With this, the affiliated union chiefs made an appeal to the rank and file urging them to remain loyal and to maintain their organizational activity. The hardships of the coming war were then graphically depicted, the clear implication being that these could be to some extent mitigated if the unions remained viable. It was also indicated that although the unions would inevitably be weakened, no attempt was expected to reduce wages or otherwise to exploit the working class.[25]

This proclamation had obviously been made as a result of some compromise with the government whereby the unions had clearly promised to break off all strikes in return for a guarantee for no lock-outs. Whether Legien's overtures had contained the proposal that was to commit the unions to the so-called *Burgfrieden* or civic truce cannot be established from the remnant of trade union records. But the meeting of 2 August had certainly taken the view that with the unemployment that must result from war, all current strikes for higher wages had become pointless and that, therefore, it would be wisest to stop them.[26]

The significance of Legien's initiative with the Ministry of the Interior was far-ranging. He had secured for the unions unexpected advantages. Far from being banned or suppressed—a contingency foreseen under the Prussian Law of Siege—the unions had manoeuvred themselves into the position of negotiating partners with the very ministry which had formerly been their sworn enemy. Thereby they had secured a guarantee that their assets were to remain inviolate and they were no longer in danger of dissolution provided that no provocation of the government occurred. Legien seems to have been at some pains to keep his part of the agreement. The effect of his action in placing the unions virtually at the disposal of the state already on 2 August certainly pre-empted any possibility of the SPD, when the parliamentary party met on the next day, from proposing any action involving union opposition to war.

What is interesting here is that the General Commission apparently thought it unnecessary to consult formally with the SPD executive before reaching its compromise with the government, a step which the Mannheim Agreement would clearly have required. As Susanne Miller reports, the decisions of the trade union leaders determined the course on social democratic policy during the war at a time when the key party bodies had not yet decided on their own course.[27] With the resolution on 2 August to cease all strike action, the civic truce policy (*Burgfriedenspolitik*) had been effectively established. The question as to why no prior consultation with the SPD executive had taken place before Legien approached the Ministry of the Interior is a significant one. And while it cannot be answered with complete certainty, the possibility cannot be excluded that Legien had fully intended to block any chance of the party deciding to adopt the more problematic course of resistance. His subsequent dogged defence of the *Burgfrieden* would indicate that he had perceived right from the beginning of the crisis the far-ranging significance of preserving the union organizations intact. Even at the cost of violating the spirit of the International, Legien and his associates could see nothing to be gained for the working class by an overt challenge to the Wilhelmine state in August 1914.

The great debate whether the German unions in August 1914 perpetrated a selfish betrayal of the spirit of the International and thus missed the historic opportunity, at least of averting what became the self-immolation of the European nations, is a sterile exercise. The past is full of examples of censorious judgments against those individuals and groups who failed to recognize their 'historic role'. In this instance, the charge of failure emanates from Marxist–Leninist inspired critics who demand that the trade union leaders of August 1914 should have had a greater vision of their task and a deeper awareness of their responsibility to humanity as a whole. This, however, is equivalent to requiring men to make sacrifices for goals they could not possibly have perceived. In their experience and world of ideas there was nothing to indicate that any self-sacrifice in the name of peace would have effected any appreciable change. Militarism, international capitalism and the chauvinism of the European masses were forces of overwhelming dimensions. These would have to be confronted by less direct means.

The problem of worker patriotism in Wilhelmine Germany is

one which requires careful analysis. While the workers felt themselves to be part of the nation, they were by no means uniformly
regarded as such even by liberal German opinion. It is, therefore,
not surprising that the union leaders wished to take advantage of
the wartime situation to acquire membership in the nation and by
so doing to modify its essentially militaristic–authoritarian
character. In view of this it is most instructive at this point to
examine the official trade union contribution to the 'ideas of
1914' which gained eloquent expression in the early months of
the Great War. This is all the more important since the German
intellectuals who were the chief spokesmen of the nation had
regarded the voting of war credits by the SPD in the Reichstag on
4 August 1914 as a miracle which fulfilled the most urgent
domestic political need of the Reich, namely the integration of
the working class into the nation. By this, of course, they assumed
that the social democratic electorate had at last given up their
opposition to the Prusso–German military state and were cheerfully submitting to it.[28] This was the naïve expression of wish
fulfilment as an analysis of the first lengthy trade union version of
the 'ideas of 1914' clearly shows. The latter were expressed in a
five-part article series in the *Correspondenzblatt* during September–October 1914, entitled *Der Krieg und die socialen Pflich-
ten* (the war and social obligations). It constitutes a major statement of proletarian patriotism in Imperial Germany.[29]

The author of the articles began by repudiating the notion that
warfare was always socially destructive, that it signified the dissolution of the existing order. On the contrary, the experience of
those weeks following outbreak of war showed that war had a
socially unifying rather than fragmenting effect. The challenge of
war had unleashed social forces whose existence no one had
previously suspected. They had produced a unified national
whole which was inspired by the same will to self-preservation and to final victory. All sections of the community had
regarded the war as a national duty arising out of the recognition that the contest of arms had become unavoidable. No
able-bodied man could withhold his contribution to national
defence without sinning against the entire community.

The author went on to contrast the class and economic war of peace time—a situation of conflict of all against all—with the social unity now engendered by the challenge of the war. This unity demanded unconditional dedication to the struggling fatherland, the highest solidarity of all countrymen (*Volksgenossen*) and the selfless support of everything that strengthened the will to resistance and self-preservation. The pressing of sectional interests was stigmatized as a crime against the nation and therefore unpatriotic.

This idea led the trade union writer to an interesting assertion. A nation struggling for its existence became highly sensitive to anything that weakened its fighting capacity. For this reason a nation at war had not only to develop a socialist ethic but must *think* and *act* socialistically—especially a nation that had made its very existence rest on the universal obligation of military service. The concept of *thinking* socialistically involved an awareness that it was not the private gain and advantage of the individual which guarantee victory but rather the sacrifice of the individual to the common weal of the nation. To *act* socialistically meant to translate into deeds the consciousness of fulfilling one's social duty so that all excrescences of egoism damaging to the common good would be suppressed: in short, to organize the awareness of the fulfilment of social duty. 'Organization is the soul of all national defence,' proclaimed the writer. Indeed, in war the victory went to the nation that was best organized. And particularly in this war, the superiority of German organization was manifesting itself in all branches of the art of war and in all theatres of the war. As proof of this, the efficiency of the massive organization needed to supply the army in the field was cited. Germany was the land of the highest developed organization in all spheres of life. Organization meant an intensification of social forces by bringing about the subjugation of personal to the common interest and of the individual to the common will.

This stream of thought culminated in the assertion that a well-organized nation was always ready for a war if it came, and thus stronger than a nation without such organization. An important factor in the German preparedness was the strong organizations of the workers. They had disciplined millions to solidarity and self-sacrifice and thereby trained them to place the common good above their own advantage.

It was with undisguised pride that the writer cited the words of the Münster professor, Johann Plenge, who had singled out the behaviour of the trade unions at the outbreak of war for special praise. The professor had told his students that whoever could achieve so much on their own initiative and had so disciplined themselves in the trade unions as the German workers had done, were truly members of the nation (*Volksgenossen*). Their patriotic behaviour had shown that they had become qualified to cooperate with the bourgeoisie in the national task imposed by the war and in the reconstruction afterwards. There could only be a feeling of happy satisfaction at the attitude of the workers, said Plenge. He concluded: 'May the war weld the nation, that is now torn by great divisions, permanently together to the common task.'[30]

Such a recognition of the indispensability of trade unions by a spokesman of the academic elite found great resonance among patriotic labour leaders who had been rather accustomed to decades of suspicion and abuse from such quarters. Certainly the wave of patriotic enthusiasm, of which the Kaiser's famous speech about the war bringing the end of party wrangling in Germany was symptomatic, generated in these men the belief that they had been finally accepted by the nation.[31] The central fact brought out by the war situation was the importance of labour organizations for the economy. With a public declaration of their readiness to subordinate their sectional interests to the common welfare, the unions had begun to fulfil what they were pleased to call their social duty. They now expected capital to do likewise:

The inner struggles between competitors, between producers and consumers, between secondary and primary industry, between employers and employees ought to be eliminated wherever possible; in place of the economic superiority [of capital] and its ruthless exploitation there should be the recognition of the principles of justice and of the protection of the weak, above all of the common welfare, and the community should move against those who do not submit to these laws of the common welfare.[32]

Such an expression of worker solidarity with the nation cannot, however, be seen merely as an emotional outburst of patriotism. The perceptive trade unionist sought to arouse the social conscience of the rich and powerful to admit the reasonableness of social, political and economic reform, since each group within the community was interdependent. This recognition ought to be followed up by practical measures. And these were enumerated by the *Correspondenzblatt*: All food supply questions ought to be treated from now on as national questions in order that the population might be adequately fed. For this reason primary industry in all its aspects needed a proper labour force, and in this regard the outmoded master and servant act ought to be reformed to allow agricultural labourers to be organized. Indeed, the modernization of this law had become a question of national defence. It was a time when agriculture ought to be making sacrifices for the national welfare particularly in view of the fact that it was winning rich profits as a result of its monopoly position. Clearly, in that sector of the economy, better treatment of labour was essential to ensure the uninterrupted supply of food-stuffs.

Secondly, the question of labour supply itself needed to be coordinated by the Reich central labour exchange, in which the labour exchanges of both management and unions would be required to cooperate for a more efficient organization of the labour market.[33] Further, those who controlled the economic structure had a giant responsibility since they disposed over the means of the economic existence of the entire nation. The mass of citizens was dependent upon the will of the entrepreneurs. For this reason the latter ought to subordinate themselves to the needs of the community to avoid unemployment, if necessary by introducing half-day shifts and the eight-hour day. The *Correspondenzblatt* warned that any continuation of anti-social exploitative practices by the employers would only advantage the enemy, so that the strictest maintenance of the civic peace was essential to the war effort.

Thirdly, therefore, current wage agreements ought to be continued and new ones reached in those industries where they did not yet exist. So the unions hoped to use the war to have collective agreements recognized by law. The advantage of this would be a concentration of the work force in urgent production rather than a wasting of energy in industrial conflict. Indeed, collective agreements thus institutionalized would protect the cultural resources (*Kulturgut*) of the nation. Thus to achieve this was a social duty, and only then would the repeated attempts of the employers unilaterally to break their agreements be countered.

Fourthly and finally, the *Correspondenzblatt* demanded an adequate unemployment insurance system. The unions, who had husbanded resources over the years, had used their accumulated strike funds after the outbreak of war to alleviate both unemployment of members and to contribute to the support of families whose bread-winner had been called to military service. It was noted that the employers had not used their strike insurance funds for some social good in view of the prevailing public peace. This would really have been an outward and visible sign of national harmony.[34]

The crucial social obligation was, however, the institutionalization of unemployment insurance by the Reich. It was inadequate to leave this responsibility to the municipalities who received occasional subsidies from the states. None of this local initiative made much impression on the overall situation. Most large cities did not provide unemployment benefits. The trade unions had had their own unemployment insurance schemes for decades but had used up their entire assets of almost eighty-eight million marks to assist those suddenly unemployed as a result of firms closing down because of the war.[35] This placing of resources at the disposal of needy members at that time was looked upon as a social obligation. Indeed, the Reich ought to regulate the entire question of unemployment benefits by requiring the municipal authorities to work hand in hand with the unions. However, the former had always tried to ignore the unions to the disadvantage of their members.[36]

To regulate all these questions, then, was the great social obligation imposed by the war upon all sections of the community for the sake of overcoming internal friction. These were eminently practical proposals, and must be understood as the trade union contribution to the 'ideas of 1914'. It is fairly clear, though, that even these modest demands for reform so rationally justified as they were, failed to make much impression upon the spokesmen of the nation. Admittedly, it was observed by leading intellectuals that the apparent confession of faith in the nation by Social Democrats at that time had signified the solution of the greatest domestic political problem of the Reich, namely the overcoming of the dangerous inner polarization. But, while this was welcomed, it was not at first accompanied by appeals to the state to meet the justified social–political demands of the Social Democrats and trade unionists.[37] This was in spite of the fact that the trade union appraisal of the war, as indicated earlier, now coincided with that of most patriotic Germans: it was now agreed by most that the war was the result of 'coldly calculating England's' determination to destroy Germany's industrial capacity and commercial rivalry.[38]

By proclaiming solidarity with the nation in this way it was expected that both the government and the employers would revise their hostility towards the unions and concede to their long-standing demands. The next chapter focuses on the convergence of the goals of organized labour with those of the Wilhelmine state, and the legislative expression of that convergence.

CHAPTER TEN
The Crucible of War

The effect of the Great War on the German social democracy has been analysed by writers of various ideological persuasions. This is understandable because, besides the communist historians who wish to account for the splits in the party, both the moderate as well as more radical Social Democrats are interested in it for their own reasons. In addition, the fate of the SPD from 1914–1918 has attracted a number of liberal writers both of German and non-German origin.[1] Naturally, these have not ignored the unions but, apart from East German and a few West German researchers there has been no attempt to trace through the aims of the German trade union leadership in this period. Most have established that all the leaders were concerned with was the strict adherence to the *Burgfrieden* or public peace, the Policy of 4 August, in exchange for legislative concessions. Little interest has been shown in examining their policies more deeply or in seeing what resulted from them. The union leaders were at worst social chauvinists, or at best, adroit pragmatists. It would appear that neither of these extremes does justice to the self-perception of the union leadership. If there had been occasionally extravagant outbursts of proletarian chauvinism they were hardly peculiar to the Germans.[2]

The overriding factor which cannot be ignored is that the union leadership remained convinced of the ability of the Prusso–German military state to wage the war successfully. In which case the old adversary, namely the industrial–military power elite, would certainly emerge strengthened from the conflict. Any head-on challenge by organized labour to that elite would thus be even more futile than it had been in the past. This realization, then, dictated a continuation of established strategy; only the situation allowed a variation of tactics. Whereas prior to 1914 the state regarded organized labour as an element to be contained, if not eliminated, from the body politic, with the outbreak of war the unions, in particular, became immediately useful to the state. It was this usefulness that the union leaders intended to exploit in order to extract those long-demanded concessions which the state had so grudgingly denied them. These legislative changes effected during the war are of central significance since they foreshadow certain revolutionary innovations of the Weimar Constitution immediately after the war; and so, in turn, point up the continuity of politics from wartime through the revolution. In short, the trade union tactics which had always aimed at improving the basic rights of workers were able in the wartime situation to secure amendments to the law. They represented *de facto* changes in the nature of the Wilhelmine Constitution, and these were then carried over into the republic, 1919 to 1933.

That the unions understood the war as being one of national self-defence in which the Reich was threatened with extinction as an industrial power determined that the leadership would uphold the public peace. The aim was that the nation might more efficiently resist these threats. But in addition, the union leaders were convinced that by upholding the public peace the government could be induced to alter legislation in favour of organized labour. Cooperation held out more hope than revolutionary rhetoric. For this reason, Legien, in particular, vigorously opposed all efforts on the part of some socialist deputies (such as Karl Liebknecht) to break the public peace by opposing the war effort in the Reichstag or by advocating wild strikes. Consequently, the union leadership began to defend the Policy of 4 August as one of vital concern to the trade union movement.

Very early in 1915 Legien had occasion to warn sections of the SPD to maintain the Policy of 4 August. He saw party solidarity on this basis as the indispensable precondition for wresting favourable concessions from the state. The radical party minority around Liebknecht was becoming ever more disillusioned with the patriotic mass of the labour movement and was threatening to destroy its unity.[3] Against these manoeuvres, Legien felt himself especially called to struggle. He had already on 2 December 1914, when Liebknecht alone in the SPD Reichstag *Fraktion* voted against the war credits, unsuccesssfully moved to have the rebel expelled from the party.[4] Legien's particularly strenuous insistence on party solidarity could only have been made from a position of moral and real strength as the unchallenged leader of the industrial wing of the labour movement in Germany. Officially, the unions were supposed to be neutral in party affairs, but as the Mannheim Agreement of 1906 had laid down, although the two wings were separate with their different tasks, they were obliged to consult each other on issues of mutual concern. This was quite apart from the fact that 46 of the 110 SPD deputies were either incidentally union officials or in some manner affiliated with unions.[5] On the issue of party solidarity over the *Burgfrieden*, Legien believed he had a definite obligation to insist on the strictest discipline of the parliamentary party. His reasoning was, that despite the fiction of union neutrality, the SPD was in practice the parliamentary representative of the trade union cause, and a threat to party unity was simultaneously a threat to the prospects of realizing those union goals which needed legislative sanction.

On 27 January 1915, Legien publicly informed the chairmen of the affiliated unions of the divisions within the SPD *Fraktion*, and at the same time repudiated charges that he had crippled and destroyed the Second International.[6] His attitude was based on the view that the unions could not stand aside to see party disunity damage the cause of the entire movement. The unions had set great store on the party being able to play an active role on their behalf in the Reichstag. If, however, the party failed to give unequivocal support to the war effort, the *Burgfrieden* would be broken and union hopes of keeping both government and industry in a conciliatory mood would be dashed. Legien was, of course, sufficiently astute not to claim an express right to make decisions over internal party matters but he stated that divisions in the SPD were a threat to the unions, and a disunited party could hardly represent the unions in parliament. And in view of the past record of independent union action and their proven capacity to command the allegiance of millions of workers, Legien's statements amounted to a thinly disguised attempt to make the SPD leadership amenable to the policies of the General Commission. It was, in fact, an invocation of the Mannheim Agreement. To prevent further deterioration in party discipline, Legien urged his union officials to play a more active part in SPD affairs; an indirect admonition to the party not to tolerate policies unacceptable to the unions or listen to the disrupting ideas of anarchists within party ranks.

Legien's unswerving conviction that socialism could be realized in Germany by the gradual winning of concessions from the Wilhelmine state and by cooperation with it was shared by the majority of the SPD. The minority who came to see the war as one of imperialist aggression on the part of Germany, and who refused to believe in the possibility of harmony between capital and labour, followed their conscience and pursued a separate line which led ultimately to the founding of the Independent Social Democratic Party (USPD).[7] Legien and his union policy of endorsing so-called 'war socialism' (*Kriegssozialismus*) had in no small measure contributed to forcing this fateful split.[8] In order to keep the SPD on its declared *Burgfrieden* policy, Legien announced in July 1915 when the intra-party debate was raging, that the unions would continue their 'positive work' (i.e. cooperation with the state). They would not be deterred by those who wanted to destroy the party. The maintenance of unity was a far more urgent necessity than unproductive and acrimonious disputes over theories of socialism.[9]

Legien's tactics and speeches reveal at every point his deep-seated mistrust for those party radicals whom he referred to as *Phrasendrechsler* (turners of phrases). German union leaders of Legien's stamp had little time for the party *Literaten* who had never really overcome either Lassalle's version of the iron law of wages or Marx's doctrine that union action alone could not prevent the immiseration of the proletariat. Nevertheless, Legien considered himself a true socialist and revolutionary, but he was convinced that the only effective and practical revolutionary activity consisted in expanding trade union organization. By concentrating all efforts to this end, the day would come when through sheer weight of numbers, both the state and industry would be forced into meeting the unions' demands. The war had produced a situation in which the indispensability of the union movement was being demonstrated every day, and the increasing extension of state control over the economy was for Legien the veritable seed-bed of socialism. Under these conditions the expansion of union influence appeared to him to be the basic prerequisite for the long-term realization of socialist goals once peace returned.[10]

These views were endorsed by the chairmen of the affiliated unions from the beginning of the dispute with the SPD radicals.[11] The most unequivocal expression of their attitude came in April 1916. The General Commission announced:

The Policy of 4 August is the precondition for the future of the trade unions, for the realization of their great goals and ideals because it is not from outside that liberation from the economic wages yoke will come; rather we must gain the strength to liberate ourselves. The nation which abandons self-preservation in the face of Tsardom and its allies has lost its decisive influence in the future of socialism.[12]

The patriotically infused determination to uphold the *Burg-frieden* on the part of the unions was not lost on such notable bourgeois observers as the economist, Gustav Schmoller who, like Werner Sombart, appreciated the essentially anti-revolutionary character of German social democracy. In reflecting on the popular SPD attitude to the war, Schmoller drew attention to the Socialists' view of themselves as the former vagabonds without a fatherland emerging as the saviours of the nation in its hour of peril. Schmoller showed keen interest in such statements which, he noted, suffered from the illusion that proclamations of socialist loyalty would eventually make socialism nationally acceptable. He warned, Socialists who believed in this would be disappointed. However, Schmoller did predict that socialist support for the war would indeed contribute to a greater cohesiveness between the classes. He even looked forward to an age of social reconciliation and honest cooperation between workers and the government which would result from the national unity engendered by the war situation. But, added Schmoller, before that could be achieved, the 'revolutionism' which had been a factor of social democracy since its beginning would have to be eliminated. This would result if the trade union wing wrested the primacy over the revolutionary–socialist element.[13]

Schmoller observed that since the Marxist ideology had gradually become the official SPD doctrine in Germany, its leaders had adopted at least a revolutionary rhetoric which gave the party its anti-patriotic reputation. If one examined the movement closely, however, it would be seen that the trade union wing had steadily acquired sufficient strength effectively to transform the character of the party. The fact that from 1890 onwards, the unions had succeeded in setting up their own centralized bureaucracy independently from the party, indicated that there would be internal tensions to overcome. These arose from the fact that the unions were pursuing practical day-to-day aims whereas the party concentrated on a utopian *Zukunftspolitik* and tried to assert its tutelage over the unions. This could hardly work in practice since the unions had a larger and wealthier organization which tended to follow the laws of *laissez-faire* economics rather than heeded the nebulous ideology of Marxian socialism.[14]

Schmoller was, of course, right when he noted in 1915 that the critical factor in the internal affairs of social democracy was the relationship between the party and the unions. This he characterized as a marriage between an impractical dreamer always waiting for the new era to dawn, and a frugal, sensible woman who steadily advanced the welfare of the household, accumulated property and preached common sense to her husband. As in most marriages, whatever was achieved was attributable to the female partner. It was, then, due to the extensive bureaucratic organization of the unions that they were not only able to survive against the hostility of the employers and the government, but could force both into making concessions. It was no wonder that the unions wished to maintain their position.

From this, Schmoller deduced, as did a number of other

bourgeois observers, that the Marxist concept of absolute class struggle had virtually been overcome within German social democracy. The future relationship between the state and labour should be one of compromise in which the justified demands of the unions were granted.[15]

Compelling evidence that these ideas were relatively widespread in the more liberal academic circles is to be found in the publication in August 1915 of a book of essays edited by Carl Legien and Friedrich Thimme, the librarian of the Prussian Upper House. The book, *Die Arbeiterschaft im neuen Deutschland*, contained ten essays by right-wing Social Democrats (mostly with trade union backgrounds) and ten by well-known academics. The thrust of the book was a clear appeal to Germany's rulers on one hand to recognize the need to integrate the working class into the nation by legalizing their organizations and liberalizing the constitution, while on the other hand it was an appeal to socialists to recognize the monarchy and abandon the doctrinaire class struggle.

That Legien emerged as co-editor in this enterprise is not surprising. His long career at the head of the unions had not gone unnoticed by the liberally minded Thimme whose chief concern was to overcome the polarization within German society. The war seemed to present a unique opportunity to promote this cause. However, what appeared to be good sense to pro-trade union socialists and bourgeois intellectuals was severely criticized by doctrinaire party radicals who saw in the attempt a betrayal of revolutionary goals. It was also rejected by nationally minded conservatives who demanded nothing less than complete acceptance by the working class of the existing constitutional order. This long and often bitter criticism did not, though, weaken Legien's resolve to continue on his course of cooperation with the state.[16]

In the Reichstag, Legien was outspoken in proclaiming the value of the union movement to the fatherland. Proudly he maintained that its effects over the decades had strengthened the people's capacity to fight the war on the homefront. The war has shown what healthy and good forces were present in the less well-off sections of the nation. A wise government should not only take advantage of these forces in the hour of danger, but seek to release them for the permanent benefit of the country.[17] In May 1916 Legien claimed in the Reichstag that the Chancellor had held up the prospect of some concessions to the unions. He reported that Bethmann had told him that the unions had developed to their present state much against the will of both the employers and the government. However, the Chancellor had said he had come to appreciate their value because they had assisted wide sections of the people to withstand the repercussions of the war. And Legien asserted that by infusing people with a socialist spirit, the unions had done a great deal in helping the people through a difficult period. It was not to be considered a foregone conclusion, he remarked, that the unions and the political labour movement should have placed themselves in the service of the fatherland. The government and the bourgeoisie had, after all, done all in their power by chicanery and oppression to crush any patriotic feelings in the working class. But if in spite of this the Social Democrats had been prepared to cooperate, then they deserved the recognition of the state.[18]

The General Commission had not been slow to press its claims. Already at a meeting with the Chancellor on 3 August 1915 a series of concessions were promised which foresaw the removal of certain legal disabilities from the trade unions.[19] The immediate result of this had led to a modification of the Law of Association (*Reichsvereinsgesetz*) whereby the unions were no longer to be considered political associations.[20] Other concessions such as the legal recognition of wage agreements were to follow. Nevertheless, the dramatic advance came with a piece of wartime legislation. The passing of the national Auxiliary War Service Bill at the end of 1916 demonstrated more than anything previously to what extent the unions had become indispensable to the nation. On 8 November 1916, the Ministry of the Interior called the General Commission to a meeting, the purpose of which was to explore means for the more efficient use of the labour force in the war effort. Appreciating that the planned legislation would curtail and violate workers' rights, Legien demanded a series of guarantees to safeguard the right of association, to maintain labour conditions and provide compensation to workers forced into service outside their home localities.

When the content of the draft bill was revealed to the unions, none of these points had been acceded to. Legien then reiterated his demands to the government.[21] The secretary of state responsible for the bill, Karl Helfferich, needed to be persuaded by the War Office that without the unions the bill could not be implemented. For their part the unions had not hesitated in accepting the principle of compulsory civilian service under the direction of the War Office but they were adamant on the issue of worker protection. The head of this new department, General Groener, had come to understand the importance of the unions and appreciated their reservations about such a bill with no safeguards for workers' rights. That the bill was ultimately revised to meet most of the unions' demands was due to Carl Legien's negotiating skill and to General Groener's practical common sense.[22] The political will of the union leadership with its stubborn demands for a labour policy which guaranteed to protect workers had won through to have far-reaching social–political consequences.

The new law, which was intended through its wide-ranging control over manpower to step up production, gave the unions not only legal recognition but also real bargaining power in dealing with management. It further showed how the military leadership could make practical compromises with that section of the population which had hitherto been relegated to pariah status in the nation. Above all, it broke 'factory absolutism', the power of management to dispose at will over their workers. From now on each factory coming under the Act was to have its elected works committee which was empowered to oversee conditions and represent workers' complaints against management in all matters including wages. Further, in each military district an office was set up to arbitrate in disputes in which works' committees could not reach agreement with management, and above these a number of arbitration courts were instituted. In these bodies sat representatives of both management and labour organizations.

For Carl Legien the institutionalization of these measures

where the state was forced to regulate the relationship between labour and capital on an unprecedented scale was the beginning of what he was pleased to call war socialism.[23] At last the state was responding to union demands.

The process of 'national integration' which Legien had been advocating for decades had in 1916–17 reached its highest point. As if to symbolize this, a large trade union conference (including the Christian and Hirsch–Duncker unions) was held in Berlin on 12 December 1916. The aim was to popularize the Auxiliary War Services Bill about to come into force. Legien chaired the meeting and emphasized that the fatherland was in dire straits. He urged all unions to fulfil the spirit of the new law so that the men at the front would be adequately equipped to meet the superior forces of the enemy. On the other hand, if the workers were to give of their best, the government must see to it that food rations were more equitably distributed. The government on this occasion was represented by none other than Karl Helfferich who, as Minister for the Interior, had initially opposed granting concessions to labour. In justifying the far-ranging powers of the new bill he conceded that it was dependent upon not only the good will and patriotism of the unions but also on their practical experience.[24]

Nothing could have pleased Legien more than such words of recognition by a man who in his person represented both the state and the world of commerce which had hitherto considered trade unionism to be virtual treason.[25] What need now of revolution when by dint of steady expansion, the goals of socialism could be achieved with the aid of the state?

While the provisions of the Auxiliary War Service Bill were interpreted by the patriotic Social Democrats as a mighty step forward towards socialism, radical socialists intensified their criticism of the obviously state-friendly attitudes of the union leaders and their parliamentary advocates. What the latter celebrated as the emergence of state socialism, the radicals condemned as state capitalism.[26] However, the majority were clearly for upholding the *Burgfrieden* as it had won them the long-desired foothold in the state. But this was purchased at the cost of splitting German labour, a split which, because of the key role played in it by

Carl Legien, can be attributed largely to the trade-unionization of the social democratic movement, a development which determined that the trade union conception of the state triumphed over that of revolutionary Marxism. It was ironic that the 'Legien concept' and that of the military had coincided to such an extent as to enable the country to prosecute the war with a higher degree of efficiency than otherwise could have been achieved. A veritable *Kriegsgemeinschaft* between labour and the army had emerged out of the pressures of war.

So the *Burgfrieden* had borne fruit for both parties. The question was now whether or not the newly institutionalized labour regulations would be maintained in time of peace. Very quickly the unions began to plan soberly for the future. At the latest by 1916 the unions had developed a very clear self-image. They saw themselves as a permanent social–political and economic factor in the life of the nation. Quite distinct from the SPD, the unions considered themselves the actual base from which the working class could win even further concessions. They were the 'natural champions of worker politics'.[27] This conviction had been growing ever since Carl Legien and the General Commission had won the right to co-exist separately from the SPD and pursue what they called *Sozialpolitik*.[28] Both the war situation and the resultant split in the SPD had reinforced this conviction to the extent that by the third year of the war, the union leadership had become quite forthright in presenting their demands to the state for the restructuring not only of social legislation but also of the very industrial order of Germany.

Nothing better illustrates the sober practicality of the union leadership which Gustav Schmoller described than the demands which were enumerated in a twelve-part article series in the *Correspondenzblatt* between 12 February and 29 April 1916, entitled *Soziale Arbeiterpolitik und Gewerkschaften*. The author was Paul Umbreit, successor to Legien as editor of the trade union organ. After tracing the growth of union independence from the tutelage of the SPD wherein the union movement was clearly dissociated from the revolutionary aims of the party radicals, Umbreit underlined the wisdom of continuing the peaceful struggle for a more liberal *Sozialpolitik*. This could only be achieved by working within the parliamentary system. And since the writer ignored the Marxist theory of revolution, the entire series of articles must be interpreted as a repudiation of it, particularly as the growing split in the SPD at the time was being followed very closely in the *Correspondenzblatt*. The latter's position was decidedly hostile to those radicals who not only destroyed party unity but preached revolution. Indeed, a trade union organization which was calling for legislation to improve worker insurance, to institute a satisfactory labour exchange, and to set up works councils (*Arbeitskammer*) clearly did not envisage the state being swept away in any worker uprising. In fact, they saw the state as the most reliable means by which conditions acceptable to the workers could be achieved because the introduction of socialism by administrative means was seen as the more realistic way.

During 1917 the General Commission began to place its demands with greater clarity before the government. The goal was the internal restructuring of the nation (*die innere Neugestaltung*). Having seen that the nation's capacity to wage war depended in no small measure upon worker cooperation, it was reasoned that the state must at the coming peace reassess the status of the working class in the nation. In order to translate these hopes into reality, the unions documented their virtually Lassallean faith in the state. They actually hoped that the state would make their social–political programme the guiding principle for the impending transition to a peacetime economy as well as for economic policy thereafter.[29] In this, the reputedly Marxist German unions were behaving very much like their British and French counterparts, since they were all in essential agreement about the responsibility of the state for the welfare of the working class after the war,[30] a fact which is eloquent comment on the reception of Marxist ideology among the German trade unionists.

The strategy of exerting pressure on the state to achieve social–political goals was most apparent in 1917 when on 30 June the General Commission presented a lengthy submission on the transition to a peacetime economy. In it the importance was stressed of taking into account worker needs and opinions in the newly established Department for Demobilization. The situation demanded that not only the industrialists be consulted by the commissioner for demobilization but also workers' representatives. These should be placed in all key departments such as the labour exchanges, housing and food supply administration and particularly where workers' rights were to be safeguarded. This was the first expression of concern that the provisions of the Auxiliary War Service Bill should be carried over into peacetime.

In order to put the position even more clearly, the union leadership drafted a works council bill (*Arbeitskammergesetz*) which was modelled on an earlier abortive attempt in 1910 to have workers' representatives elected to works committees in which they would enjoy parity of representation with management. Such a provision had been strenuously resisted by industry, but in 1917 the chances were justifiably greater as such councils already existed under the War Service Act. However, the new draft legislation was resisted so long in committee that it could not be tabled before October 1918, by which time events at the front had overtaken the normal working of the Reichstag.

The degree of control over the economy expected by the works councils would have guaranteed in their view a harmonious transfer from war to peace. Simultaneous to the unions' efforts to promote the legislation for works councils was their eighteen-point social–political programme published in January 1918. This was formulated in the conviction that the nation owed a debt of gratitude to the working class since they had made great sacrifices for the Reich.[31] In presenting such demands at that time it is important to bear in mind the rationale of the union leadership. Uppermost in their thinking was the competitiveness of the national economy. This was the first precondition for a well-fed and adequately housed working class. The cost of production must be kept to a minimum because increased production costs would lead to increased food prices and rents and then to demands for higher wages. The wage–prices spiral must be prevented. It was a matter of national importance that wage struggles should be avoided since these affected labour and management alike, and ultimately would harm the economy during the critical transition. The way to keep industrial peace was to institute works councils coupled with arbitration and conciliation courts.

Ultimately there should be a national arbitration and conciliation department (*Reichseinigungsamt*).

These proposals early in 1918 were made by way of a serious warning to both government and industry. To disregard them would be to hinder the reconstruction of the economy.[32] But, despite their rationality and common sense, the proposals had little immediate impact. They were rejected by heavy industry because industrialists believed that such measures would lessen their control of the economy. The industrialists were against surrendering any independence to the unions unless it was absolutely unavoidable. Their two views of the state conflicted here: the one believing in the state's duty to uphold the dignity of the individual worker and to promote a more cohesive integration of the classes; the other concerned with maintaining what they imagined to be German power and prestige based on the old social–political and economic structure.

As will be discussed in the following chapter, the crisis which accompanied the end of the war contributed to a temporary drawing together of the forces of capital on the one hand, and of union organized labour on the other. However, before concluding this chapter, it is essential to observe that although the Policy of 4 August had been pursued conscientiously by the union leadership with the aim of improving conditions for the working class it only achieved limited success in this regard. All the efforts to improve *Sozialpolitik* as well as the numerous day-to-day 'bread and butter' tasks in the sphere of welfare for war widows and their families as well as overseeing food supplies were insufficient to prevent an alienation of the union leadership from the mass of the working class.

This gained expression in the number of unauthorized strikes which occurred, indicating that as far as large groups of workers were concerned, the Policy of 4 August was not working.[33] In other words, it had proved impossible for the General Commission to prevent the immiseration of all wage earners. This, as Jürgen Kocka has pointed out, had negative repercussions for the union leadership. By virtually abandoning any form of class struggle, by identifying themselves with the military state and supporting its war effort, they could not give vent to the class tensions that had accumulated as the war endured. Indeed, whatever class militancy the unions demonstrated before the war had been largely abandoned after 4 August 1914, and so the union leadership did not keep abreast of the social–psychological changes in the rank and file.[34]

These changes were the inevitable consequence of the privations inflicted on the civilian population in the wartime economy. But it is important to bear in mind the complex motives of the union leadership. At the beginning of the war they were genuinely afraid of the effects of unemployment on the union membership. There had been, too, a fear of repressive measures; it was better to display a cooperative rather than a hostile spirit to the government. Associated with this there was the genuine patriotism of many unionists and the hope that cooperation with the state would bring the longed-for recognition and thus terminate the 'outsider' status of organized labour in Wilhelmine society. All this, it was expected, would certainly result in real social–political reforms.

As has been seen, none of these motives, despite the partial success of the calculation behind them, could ward off the ultimate alienation of the union leadership from the rank and file. Again, as Kocka stresses, the world of the trade union bureaucrat, which even before the war, had always been so different from that of the worker on the factory floor, now, because of the effects of the war, became doubly so. From August 1914 until 1916 the unions had lost more than half of their membership, mainly because of enlistment in the armed forces as the following table indicates:[35]

Membership Fluctuation in the Trade Unions (in 1000)

	SOCIALIST	LIBERAL	CHRISTIANS
1913	2574	107	343
1914 1st half	2511	78	283
1914 2nd half	1664		
1915	1159	61	176
1916	967	58	174
1917	1107	79	244
1918	1665	114	393
1919	5479	190	858

Proportionately the socialist unions suffered the greatest losses. The gradual improvement then in 1917 is attributed by Kocka to the role unions were playing in the war economy, especially after the Auxiliary War Service Bill had come into force. Also the amendment to the *Reichsvereinsgesetz* in 1916 had allowed minors under eighteen years to be organized. In addition to these previously unorganized workers in place of those in the forces, there came many more thousands of women, so that the membership in 1918 was essentially quite different sociologically from that of 1913. In contrast to the old style of unionists, the new ones, lacking the years of schooling, were more impatient and radical. All this meant that while the basis of the union movement had been transformed, the old bureaucracy remained the same, bent on pursuing its well-established goals in the old style, namely a continuation of their integrationist, revisionist and non-militant tactics.[36]

It is this shift in the structural relationship between leadership and rank and file which heightened tensions at the time of the revolution and during the months immediately following the war.[37]

CHAPTER ELEVEN

The Trade Unions between Capitalism and Bolshevism

The trade unions have thoroughly paved the way for the revolution and they have secured its economic achievements without endangering the total economic process.[1]

The successful tight-rope act performed by the socialist trade union leadership (indicated in the above quotation) during the dying months of the old Reich and the actual revolution of 1918–19 was one of the basic preconditions for the emergence of the Weimar Republic founded upon a parliamentary constitution.[2] It has been seen that their wartime policy was motivated by a largely rational attempt to preserve their organization intact in the belief that by doing so the best interests of the working class would be served. The Policy of 4 August had been inspired by the determination to resist national extinction at the hands of the Entente; and as that possibility loomed even larger in October–November 1918, it is not surprising that the General Commission took steps to see that as far as possible the economic viability of the Reich would be maintained.[3]

Throughout the latter part of the war, the trade union leaders had been most persistent in warning the government about the need to plan an efficient transition from a war to a peacetime economy. But the Reich government failed to respond to these appeals until it was too late. A demobilization office which complied with the wishes of both the unions and management was not established until 7 November, two days before the revolution broke out.[4] The basic concept behind a demobilization office was naturally the prevention of industrial chaos and widespread

economic dislocation. In the heat of the revolution, then, this
need was intensified for both unions and management because
of the additional danger of bolshevism. Neither side, for their
own reasons, wanted a repetition of the Russian experience in
Germany.

The national defeat and the revolution in Germany had produced curious bed fellows: trade union leaders dedicated to the
attainment of socialism, and industrialists equally pledged to the
maintenance of the capitalist system. Negotiations between them
had been developing over the course of a year and had reached
maturity in the very days of the revolutionary disturbances
towards mid-November 1918. Obviously, the union leaders had
exposed themselves to the charge of opportunism by appearing to
come to terms with management on the same day that the
revolutionary government had abrogated the Auxiliary War Service Law. This piece of imperial legislation, through its wide ranging powers, had severely limited personal freedom. However, its
provisions for the mediation and arbitration of industrial disputes
were retained, a factor which institutionalized the power of
organized labour in the postwar situation.[5] But the independent
negotiations between industrial management and unions which
had been finalized on that day (12 November) were effectively to
frustrate any chances of the new socialist government of really
developing a programme of socialization. For this reason the
background to, and the provisions of, the famous November Pact
between industry and unions is an important aspect of the latter's
struggle for economic democracy in Germany.

It must be stressed that the November Pact, as far as the trade
union leaders were concerned, was merely the end result of their
wartime efforts to bring management to the negotiating table.
Their aims were firstly to secure better conditions for labour
within a more efficient war economy, and secondly as the war
endured, to ensure a smooth change over to a peacetime
economy. It was not primarily the threat of bolshevism which had
driven the unions to negotiate, but the fear of the breakdown of
the national economic structure; and that possibility appeared

more acute at the end of 1918 than at any time during the war. It is this concern to maintain national economic viability which provides the key to understanding the apparently schizophrenic attitude of trade unions towards the revolution.

As G. D. Feldman has shown, this concern from the union leadership came to the aid of German industrialists who also were naturally worried by how military defeat and an over-hasty demobilization might affect German industrial competitiveness after the war. This was the thought which led ultimately to the creation of the famous *Zentralarbeitsgemeinschaft* (ZAG) or joint industrial alliance after the revolution. The idea of labour–management cooperation had been, however, conceived well before the second week of November 1918. As has been seen, the socialist trade union leaders had made the offer to management at the very beginning of the war to establish a joint industrial alliance to combat unemployment with a view to keeping the economy buoyant.[6] This approach, however, had been ignored by the Association of German Employer Organizations, and the aim of getting joint industrial alliances to work was only achieved in isolated instances prior to the end of 1918. It had been possible for the unions in the printing, wood and building industries to convince management in those sectors of the wisdom of cooperation. And it is significant here that these industries had entered collective agreements to some extent already before the war. Other instances of union–management cooperation were limited to 'medium sized finishing industries and large scale firms in urban areas like Berlin and Stuttgart where the workers were highly skilled and well organized'.[7] Beyond this, no industrial magnates had shown any inclination to cooperate with organized labour until they could be convinced of the prudence of doing so.

The germ of the idea for an across-the-board industrial alliance grew out of meetings of the wartime Berlin club, *Deutsche Gesellschaft 1914* where the social democratic public servant, Dr. August Müller, and Professor Hermann Schumacher began to ventilate ideas about the economic and social problems that must inevitably accompany demobilization and the postwar economy. These discussions began early in 1917, the basic concept of which was the collaboration of management and organized labour to solve economic and social problems. The outcome was that Schumacher was able to arrange a meeting between Müller and the mine-owner, Hugo Stinnes, to prepare direct discussions between the latter and the industrial trade union leaders, the first on 9 August and the second in October 1917.[8]

At this point there was, of course, no thought that the war might be lost. On the contrary, Stinnes was still thinking in terms of the fatherland securing annexations of industrially valuable regions in Briey–Longwy and in Belgium. The priorities of this spokesman of German heavy industry are significant. Stinnes was desirous of collaboration with the union leaders because he had become disillusioned with the state's interference in the economy. He preferred to negotiate directly with those circles which could bring the most efficient results. At that time it appeared tactically wise to enlist the support of the unions by offering them the recognition they had so long been denied. For their part the unions were expected first to acquiesce in Stinnes' annexationist plans. This, of course, was tantamount to demanding that they betray the July 1917 Reichstag peace resolution which as Social Democrats they had endorsed.[9]

As Feldman reports, it is not possible to determine how far the unions were prepared to go in order to gain the desired recognition and the accompanying concessions on wages and conditions. However, one thing is clear: although both sides expressed a desire to continue discussion, no further meetings seem to have been arranged. All that had been achieved was a contact between key personalities which might later be revived. It is clear that the industrialists had only been thinking in terms of exploiting the unions for their own ends. They had only given thought to the 'social question' in so far as it might aid their efforts to gain more freedom from state controls at times when German military superiority seem to be winning spectacular success.[10] When fortune turned against the German military machine, however, negotiations between management and labour on the demobilization problem were resumed. This was in the summer of 1918.

Impending defeat had caused Hans von Raumer as Business Manager of the Association of the German Electro–technical Industry to begin the new wave of talks on behalf of a number of important industrialists for the purpose of bringing about an 'organic collaboration with the unions'.[11] By the time actual meetings had begun on 2 October the spectre of collapse had inspired fear in both industrialists and trade unionists alike. The constitutional changes made in response to the Wilsonian peace formula which led to the formation of the first government responsible to the Reichstag had begun to take effect. On 3 October the government of Prince Max von Baden had taken office and this included social democratic leaders from among whom the trade unionist, Gustav Bauer, was named Secretary of State for Labour.[12] There was an undoubted panic atmosphere surrounding all these events, but the trade unions were convinced of the good will behind the approach of von Raumer, because they believed his overtures had been made at a time when the military situation was favourable,[13] although it is clear that the industrialists had had a better appreciation about the real state of affairs than the labour leaders.

While the true motivation behind the industrialists' desire to befriend the trade unions at this time is quite transparent, that of the trade union leaders needs more investigation. At a meeting held on 4 October 1918, the trade union chiefs discussed the military situation as it had been revealed to the SPD parliamentary party on 2 October when social democratic politicians were included in the government for the first time. Carl Legien explained that he believed Germany was in a predicament very similar to that of 2 August 1914, though with certain differences. At that time the unions had been completely in the dark about the situation and had been unable to calculate what the future would bring. But in early October 1918 the likelihood of military collapse loomed very clearly indeed. This would bring with it not only reparations demands from the enemy but also the partition of Germany. 'In any case the conditions will be so hard that we will all have difficulty in getting to the top again.'[14] The context of this report indicates that Legien was referring to the favourable negotiating position the unions had won for themselves vis à vis management in the course of the war. Such a critical situation demanded that everything be done to rescue what could be rescued. This meant not only the political collaboration of the

SPD in the government but also the economic collaboration of the unions with industry to maintain viability while the war was being terminated.

That the union leaders perceived Germany to be fighting the most crucial struggle of all for her very existence is evidenced by their reaction to the news that the Western Allies wished to achieve an 'absolute victory' over Germany before peace was made. It was understood that the Allies wanted an enforced or dictated peace (*Gewaltfrieden*) rather than a negotiated peace (*Verständigungsfrieden*). 'The German people are supposed to become the proletarian nation of the world which will pay tribute to the imperialistic capitalism of England and France. For the German working class, these peace terms represent an intolerable enslavement which must permanently hinder its resurgence.'[15] This conviction was strengthened by the assertion that the German working class had been struggling over the decades to break the power of reaction in Germany and to achieve the right of self-determination for the entire German people. For this reason, the trade unions would oppose a dictated peace:

> We do not shake off the domination of our own reaction to bow to that of the French and English imperialists. We are by no means inclined to replace the German by a French military caste . . . It follows that we may not allow our strength to be crippled but rather must concentrate everything to ward off the defeat which the imperialistically enforced peace of the Entente has planned for us.[16]

The belief that the Western Allies were out to destroy the basis of Germany's industrial power and thereby the livelihood of millions of German workers was one that clearly dominated the thinking of the German trade union leadership in 1918/19. Their subsequent propaganda against the Treaty of Versailles bears eloquent testimony to this.[17] And in the closing weeks of the Great War the determination of the union leaders to do all in their power to prevent industrial chaos overwhelming the nation as a result of a dictated peace caused them to throw in their lot with German industry.[18] The first precondition for the emancipation of the working class was, after all, a viable national economy. How the national wealth ought to be managed was for the moment a secondary question. This is why there was no demand for immediate socialization. The sudden restructuring of the economy at a time when four million men were about to be demobilized could only create widescale dislocation. It was better to allow management to contribute their expertise to the task of accomplishing the smoothest transition of the economy from a wartime to a peacetime footing. This did not mean, however, that organized labour should not exploit the situation to realize long-standing aims by extracting concessions from management. While the labour leaders were clear in their own minds that the first priority was the continued existence of German industry, they quickly appreciated that key sections of management had come to realize that the trade unions represented focal points of power which demanded recognition if industry was to remain viable. In other words, organized labour was seen at last to be a crucial factor in the capitalist economy. Indeed, it had been recognized in industrial circles that a rapprochement with labour had become more economically and hence politically important than the link with the Junker agrarian elite.[19]

For this reason industry had abandoned its formerly insular attitude toward the trade unions and had become eager to negotiate. This change had been induced by the wartime conditions when industry had felt acutely the clumsy hand of state intervention in the economy. It was, however, not until as late as October 1918 that industry seriously attempted to take the necessary steps. The initiative was taken by the aforementioned Hans von Raumer of the electro-technical industry based in Berlin who urged upon leading personalities in the industry the wisdom of negotiating with trade union leaders as equal partners. On 8 October 1918 he considered it timely to make this recognition of the unions because any delay would put the industrialists at an even worse disadvantage.[20] Similarly the representatives of Rhenish–Westphalian heavy industry were concerned to come to terms with the unions. At a meeting in Düsseldorf on 9 October they had estimated that the new government of Prince Max von Baden would not hold out more than four or five weeks, and that an alliance with the unions was necessary to save the economy. They delegated the redoubtable Hugo Stinnes to negotiate with the trade union leaders.

The first meetings were only with the coal miners' union. This was, of course, crucial since this industry was of central economic importance and most vulnerable to extreme left-wing agitation. As Feldman points out, the nature of the negotiations here were very much determined by the significance of the coal industry to the economy. There was a great demand for coal and therefore no danger of unemployment in that sector. However, there was the fear that decreased production would lead to unemployment and general dislocation in dependent industries and services during demobilization. Therefore, both industrial and labour leaders were equally concerned to keep the miners from becoming militant at this time. Yet, the anxiety on the part of the union leaders about the effects of left-wing agitation, coupled with their patriotic concern to keep the national economy viable, weakened their negotiating position vis-à-vis management.[21]

At this pre-revolutionary stage where negotiations were in progress the unions in general were trying to press a range of practical questions as well as the specific issues of the eight-hour day and collective wage agreements.[22] Underlying all these discussions was the basic issue of the impending demobilization and how to tackle it. The union–management discussions that had been taking place in Berlin and in the Ruhr over the last ten days of October had resulted in both a coordination of efforts from industry to industry and the evolution of an agreed programme for demobilization. The latter was based on the principle that both industry and labour were to be free to influence decision-making in the agency to be set up for this purpose, and that they should then be responsible for carrying out the policies they had helped to mould.[23]

This bore fruit, as indicated at the outset, in that the new Chancellor was constrained to listen to the industrial and labour leaders who made no secret of the fact that they regarded the government bureaucracy as incompetent. A demobilization office was set up to comply with these joint demands on 7 November.[24] This entire process was characterized by more conciliatory overtures made from the trade union side who by early November had still not won any crucial concessions from industry. The unions had agreed through Carl Legien's mediation that there should indeed be a demobilization office in which both labour and management equally should cooperate on the following problems:

(a) establishment of principles on the return and distribution of labour
(b) the setting up of a labour exchange
(c) unemployment benefits
(d) the creation of contracts and demands for relief work
(e) the adjustment from the wartime to a peacetime economy[25]

While this general scheme gained the approval of both camps, the General Commission remained uncommitted until the question was decided of which trade unions should contribute to the envisaged administration of demobilization. The employers had still wished to retain the yellow or non-militant, strike-breaking unions whom they had employed in the past to resist the demands of the socialist unions. Legien was adamant on the principle that from then on the employers had to abandon the fostering of company unions. Even the Christian and Hirsch–Duncker union leaders who were also involved by this time sided with Legien in insisting that the employers withdraw financial support from the non-militant unions and allow full freedom to workers to join whatever union they liked.[26]

But, while this was a partial concession gained prior to the establishing of the demobilization office on 7 November, there was still no uniform concession on either the eight-hour day or on collective wage agreements. All that had been achieved essentially was recognition of the trade unions as the representatives of the work force and as such of their importance to the economy. There was still much to be negotiated. As Theodor Leipart reported, as late as 8 November, the employers had still refused to admit the principle that recognition of the unions implied acceptance of collective wage agreements; and neither were they ready to concede the eight-hour day. Only on the question of the setting up of a labour exchange administered jointly by labour and management had there been satisfactory agreement. Prior to the actual revolution, the chief issue under discussion had been that of a joint industrial alliance within the new demobilization office.

Then came the days of upheaval. The discussions had been thereby interrupted. But, on Monday 11 November, they were to be resumed. Theodor Leipart claimed that he had advised his chief, Carl Legien, that with the new political situation, the unions might easily increase their demands for further concessions. These would be the eight-hour day, the institution of collective agreements for all branches of industry, as well as the demand that the employers include all employer associations in these negotiations. Up to that time only the metal and heavy industry of the Rhineland had been represented. Legien had agreed to press these demands in association with Adam Stegerwald, the chairman of the Christian trade unions. Leipart then drew up a draft of an agreement.[27]

The final form of this was in fact the work of Leipart in collaboration with Hans von Raumer, the text of which is in Appendix I. As Feldman reports, this had been completed and discussed by 12 November and it was virtually all written in Berlin. Stinnes, as chief spokesman for the Ruhr industrialists, pressed his colleagues for full powers to act on their behalf, recognizing that otherwise valuable time would be lost, and the unions could lose control over their own people.[28] To this extent the revolution did have a direct influence on the content of the so-called *Magna Carta* of German labour.[29] The industrialists, of course, had signed the Stinnes–Legien Agreement as a tactical manoeuvre at a time when they and organized labour feared for the continued existence of the national economy. Certainly, just before and after the revolution, the unions and management shared a common interest in maintaining full employment and industrial peace.

Out of this grew the ZAG, the constitution of which was drawn up in the days after the above agreement of 15 November was signed. Its *ad hoc* character was evident from the start. Having been hammered out in a situation of acute political tension, it presumed a harmony of interests instead of conflicts in labour and management collaboration and 'thus went far beyond the requirements of collective bargaining or the realistic perceptions of conflict of interests which normally underlie it'.[30] The actual constitution of the ZAG was finally agreed upon on 4 December 1918. Its short preamble stated:

Conscious in the knowledge and of the responsibility that the reconstruction of our national economy requires the coordination of all economic and intellectual forces and cooperation on all sides, the organizations of the industrial and business employers and employees join together in a common industrial alliance.[31]

The purpose of this was to achieve a common solution to all economic and social questions affecting industry and commerce in Germany as well as all legislative and administrative matters pertaining thereto. And in order to achieve this an elaborate organizational apparatus was set up. This was intended to ensure the closest cooperation of management and labour in each branch of industry. Three organs constituted the ZAG:

(1) the Central Executive and Central Committee
(2) the Industry or Branch Group with Group Executive and Committee
(3) the Sub Groups with Sub Group Executives and Committees

It was intended that in each branch of industry or business a so-called Industry Group would be formed consisting of an equal number of elected workers and management personnel. This unit would constitute the actual joint industrial alliance of the organized employers and employees of a particular section of industry. Its task was to regulate autonomously all matters affecting the industry in line with the resolutions of the Central Executive and Committee. In matters affecting areas outside the industry, the

Industry Group could appeal to the Central Executive and Committee. This latter body (the Committee) had the task of advising and regulating all those questions which the Industry Groups of the entire nation would direct to it. Its personnel were elected by the associated industry groups for a period of three years. Also to this Central Committee, six representatives of the central trade union as well as employer associations were delegated. The Central Executive consisted of twelve representatives each of employers and trade unionists elected from the ranks of the Central Committee. This body was the national organ of the ZAG. It implemented the resolutions of the Central Committee and was empowered to interpret collective agreements as well as to act as an arbitration court in industrial disputes provided that arbitration was foreseen in the collective agreement.[32]

This outline of the organization and competencies of the ZAG serves to illustrate its wide-ranging intention. It constituted a remarkable, though in the circumstances utopian, attempt to avert political and economic chaos in Germany at the end of the Great War. That it could not succeed in the long term is not surprising, particularly in view of the ideological differences between the so-called social partners. The industrialists clearly entered into the November Pact and the ZAG in the first instance to escape governmental controls and then to save industry from bolshevism.[33] It was purely a temporizing manouevre. Subsequent events showed that a real conversion to the idea of collective agreements had not taken place in capitalist circles. For their part, the unions could be accused of selling out their socialism because by their consistent stand they clearly enabled the survival of capitalism. That, however, would be a far too superficial assessment if one is to accept Carl Legien's rationale: none other than Walter Rathenau who had been a representative of industry during the discussions with the unions had asked Legien on the second day after the revolution whether he felt that entering such an agreement with capitalists had in fact compromised his socialist principles. Rathenau had suggested that the unions could possibly lose credibility thereby. Legien had replied that the union leaders had certainly considered this aspect but had concluded that the agreement was absolutely necessary for the working class in order to avoid unemployment, and want. But beyond this the union leaders had drawn support from views current in social democratic circles about socialization which were attributable to Karl Marx himself, namely that whereas a political restructuring could be effected in a few hours or weeks, socialization which had to come after such a political reformation would take months and years. Legien had then informed Rathenau that he considered the November Pact to have contributed essentially to the preparation of socialism.[34]

There is no cause to doubt Legien's sincerity regarding this belief. His entire background and development had indicated that he preferred to try and transform the existing power structure by the gradual application of trade union organizational strength at points where it had some chance of getting tangible results, however modest they might be for the present. The same attitude is true of the succeeding trade union leaders. A sudden, violent and disruptive attempt to realize socialism would have been unthinkable for the men around Legien. They therefore looked upon the ZAG as means of educating the 'social partners' towards socialism.[35] It was in their view the logical extension of the Policy of 4 August, the public peace of the war, and of the social–political provisions of the Auxiliary War Service Law. The motivation of the trade union leaders was based on a very pragmatic analysis of the social and economic situation. Always concerned to struggle only for the attainable in a given context, the trade union leaders could see no rational alternative to the kind of economic–political cooperation that the ZAG represented.

However, most importantly, while the ZAG functioned, as Legien clearly recognized, to perpetuate capitalism, it ensured that capitalism could no longer ignore organized labour in its planning. But in this the trade unionists over-estimated their success and the possibilities for the future. With the institutionalization of industrial alliances on a parity basis for deliberating and deciding upon general economic and social issues, they believed they had taken a gigantic step towards the realization of economic democracy. They could be forgiven for thinking in this way. After all, the unions had manoeuvred themselves into a situation where they replaced the Junker class as the social partners with the industrialists as the determining socio–economic force in the nation. Unfortunately, however, the ZAG machinery did not adequately cover the important sectors of the management and administration of individual enterprises. The power of the employers remained virtually unchallenged and largely unchecked. Here, as Friedrich Zunkel explains, the unionists underestimated their power and actually shied off pressing this issue with the spokesmen of industry prior to the agreement for fear of risking the collapse of the negotiations.

Because of the resistance of the industrialists on the question of codetermination in the factory, the unionists were satisfied with relatively vague regulations intended to safeguard worker welfare, namely that there would be collective agreements in factories employing more than fifty persons and that these agreements would be negotiated by a workers' committee with management. But that this could be interpreted as allowing the workers the right to interfere in the running of an enterprise had been strictly repudiated by the industrialists.[36] And for reasons that have been made apparent, the union leaders steadfastly refused to admit the principle that the workers alone should assume sole responsibility for production. A successful socialization in their view could not have been brought about at that time by the councils' movement. The economy would first of all have to emerge from the critical situation it was in as a result of the lost war before steps in that direction could be taken. And in this respect the ZAG would perform its historic role. Through its machinery it was expected that workers would learn the skills required to assume the control of the economy. But until that was accomplished the employers were needed in their key positions. Nevertheless, the ZAG constituted a virtually revolutionary breakthrough for the union leadership. It promised to provide the basis for the future realization of socialist goals by virtue of the principle of codetermination built into the organization. With this, the previous policy of collective agreement could not only be continued and expanded but it offered the hope of securing trade union codetermination in all social and economic questions. Indeed, the possibility of an organized economy seemed to present itself in which the trade unions in cooperation with the employers' organizations regulated production and therewith the preconditions for a future social and economic transformation. This was, in the event, a far too optimistic expectation in a situation where the employers still controlled productive capital, had access to better information and possessed in any case a more sophisticated economic education.[37]

As Feldman rightly points out, it is unhistorical to judge the union leaders at this time in terms of what happened in 1933.[38] Their conception of their immediate tasks in 1918/19 was determined by a range of factors: these included their historically developed stance vis-à-vis the state and industry; the intimately related appraisal of the combined effect of a rigorous peace treaty; and the disruptive effect of a councils movement on the economy. The General Commission's spirited defence of the ZAG at the Nuremberg Congress of the free trade unions in 1919 revealed this thinking. For them, as their spokesman Adolf Cohen observed, the ZAG constituted the best possible solution in the context of the time, without in any way blocking the way to socialism.[39] In underpinning this evaluation Cohen had stated:

August Bebel and other leaders have often enough emphasized that no greater misfortune could befall the working class than if the bourgeois society one day simply left the running of things to it alone before the working class was adequately prepared. [Lively approval.] The correct running of economic matters must be learned just as much as the trade of a fitter and turner or a wood worker, and if you believe that it would be a triviality then you are sadly mistaken and prove that you are most unsuitable to solve economic questions; for the time being we cannot dispense with the cooperation of the employers before we have ourselves trained the relevant experts. [Lively approval.][40]

The self-imposed reliance of the trade union leaders on the expertise of the employers was a dilemma which it was hoped the passage of time would resolve in favour of the unionists. The employers for their part were clearly not interested in socialism or even the high sounding schemes of a Walter Rathenau for a so-called *Gemeinwirtschaft* (collective economy).[41] It was primarily the anxiety of the industrialists about the incompetence of the imperial government to handle the demobilization plus their fear of bolshevism that led them into the ZAG. As Zunkel observes, the majority of the employers accepted these new social and political developments as unavoidable but as certainly unwelcome changes.[42] Perhaps the best characterization of the industrialist attitude to the ZAG is summed up in the words of Jakob Reichert, the business manager of the Association of German Iron and Steel Industrialists during a lecture on 30 December 1918:

> So it became clear to everyone that we were now confronted with ruins of our entire policy and that it was necessary in the field of rubble to find the corner stone, the fundament upon which we can build the basis of our new economy, one upon which private enterprise [*Unternehmertum*] as such can continue to exist. Indeed, the situation was already clear in the first days of October. The crucial question was: How can industry be saved? How can private enterprise be preserved from socialization, nationalization and the approaching revolution which threatened to sweep all branches of the economy away?[43]

Having made this depressing observation the industrialists 'discovered' organized labour and drew the conclusion that in the midst of the general chaos, in view of the tottering power of the state and government, there was only one reliable ally left for industry and that was the trade unions![44] In carrying out the role assigned to them by industry the unions performed well, though this does not at all mean that the ZAG functioned in a positive sense. It merely served for a time as a suitable vehicle in which to ride out the rapids of revolution. This latter event had merely interrupted the dialogue with the unions for two days so that there was no real danger that industry would be isolated. Certainly, concessions had had to be made but they in no way endangered the economic dominance of the employers. Rather, this had been squarely recognized by the November Pact which in turn received the endorsement of the revolutionary government.

This agreement not only confirmed the recognition of the trade unions by the employers' organization but also the recognition of the latter by the socialist government. Private enterprise could not now be abolished. For the above mentioned Reichert, the ZAG signified nothing more than means of preserving private enterprise, thereby securing the economic order and the maintenance of the bourgeois society. This attitude emphasizes the putatively defensive function attributed to the ZAG by industry. However, other industrialists thought to exploit it in a more positive fashion by forming a so-called working bloc which could be employed to exert capitalist influence upon the now socialist government. A signal success for this kind of thinking was the nomination of the industrialists' candidate to head the Reich office for economic demobilization through whom a policy favouring private enterprise would emerge resulting in the rapid restoration of industrial autonomy. Indeed, it was hoped that the ZAG might become the means by which the more radical and undisciplined sections of labour might be forced to confront economic realities and thereby recognize that there were limits to their social welfare demands as well as negative aspects to socialization.[45]

Clearly, the ZAG was nothing more than a marriage of convenience which in practice achieved very little, even with regard to the demobilization. As Feldman trenchantly observes:

Right from the beginning the ZAG was founded on assumptions and conditions which made its failure unavoidable. The idea that the political conditions in Germany were of a kind that the industrial and trade union organizations could pursue an autonomous policy was a distorted and unrealistic outgrowth of the "unpolitical" arrogations of pressure groups as they had been nourished under the old regime. In the final analysis the ZAG was unable to prevent the government from reasserting its authority in the socio–economic sphere and to introduce legislative measures independent of the advice of the ZAG.[46]

If the ZAG did not in the event attain any real economic significance it certainly had a far-ranging political effect on the German revolution. Through its steadfast support of the ZAG, the General Commission had helped essentially in the revolutionary situation by warding off both the threat of the councils movement and the possibility of immediate socialization. Indeed, as Hans Schieck affirms, if one examines the attitude of the Majority Socialists in the council of the People's Commissars (Ebert, Scheidemann and Landsberg) to this problem, it will be seen that they agreed with the General Commission. This latter body had been instructed by the SPD leadership to keep in the background after 9 November so that the Majority Socialists could work in with the USPD people who were inimical to the General Commission because of its wartime policies. In compliance with this shrewd tactical manoeuvre, the General Commission had let it be known (23 November) that in view of the previous accord between SPD and unions on economic questions it was expected that the party would continue to make use of trade union experience and knowledge.[47]

This was made a bare week after signing of the November Pact and was tantamount to a directive to the government to pursue a course to suppress the disrupting influence of the workers' and soldiers' councils. But even prior to this, on the very day after the signing of the November Pact, Legien had affirmed in reply to the question from the soldiers' councillor of the army concerning what the chief task before the Councils Congress in fact was:

> . . . working together for the continuation and reconstruction of our economy, for the time being on the existing basis of private property in land and means of production. Once the continuation of the national economy is ensured then the transfer to public ownership of those branches and enterprises which are ripe for it can be made. This can take place not according to theoretical considerations but after practical examination of whatever is of best service to the nation. Socialization of a national economy which has been shaken and disorganized by a wartime economy is not possible.[48]

Declarations of the same content were frequently made in the pages of the *Correspondenzblatt* in the ensuing months while the debate on socialization and the councils question raged. Above all, the trade unions (including the Christian and Hirsch–Duncker unions) were urged to cooperate with the central employers' organizations 'to secure the transition economy'.[49] From this base then, the General Commission with accustomed tenacity proceeded to close its ranks against the onslaught of the councils' movement. From what occurred until the National Assembly passed the Works Council Law 4 February 1920, it is evident that the General Commission regarded all attempts from the extreme left to engage in any form of economic action as endangering the real achievements of the revolution. This is certainly one of the most tragic misunderstandings to be found among the diverse protagonists of the German revolution. The trade unions had been agitating for decades for the radical transformation of the monarchical, bureaucratic and military state that was Wilhelmine Germany into a *Volksstaat*—a people's republic. However, bound by their trade union concepts they were never able to take the initiative to bring about the desired change. When it came in November 1918, it was effected by soldiers' and workers' councils, who, as Ulrich Kluge rightly points out, did not want themselves to implement the widely desired political and economic reforms, but rather expected them to be carried out by the established and recognized institutions (parties and trade unions) within the framework of the new parliaments.[50]

The total effect of the councils movement had been virtually to ensure a social democratic leadership in the Reich even though many of the revolutionary soldiers in particular were not ideologically committed to pursuing specifically socialist goals.[51] In short, it was a mistake on the part of the trade union leadership to see in the entire councils movement a tendency hostile to themselves. This was, in fact, the result of the virulent criticism by radical Socialists of the entire ZAG policy which the employers supported for the express purpose of preventing socialization.[52] Understandably, since millions of German workers had over the years been led to expect socialization once the monarchy had been removed, the failure of the revolutionary government in 1918/19 to implement forthwith a programme of socialization came as a bitter disappointment to many. Beyond this there prevailed diverse opinions among the Socialists as to how and when to begin it.[53] The trade unions must, of course, be numbered among the advocates of socialization but they were committed firstly to the principles of the ZAG and secondly to the concept of parliamentary democracy whereby socialization, if it were to come, would be the result of democratically evolved legislation. By examining, then, the response of the trade union leadership to the perceived threat of the councils movement much is revealed that explains why the parliamentary system survived its birth in the postwar situation.

Having been instructed to keep in the background during the revolution, the trade union leadership contented itself with restrained comment from the side-lines and earnest discussion in trade union headquarters. However, the public statements (in the *Correspondenzblatt*) made very plain what their priorities were. Already on 16 November it was noted:

> It appears understandable that revolution cannot be carried out everywhere with the strictest observation of all democratic guarantees, and it would be senseless to be angered by it or to complain. One essential requirement is that as soon as it is at all possible a democratic popular assembly be created in the Reich which will instal an ordered leadership to assume the business of the state. As soon as this occurs the revolution has fulfilled its great historic task.[54]

Like the policy which led the unions into the ZAG, this statement bears witness to the consistency and continuity in trade union political thought. There were clearly no alternatives to popularly elected national assemblies which maintained the highest possible degree of order and justice, both politically and economically. The government of the People's Commissars had immediately righted all the political wrongs of the imperial regime with an impressive list of decrees guaranteeing basic freedoms.[55] It remained simply to regulate the national economy so that these political freedoms might be realized to the full. And for this the trade union formula had already been worked out in collaboration with the employers. For this reason, the emergence of workers' and soldiers' councils, who not only claimed political power but in many instances also the right of economic control, was an unwelcome disturbance. But since it was an inescapable fact that they had 'made' the revolution, it was impossible to deny them recognition. This situation led the unions to assert their role in the revolution as the true representatives of the workers' economic interests while the councils were recognized as the provisional bearers of political authority. In this way the trade unions, who were supposed to keep in the background during the revolution, became a central factor. It was their insistence on continuing their role as economic leaders of the working class that was the basis of the bloody conflict with the Spartacist movement.

The trade union self-perception was that until the revolution there had never been any doubt concerning the function of trade unions to represent the economic interests of the workers.[56] The role of the works committees in the factories had never displaced the function of trade unions. In the isolated instances where that had happened in the past it was usually due to chicanery on the part of the employers who had sought to play off works committees against the unions. The normal practice had been that the unions were the recognized worker representatives and the works committee had to collaborate with them if it wished to avoid confrontations with the unions and the possibility of its own elimination as a negotiating factor.

Indeed, there was a division of functions within the labour movement. The party had the task of political representation whereas the unions had social–political and economic roles to fulfil. Wherever issues arose which clearly involved both wings of the movement, a consensus was reached on the basis of the 1906 Mannheim Agreement between party executive and General Commission. Since that time there had never been any doubt that the unions were the economic organs of the working class. In a tactfully worded protest about the actions of some councils in

November 1918, the General Commission observed that the emergence of councils with dictatorial powers had led to occasional disruptions in factories that were not in every case very productive.

It was further noted that where this happened, the intention of the councils had been not to eliminate the unions but that they had been approached by the workers of isolated factories over some specific issue. That was explainable because masses of workers were not yet organized in unions and therefore unused to turning to the trade union representatives when disputes suddenly arose. In such cases, workers had turned to the councils who in turn invoked the authority of dictatorial revolutionary power. In many cases, commented the *Correspondenzblatt*, it may have been that the workers were stirred up in an anarcho–syndicalist sense, a feature which had played no part in industrial relations in Germany prior to the revolution. The General Commission then stressed that any further examples of this kind of activity would jeopardize the achievements of the revolution. The working class was confronted with the task of building a new social order and could not now afford the luxury of a dispute over areas of responsibility. This would impede the establishment of a permanent centre of governmental power. If an uncoordinated, fragmented pattern of rule emerged in Germany it would be a total fiasco.

The General Commission then sought to win the confidence of the masses by stressing the democratic structure and history of the unions. They had always tried to work within the framework of existing possibilities. The virulent hostility in some sections of the working class towards the democratically elected trade union leaders was working against the interests of the revolution. This occurred when councils interfered in spheres which were exclusively the preserve of trade unions.[57] Such actions unnecessarily disturbed industrial productivity. It was also pointed out that the revolutionary government had publicly declared that an immediate nationalization of the economy was not intended because of the confusion it would cause. The present situation demanded the utmost orderliness to enable the re-integration of the millions of returning soldiers into paying jobs.

All this reasoning was directed towards giving to the ZAG the credibility it needed among the masses in order to carry out the demobilization and reorientate the economy to compete with its international rivals. For the General Commission, as well as for the People's Commissars, the sustaining of German industry, the uninterrupted supply of goods and raw materials from abroad, and the maintenance of all banks and institutes of credit were all linked inextricably with the survival of the new republic. And because a councils' system would have disrupted all these things, it was doubly imperative to clarify the still open question of the ultimate nature of the form of government, i.e. parliamentary or councils.[58]

The core opposition to the trade union leadership, the ZAG and the idea of a National Assembly had crystallized in the Spartacist movement. Its basic aim was to mobilize the masses into action to fight for the ideals of international socialism. The major hindrance to this goal was the free trade union organization and its insistence on full cooperation with capital to restore the German economy. This attitude was the supreme betrayal of the German people, and therefore the Spartacist League (afterwards the Communist Party) regarded the destruction of the traditional trade union movement as their primary task.[59] The Spartacists were still at this time linked with the USPD but because the latter party suffered from internal divisions on how best to pursue the revolution—the majority favouring elections to a National Assembly—the Spartacists led by Rosa Luxemburg dissociated themselves from the parent body. Already on 18 November 1918 she declared their aims in the *Die Rote Fahne* with an article entitled 'The Beginning'. The great revolution must be realized by the masses taking it into their own hands. As she wrote, 'The path of the revolution follows clearly from its objective, its method derives from its mission: *All power into the hands of the toiling masses, into the hands of the workers' and soldiers' councils . . .* this must be the guiding principle for all measures taken by the revolutionary government.'[60]

As has been indicated, however, the councils of soldiers and workers that had made the revolution did not by any means constitute an ideologically homogeneous mass. And so the Spartacist

League set out to capture the mind of the councils movement. In the 14 December 1918 issue of *Die Rote Fahne* the programme of the Spartacists was clearly enunciated in the article 'What Does the Spartacist League Want?' The key section represented concepts which were diametrically opposed to those of the General Commission, as this passage illustrates:

> The essence of a socialist society consists in this, that the great toiling mass ceases to be a regimented mass, and instead lives and directs the whole political and economic life in conscious and free self-determination. . . . The proletarian masses must learn to become the thinking, free, and active guides of this process [of production] rather than remain dead machines employed by the capitalists. . . . They must acquire the sense of responsibility of active members of the commonweal, which is the sole owner of all social wealth. They must develop zeal without the employer's whip, highest productivity without capitalist drivers, discipline without a yoke, and order without regimentation. Highest idealism in the interest of the commonweal, strictest self-discipline, a true civic spirit of the masses, these constitute the moral basis of a socialist society.[61]

As W. T. Angress has noted, this assessment of the German situation evidenced a

> curious absence of a sense of reality and proportion. They [the Spartacists] chose to ignore the true state of mind of the masses to whom they appealed, an attitude which was to become a chronic feature of German Communism. They failed to appreciate the fact that the German people in 1918 were convinced that the revolution had already established a new order of society, and that the people, after four years of war which had ended in defeat, were tired of strife and chaos. Under these circumstances the Spartacist programme was utopian and the determination of the leaders to put it into practice quixotic.[62]

The reaction of the trade union leadership to this practice which gained its expression in a series of wild strikes culminating in virtual civil war is most instructive and helps to explain their determination to keep the upper hand against the councils movement since this was seen to be the means by which the Communists would carry out their work.[63] In response to the so-called Spartacus Putsch or January uprising in Berlin the General Commission spelt out its understanding of the ideology behind these bloody events.[64] The somewhat oversimplified analysis of the background made it clear that it was the culmination of years of insidious and deleterious action against the unity of the German labour movement organized by the radical wing. And just as the revolution had triumphed in the Reich, these people had proclaimed a reign of terror against the socialist government, against the state, law and order, against democracy and social welfare, in short, against everything that would lead to a rapid cementing of the achievements of the revolution. They had been ruthlessly striving for the overthrow of everything thereby plunging the nation into limitless misery. The guiding precept appeared to be the eternal revolution. Everything had to be destroyed before it could be rebuilt in accordance with the principles of a completely pure socialism.

The General Commission observed that there were scarcely two comrades on the left of the USPD who could reach an agreement on what these principles might be, there being three or four different revolutionary groups. One might well wonder how long the revolution should be continued until the final goals of their most radical adherents were achieved. There was even the revelation of the Bolshevik propaganda chief Karl Radek, that the Soviet red army was prepared to march with a German revolutionary army together to the Rhine to fight against the capitalist West and to carry through the world revolution. The prospect thus conjured up of a Germany plunged into another war, of the shattering effects of bolshevism as witnessed in Russia to be played out again in Germany was too much for the trade union leaders. Germany was no place for such unrealistic experiments. The Spartacists like the Bolshevists were ridden with

238 *Trade Unionism in Germany: Volume One 1869–1918*

irreconcilable factionalism. Internecine conflict such as that between Lenin and Trotsky was a good example of what would be
in store for Germany if the Spartacist Putsch had succeeded in
toppling the Socialist government.

In particular, the General Commission attacked the Spartacists' attempt to destroy the principle of true democracy in Germany, namely the concept of majority rule which was the basis of
parliamentarism. Parallel to this the Spartacists sought continually to foment unrest in the factories and to capture the works
councils. They were continually seeking to stage strikes which
were not democratically decided upon. Indeed, the national conference of Spartacists on 30–31 December 1918 had adopted two
resolutions against the trade unions which illustrate graphically
the gulf separating the General Commission and their bitterest
opponents. These stated:

(1) The collective wage agreement policy of the central trade
union bodies, the strangling of strikes and the systematic prevention of the struggle for social emancipation of the proletariat by the trade union bureaucracy as well as the contrary,
indeed hostile attitude of the trade union leaders to the
immediate socialization of the means of production is in its
effect conservative of the present state [*staatserhaltend*] and
therefore hostile to the revolution. Membership in such trade
unions is therefore irreconcilable with the goals and tasks of
the Communist Party of Germany. For the organization of
economic struggles and for the taking over of production after
the victory of the social revolution the formation *of revolutionary locally based workers' organizations* is required [unity organ-
izations]. These fighting organizations have to exercise their
functions in the closest liaison with the Communist Party and
the central strike committees and help to prepare and implement a communistic production.
(2) The tactics of the trade unions both before and during
the war has led to a complete crippling of the revolutionary
class struggle. To attempt to reform the trade unions from
within is, as all previous experience has shown, a hopeless task.

Therefore, the Conference of the Communist Party resolves to take up the struggle against the trade unions from without and demands that the affiliated organizations begin without delay the most energetic propaganda to desert the trade unions. The conference makes it obligatory upon its members to effect their withdrawal from the trade unions immediately.

In the present situation the standpoint that the economic and political struggle be kept separate is completely outdated. What is required for the revolutionary proletariat is the economic–political unity organization. This is the Communist Party of Germany.[65]

That these resolutions discussed at the founding conference of the KPD were immediately inspired by a repudiation of the General Commission's ZAG policy is self-evident. Rosa Luxemburg summarized the KPD attitude epigramatically as follows: 'The question of the struggle for liberation is identical with the fight against the trade unions.'[66] But, although the debate over the two resolutions indicated a uniform agreement condemning the policies of the General Commission there was divided opinion on the wisdom of demanding the exodus of KPD members from the unions. On the other hand the idea was ventilated that it was better to leave things as they were and rather promote the works councils since these could be relied upon to support the workers against the unions and the employers. After the debate the resolutions were not voted upon but transferred to a commission. This indicates that the age-old problem of first requiring ideological submission from workers who wish to join a trade union had still not been overcome.

The drive to organization in trade unions continued to be quite independent from party political considerations. The situation in which the Spartacists found themselves in 1918/19 with regard to the trade union problem was the reverse to that in the pre-1918 period. At that time membership in a union was expressly independent of party or religious affiliation. Now the idea was that ideological commitment was a prerequisite to waging the unified political–economic struggle because the two factors were really inseparable. The 'exodus propaganda' was in practice a demand for unconditional loyalty to the new KPD; but it was recognized by Rosa Luxemburg that to set up a completely new unity organization was impractical. All that was required was for the workers' councils to oversee the economic struggles in each factory. The individual works councils were to be elected by the works' staff in collaboration with the workers' councils, the latter being drawn from the factories. All these were to coordinate in a Reich economic council. The effect of this would be a complete undermining of the trade unions. 'We will ursurp the trade unions' functions which were entrusted to them by the workers, and which they have betrayed. We will replace the trade unions by a new system on a completely new basis.'[67]

As indicated, the reaction of the conference to Luxemburg's analysis was, to use the phrase from the *Correspondenzblatt*'s report, to bury it in a committee (*Kommissionsbegräbnis*).[68] It nevertheless caused great indignation in the trade union camp because it illustrated beyond doubt to what extent they were despised and rejected by the Communists and how the latter would seek to continue to frustrate the unions by exploiting the councils movement. It convinced the trade union leaders that there was no room for both councils and union in the future of the labour movement, and overcoming this problem formed the greatest internal task for the union leadership in the first half year of 1919.

All actions undertaken against the policy of the General Commission were seen to be in the anarcho–syndicalist tradition of the earlier localists.[69] The niceties of debate within the newly founded Communist Party on the trade union question were without meaning to the trade union leaders. For them disruption remained disruption, and the vehicle for it was the councils movement. The essential task for the unions was clear, namely to solve the problem of how this movement was to be rendered harmless. It was recommended at the beginning of February 1919 that this should be done at a trade union congress to be convened as rapidly as possible.[70] By the end of April 1919 the requisite preparation had been made on the assumption that since the councils movement was not going to disappear, it must be somehow integrated into the broader trade union movement. For this purpose a committee had been set up with the following brief: 'How can the workers' councils be incorporated into the economic process, what practical functions can they discharge?'[71]

The first step in solving this problem was the gaining of clarity over the concepts workers' councils (*Arbeiterräte*) and works councils (*Betriebsräte*). These had been confused and were in reality two distinct organs. The former was a communal council of workers being the representation of workers within a district whereas the latter was more in the nature of an elected works committee within an individual factory.[72] And while the trade unions had always advocated workers committees (*Arbeiterausschüsse*) and could envisage a useful liaison between them and the trade unions, they were exceedingly cautious regarding the workers councils which, as products of the revolution, claimed political as well as economic functions. How this confused issue ought to be resolved was spelled out at the trade union congress planned for Nuremberg at the end of May 1919.

NOTES

Full publication details to the works cited to be found in the bibliography

Chapter one

1. In his introduction to Ossip K. Flechtheim, *Die KPD in der Weimarer Republik*, p. 16.
2. See Ernst Nolte, 'The Relationship between "bourgeois" and "Marxist" historiography'.
3. See the collective authorship volume, *Unbewältigte Vergangenheit. Handbuch zur Auseinandersetzung mit der westdeutschen bürgerlichen Geschichtsschreibung*, Gehard Losek, Helmut Meier, Walter Schmidt & Werner Berthold, pp. 413–16 cited hereinafter as *Handbuch*.
4. *Ibid.*, p. 337.
5. *Ibid.*
6. Heinz-Joseph Varain, *Freie Gewerkschaften, Sozialdemokratie und Staat 1890–1920*.
7. Heinz Langerhans, 'Richtungsgewerkschaft und gewerkschaftliche Autonomie 1890–1914', 21–51, 187–208.
8. *Ibid.*, p. 22.
9. *Ibid.*, p. 23.
10. *Handbuch*, p. 312.
11. See the collective authorship work under the chairmanship of Walter Ulbricht, *Geschichte der deutschen Arbeiterbewegung in Acht Bänden*, III, p. 31. Edition used here is that in fifteen so-called chapters, cited hereinafter as *GDA*. See Dieter Fricke, *Die deutsche Arbeiterbewegung 1869–1870*, p. 295.
12. Wolfgang Schröder, *Partei und Gewerkschaften 1868/69 bis 1893*, p. 355.
13. Paul Merker, *Sozialdemokratie und Gewerkschaften 1890–1920*, and Werner Richter, *Gewerkschaften, Monopolkapitalismus und Staat im ersten Weltkrieg und in der Novemberrevolution (1914–1918)*.
14. Dieter Groh, *Negative Integration und revolutionärer Attentismus*.
15. *Ibid.*, p. 21. Guenther Roth, *The Social Democrats in Imperial Germany—A Study in Working-Class Isolation and National Integration*, pp. 8–10.
16. *Ibid.*, p. 503.
17. Klaus Saul, *Staat, Industrie und Arbeiterbewegung im Kaiserreich zur Innenund Aussenpolitik des wilhelminischen Deutschland 1903–1914*.

18. Jürgen Kocka, *Klassengesellschaft im Krieg 1914–1918*.
19. See Helga Grebing, 'Konservative Republik oder soziale Demokratie' in *Vom Kaiserreich zur Weimarer Republik*, ed. Eberhard Kolb, pp. 386–403. The author investigates the various interpretations placed on the November Revolution by West German historians. Particularly interesting is that of the conservatives who stressed the 'state conservatism' of the moderate Social Democrats.
20. *Handbuch*, p. 392.
21. *GDA* VI, p. 195.
22. *Ibid.*, p. 196.
23. *Ibid.*, p. 197.
24. *Ibid.*
25. See Walter Tormin, *Zwischen Rätediktatur und sozialer Demokratie* (Düsseldorf, 1954), Eberhard Kolb, *Die Arbeiterräte in der deutschen Innenpolitik 1918–1919*, Peter von Oertzen, *Betriebsräte in der Novemberrevolution*, and Wolfgang Elben, *Das Problem der Kontinuität in der deutschen Revolution*. See also Reinhard Rürup, 'Problems of the German Revolution 1918–19', *JCH*, III (1968), pp. 109–135 for a comprehensive survey of writing on this subject.
26. See Gerald D. Feldman, Eberhard Kolb & Reinhard Rürup, 'Die Massenbewegung der Arbeiterschaft in Deutschland am Ende des ersten Weltkriegs (1917–1920)'.
27. See Gerhard A. Ritter & Susanne Miller, *Die deutsche Revolution 1918–1919. Dokumente*, pp. 243–45.
28. Oertzen, *Betriebsräte*, p. 183.
29. *Handbuch*, pp. 399–401.
30. *Ibid.*
31. *Ibid.*, p. 413.
32. *GDA* IX, pp. 177–87.
33. Erich Kosthorst, *Von der Gewerkschaft zur Arbeitsfront und zum Widerstand*, p. 7, Hans-Gerd Schumann, *Nationalsozialismus und Gewerkschaftsbewegung*, p. 16, Rolf Thieringer, *Das Verhältnis der Gewerkschaften zu Staat und Parteien in der Weimarer Republik*, pp. 79–87.
34. Lewis Edinger, 'German Social Democracy and Hitler's "National Revolution" of 1933: A Study in Democratic Leadership', & *Social Democracy and National Socialism*, p. 13.
35. *Die Gewerkschafts-Zeitung* (30.IV.1932), p. 273, cited hereinafter as *GZ*.
36. Thieringer, *Das Verhältnis*, p. 141 and Erich Matthias, 'Die Sozialdemokratische Partei Deutschlands' in *Das Ende der Parteien*, ed. Erich Matthias & Rudolf Morsey, p. 176.
37. See *GZ* (18.I.1933), p. 149.
38. Franz Josef Furtwängler, *Die Gewerkschaften-Ihre Geschichte und internationale Auswirkung*, p. 76, and Hannes Heer, *Burgfrieden oder Klassenkampf*, p. 75.
39. Schumann, *Nationalsozialismus*, pp. 53–5.
40. See Edinger, 'German Social Democracy', p. 338 and Matthias, 'Die Sozialdemokratische Partei Deutschlands', pp. 178–79.

Chapter Two

1. Hans-Josef Steinberg, *Sozialismus und deutsche Sozialdemokratie. Zur Ideologie der Partei vor dem ersten Weltkrieg*.
2. The question of revisionism was thrashed out at the SPD conferences at Hanover 1899 and Dresden 1903. At the latter Bernstein's views were condemned by the party. See *Protokoll der Verhandlungen der Sozial-demokratischen Partei Deutschlands 1903 zu Dresden*, pp. 418–9.
3. Friedrich Engels, *The Condition of the Working Class in England*, trans. and ed. W. O. Henderson and W. H. Chaloner. See especially ch. IX, 'Working Class Movements', pp. 241–73 *passim*.
4. Ursula Herrmann, *Der Kampf von Karl Marx um eine revolutionäre Gewerkschaftspolitik in der 1. Internationale 1864 bis 1868*, pp. 24–5.
5. Karl Marx, *The Poverty of Philosophy*, with an Introduction by Friedrich Engels, p. 167.
6. *Ibid.*, p. 168.
7. *Ibid.*
8. *Ibid.*, p. 172.
9. *Ibid.*
10. Karl Marx and Friedrich Engels, 'Manifesto of the Communist Party' in Marx and Engels, *Selected Works in Two Volumes* (MESW), 1962, vol. I, p. 45.
11. *Ibid.*
12. Karl Marx, 'Wage Labour and Capital' (MESW), 1962, vol. I, p. 104.
13. Cited by Henry Collins and Chimen Abramsky, *Karl Marx and British Labour*, p. 31.
14. Karl Marx, 'Inaugural Address of the Working Men's International Association' (MESW), 1962, vol. I, pp. 382–83.
15. *Ibid.*, p. 384.
16. Karl Marx, 'Provisional Rules of the Association' in *The General Council of the First International 1864–1866—The London Conference Minutes—Documents of The First International* (DFI), p. 16.
17. Herman Müller, *Karl Marx und die Gewerkschaften*, p. 54. See Hermann Oncken, *Lassalle–Zwischen Marx und Bismarck*, pp. 363–65.
18. Ferdinand Lassalle, 'Offenes Antwortschreiben' in *Lassalles Reden und Schriften*, pp. 421–22. Cited by Müller, *Karl Marx und die Gewerkschaften*, pp. 55–6. Edward Bernstein, *Ferdinand Lassalle as Social Reformer*, pp. 123–24.
19. Müller, *Karl Marx und die Gewerkschaften*, pp. 56–7.
20. Karl Marx, *Capital*, vol. I (Moscow 1961), pp. 637–38. 'Taking them as a whole, the general movements of wages are exclusively regulated by the expansion and contraction of the industrial reserve army, and these again correspond to the periodic changes of the industrial cycle. They are, there-fore, not determined by the variations of the absolute number of the working population, but by the varying proportions in which the working-class is divided into active and reserve army, by the increase or diminution in the relative amount of the surplus-population, by the extent to which it is now absorbed, now set free.'

21. J. B. von Schweitzer, in *Der Social-Democrat*, no. 16, 1 Feb 1865 cited by Müller, *Karl Marx und die Gewerkschaften*, p. 60.
22. Marx's letter to von Schweitzer of 13 Feb 1865 is not extant. However, Marx quoted it in a letter to Engels 18 Feb. 65. See *Marx–Engels Werke* (MEW), vol. 16 (Berlin, 1971), pp. 88, 621. The text given here is translated from the German cited by Müller, *Karl Marx und die Gewerkschaften*, p. 61.
23. Karl Marx, 'Wages, Price and Profit' (MESW), p. 447.
24. Karl Marx, 'Instructions for the Delegates of the Provisional General Council. The Different Questions', *DFI* (1864–66), pp. 347–48.
25. Carlo Schmidt, 'Ferdinand Lassalle und die Politisierung der deutschen Arbeiterbewegung' in *Archiv für Sozialgeschichte*, III (1963), 8–10.
26. *Ibid.*, p. 11.
27. *Ibid.*, p. 12. August Bebel, *Aus meinem Leben*, vol. I, p. 51.
28. Schlomo Na'aman, 'Lassalle—Demokratie und Sozialdemokratie', 21. See also Franz Mehring, *Geschichte der deutschen Sozialdemokratie*, vol. II, pp. 46–52, 56.
29. Hermann Müller, *Karl Marx und die Gewerkschaften*, p. 67. See also Roger Morgan, *The German Social Democrats and the First International 1864–1872*. 'Thus Bebel in 1868 presented the International as a *working-class* organisation—its precise programme being relatively immaterial—whose name would consolidate the *Verband Deutscher Arbeitervereine* and separate it from the Liberal democrats; Liebknecht in 1869 represented it as a *democratic* organisation, which would as a matter of course share his opposition to the dictatorial power of Schweitzer. . . .', p. 237.
30. Werner Conze, and Dieter Groh, *Die Arbeiterbewegung in der nationalen Bewegung*, pp. 78–86.
31. See GDA II, p. 114 and Gustav Mayer, 'Die Trennung der proletarischen von der bürgerlichen Demokratie in Deutschland, 1863–1870, in *Radikalismus, Sozialismus und bürgerliche Demokratie, passim.*
32. Hermann Müller, *Karl Marx und die Gewerkschaften*, p. 66.
33. *Der Volksstaat*, 27 Nov. 1869.
34. August Bebel, *Aus meinem Leben*, vol. I, p. 225.
35. Hermann Müller, *Geschichte der deutschen Gewerkschaften bis zum Jahre 1878*, p. 137.
36. See Wilhelm Mommsen, *Deutsche Parteiprogramme*, p. 313.
37. See John A. Moses, 'The Trade Union Issue in German Social Democracy 1890–1900', pp. 1–19 *passim*.
38. *Ibid*.
39. As illustrated particularly in the party–union confrontation on the use of the mass or general strike weapon which reached its culmination at the 1906 Mannheim Conference of the SPD.
40. *Protokoll über die Verhandlungen des allgemeinen deutschen sozial—demokratischen Arbeiterkongresses zu Eisenach 7, 8, und 9, August 1869*, p. 29.
41. Hermann Müller, *Karl Marx und die Gewerkschaften*, p. 68.
42. Richard W. Reichard, *Crippled from Birth—German Social Democracy 1844–1870*, p. 237.

43. Hermann Müller, *Karl Marx und die Gewerkschaften*, p. 69.
44. John A. Moses, 'Das Gewerkschaftsproblem in der SDAP 1869–1878', in *Jahrbuch des Instituts für Deutsche Geschichte*, III (1974), 172–202 *passim*.

Chapter Three

1. Recent studies on the history of trade unionism in Germany prior to 1890 include: Elisabeth Todt, *Die gewerkschaftliche Betätigung in Deutschland von 1850–1859* (Berlin, 1950); Elizabeth Todt & Hans Radandt, *Zur Frühgeschichte der deutschen Gewerkschaftsbewegung 1800–1849* (Berlin, 1950); Ursula Herrmann, *Der Kampf von Karl Marx um eine revolutionäre Gewerkschaftspolitik 1864–1868* (Berlin, 1966); Werner Ettelt & Hans-Dieter Krause, 'Die Durchsetzung der marxistischen Gewerkschaftspolitik in der deutschen Arbeiterbewegung 1869–1878', ZFG, XVIII (1970), 1023–1046. The work of Ulrich Engelhardt, *Die Anfänge der Gewerkschaftsbewegung in Preussen–Deutschland* was not available to me at the time of writing.
2. On Stefan Born's activity see P. H. Noyes, *Organisation and Revolution. Working Class Associations in the German Revolution of 1848–1849*.
3. Frolinde Balser, *Sozial–Demokratie 1848/49–1863* (Textband), p. 33.
4. Hermann Müller, *Geschichte der deutschen Gewerkschaftsbewegung bis zum Jahre 1878*, pp. 12–3, and Todt, *Die Gewerkschaftliche Betätigung*, p. 33.
5. W. H. Dawson, *Germany and the Germans*, vol. II, p. 6.
6. Balser, *Sozial–Demokratie*, p. 38.
7. Siegfried Nestriepke, *Das Koalitionsrecht in Deutschland. Gesetze und Praxis*, p. 230.
8. *Ibid.*, pp. 230–31.
9. On von Schweitzer, see the standard biography by Gustav Mayer, *Johann Baptiste von Schweitzer und die Sozialdemokratie*.
10. August Bebel, *Aus meinem Leben*, part I (Stuttgart, 1911), p. 213.
11. Hermann Müller, *Geschichte*, p. 45 and Richard W. Reichard, *Crippled from Birth—German Social Democracy 1844–1870*, p. 219.
12. Mayer, *von Schweitzer*, pp. 226–27.
13. *Ibid.*, p. 240. The ADAV was reconstituted in October 1868.
14. *Ibid.*, p. 256.
15. Hermann Müller, *Geschichte*, pp. 61–65. The congress referred to here convened 205 representatives of 56 trade organizations encompassing 142,008 members from 105 localities.
16. Mayer, *von Schweitzer*, p. 265 and Bebel, *Aus meinem Leben*, vol. I, pp. 221–23.
17. The Progressive Party (*Fortschrittspartei*) via the efforts of Dr Max Hirsch and Franz Duncker had also founded a trade union federation with the aim of winning the workers for liberalism. The Hirsch–Duncker unions have therefore the reputation of being the oldest since their constitution goes

back to October 1868. However, though a viable organization, it did not attract more than minority support among the workers. See Hermann Müller, *Geschichte*, pp. 78–83.

18. See *Protokoll über die Verhandlungen des allgemeinen deutschen sozial–demokratischen Arbeiterkongresses zu Eisenach 7., 8. und 9. August 1869*, pp. 65–6. (Hereinafter cited as *Protokoll* with location).
19. Fritz Opel & Dieter Schneider, *Fünfundsiebzig Jahre Industrie-gewerkschaft, 1891 bis 1966*, p. 56.
20. *Protokoll*, Eisenach, p. 66.
21. *Ibid.*, p. 26.
22. *Ibid.*, pp. 70–71.
23. See Jürgen Kuczynski, *Die Geschichte der Lage der Arbeiter in Deutschland 1789–1870*, 6th edn, vol. I, part I, pp. 283–39. (The details of strikes and demonstrations during this period as well as of the spread of worker organizations are supplied in *Geschichte der deutschen Arbeiterbewegung CHRONIK Teil I von den Anfängen bis 1917*, pp. 52–86.) Kuczynski reports that such strikes were the climax of the class struggle which led to the formation of numerous workers' organizations.
24. Hermann Müller, *Geschichte*, p. 137.
25. *Protokoll*, Eisenach, pp. 70–71. See also John A. Moses, 'Das Gewerkschaftsproblem in der SDAP 1869–1878', 178.
26. *Ibid.*, pp. 19–21. Moses, 'Das Gewerkschaftsproblem', p. 176.
27. Hermann Müller, *Karl Marx und die Gewerkschaften*, p. 69.
28. Arthur Dissinger, *Das freigewerkschaftliche Organisationsproblem*, p. 125. See also *Protokoll*, Stuttgart (1870), p. 6.
29. *Protokoll*, Stuttgart, p. 40.
30. *Protokoll*, Dresden, pp. 6–7.
31. *Ibid.*, p. 31.
32. *Ibid.*, p. 9.
33. *Der Volksstaat*, 8 June 1872.
34. See Opel & Schneider, *Fünfundsiebzig Jahre*, p. 52.
35. See Bebel, *Aus meinem Leben*, part I, pp. 223–25. Here Bebel gives his account of the efforts to establish a trade union federation in Germany.
36. *CHRONIK*, p. 99.
37. Hermann Müller, *Geschichte*, pp. 142–3.
38. See York's explanation in *Protokoll*, Mainz, (1872) p. 52.
39. Josef Schmoele, *Die sozial–demokratischen Gewerkschaften in Deutschland seit dem Erlass des Sozialisten–Gesetzes* (1 vorbereitender Teil), p. 45.
40. *Der Volksstaat*, 24 May 1873.
41. *Ibid.*
42. *Der Volksstaat*, 31 May 1873.
43. *Ibid.*
44. *Der Volksstaat*, 11 June 1873.
45. *Ibid.*
46. Schmoele, *Die sozial–demokratischen Gewerkschaften*, pp. 44–6.
47. *Der Volksstaat*, 22 May 1874.
48. *Ibid.*
49. *Ibid.*

50. *Ibid.*
51. Hermann Müller, *Geschichte*, p. 145.
52. *Ibid.*, pp. 145–46.
53. *Ibid.*
54. *Ibid.*, p. 147.
55. *CHRONIK*, pp. 106–7.
56. Siegfried Nestriepke, *Die Gewerkschaftsbewegung*, 2 vols. vol. I, p. 209.
57. Dieter Fricke, *Die deutsche Arbeiterbewegung 1869–1890*, p. 302.
58. Hermann Müller, *Geschichte*, p. 168.
59. *Ibid.*
60. *Der Volksstaat*, 2 July 1875.
61. See Hermann Müller, *Geschichte*, p. 178.
62. *Ibid.*, p. 179.

Chapter Four

1. Wolfgang Schröder, *Klassenkämpfe und Gewerkschaftseinheit*, p. 17.
2. See Vernon L. Lidtke, *The Outlawed Party*, pp. 70–104 for the immediate effect of the Anti-Socialist Law on the SPD. The law gave the police extreme coercive powers which are contained in section 28 of the act. It was intended to apply to areas within which socialism was suspected to have spread to such proportions as to be a danger to public security. The special provisions here applicable constituted what was known as the 'minor state of siege'. These were:

   (1) Meetings may only take place with the previous sanction of the police, but this restriction does not extend to meetings held in connection with elections to the Reichstag or the Diets;

   (2) the circulation of publications may not take place without permission in the public roads, streets, squares or other public places;

   (3) persons from whom danger to the public security or order is apprehended may be refused residence in a locality or government district;

   (4) the possession, carrying, introduction, and sale of weapons within the area affected are forbidden, restricted, or made dependent on certain conditions.

   Penalties for breaches of these regulations consisted of either a heavy fine of 1,000 Marks or up to six months imprisonment. The law was at first only passed for two-and-a-half years and was thereafter presented to the Reichstag for prolongation. See W. H. Dawson, *Germany and the Germans*, vol. II, p. 188–9.
3. Hermann Müller, *Geschichte der deutschen Arbeiterbewegung bis zum Jahre, 1878*, p. 180. A conservative contemporary estimate of the number of trade union organizations affected by the Anti-Socialist Law counted a total of 332 organizations banned. Among these were seventeen centralized unions, seventy-eight local trade unions, three central and twenty local assistance fund societies, 106 political branches and 108 social clubs. A total of 1,299 publications were banned. The number of persons exiled totalled 893. Minor variations in these figures will be found in more

recent publications such as the work of Wolfgang Schröder and Alfred Förster.

4. Reinhard Höhn, *Die vaterlandslosen Gesellen*, vol. I, p. xix and Alfred Förster, *Die Gewerkschaftspolitik der deutschen Sozialdemokratie während des Sozialistengesetzes*, p. 14.
5. Characteristic of the Social Democratic trade unionist attitude to the Reich are the words of Julius Motteler in *Der Volksstaat* (20 May 1875) when he wrote:

> 'We are opponents of the Reich in so far as the Reich represents certain institutions under which we feel oppressed and under which we suffer. . . We are not opponents of the Reich because it is a Reich and because it is a national whole, but rather because in its present condition it cannot fulfil the purpose of its existence.'

(quoted in Hans-Josef Steinberg, 'Sozialismus, Internationalismus und Reichsgründung', 45.
6. Förster, *Die Gewerkschaftspolitik*, pp. 14–33 for details of police action against trade unions.
7. *Ibid.*, p. 17. For example, the Braunschweig police dissolved the local metal workers for striving to overthrow the existing order on the charge that they had set up productive cooperatives for the purpose of replacing the wages system.
8. *Ibid.*, p. 18. The effect of closing down a centralized union and its affiliated local branches was that almost all their sickness and funeral expenses schemes as well as their newspapers were suppressed.
9. *Ibid.*, p. 19. For example the glove-makers and the tanners.
10. *Ibid.*, p. 19. For a most comprehensive study of the printers see Gerhard Beier, *Schwarze Kunst und Klassenkampf.*
11. Förster, *Die Gewerkschaftspolitik*, pp. 23–24.
12. *Ibid.*, pp. 26–27.
13. It is an interesting characteristic of recent Marxist–Leninist literature to try and interpret this movement as 'opportunistic' and 'bourgeois-reformist' in virtual distortion of the facts, clearly with a view to discrediting *post hoc facto* those leaders to whom much credit is due for keeping the movement alive at all.
14. Wolfgang Schröder, *Partei und Gewerkschaften 1868/69 bis 1893*, p. 163.
15. *Ibid.*, p. 168. See Bismarck's policy in the speech from the throne 17 Nov 1881 in the Reichstag. The cure of the social damage was not to be sought exclusively by way of repression but equally in promoting the welfare of the workers.
16. For studies on Bismarck's 'state socialism' see the work of that title by W. H. Dawson (1890) and the more recent study by Walter Vogel, *Bismarcks Arbeiterversicherung* (1951).
17. Schröder, *Partei und Gewerkschaften.*
18. Dieter Fricke, *Bismarcks Prätorianer*, p. 145.
19. For example the cited works of Fricke, Förster and Schröder.
20. Lidtke, *The Outlawed Party*, p. 181 and Fricke, *Bismarcks Prätorianer*, p. 148. At the end of 1884 the Berlin police reported in a memorandum that by far the most craft unions were focal points for Social Democratic

elements and that a great number of the craft unions were virtually SPD agitation organs.

21. Fricke, *Bismarcks Prätorianer*, pp. 150–151. Others had of course been banned under the old Prussian Law of Association of 1850.
22. *Ibid.*, pp. 152–53.
23. Höhn, *Die vaterlandslosen Gesellen*, p. 145.
24. Förster, *Die Gewerkschaftspolitik*, p. 209.
25. *Ibid.*, p. 325.
26. CHRONIK, p. 136.
27. Fricke, *Bismarcks Prätorianer*, p. 311 and Förster, *Die Gewerkschaftspolitik*, p. 326.
28. Schröder, *Klassenkämpfe*, p. 23.
29. *Ibid.*, p. 29.
30. *Ibid.*, p. 24.
31. See Carl Legien's obituary for Karl Kloss in *Correspondenzblatt* No. 7 (15 Feb. 1908), according to which Kloss was the most energetic champion of the centralized organization form for trade unions in the decade after 1880.
32. *Protokoll des 1. Verbandstages des Central-Verbandes von Vereinen der Tischler (Schreiner) Deutschlands*, in Offenbach a.M. 29–30 Juni & 1 Juli 1885 (Stuttgart, 1885), pp. 41–2.
33. *Ibid.*
34. *Ibid.*, p. 43.
35. *Ibid.*, p. 44.
36. *Ibid.*, p. 45.
37. *Ibid.*, p. 46.
38. *Ibid.*, pp. 46–7.
39. The printers' union was in fact an earlier example but it religiously avoided association with social democratic ideas.
40. Lidtke, *The Outlawed Party*, p. 181 cites the case of a Berlin gilder, Ferdinand Ewald, in 1882 who was chairman of his union not previously oriented to the SPD. However, 'Ewald soon learned that if he wished to attract a mass following for his plan he could not pursue his middle-of-the-road policy. By February 1883, Ewald was moving towards the Social Democrats, and in 1884 he became one of the party's first elected deputies to the Berlin *Stadtverordnetenversammlung* [Municipal Council].'
41. Schröder, *Klassenkämpfe*, p. 23.
42. Printed in the *Protokoll des II Verbandstages des Verbandes von Vereinen der Tischler (Schreiner) und Verwandten Berufsgruppen Deutschlands in Gotha 27–31 Dezember 1886*, p. 64.
43. Schröder, *Klassenkämpfe*, pp. 27, 46.
44. *Ibid.*, p. 46.
45. Schmoele, *Die sozial-demokratischen Gewerkschaften*, pp. VII–VIII.
46. Schröder, *Klassenkämpfe*, p. 29.
47. Max Koch, *Die Bergarbeiterbewegung im Ruhrgebiet zur Zeit Wilhelm II*, pp. 33–51.
48. Schröder, *Klassenkämpfe*, p. 34.

49. *Ibid.* It is important to note that the strike was not organized by Social Democrats. Indeed the police had tried to establish a connection between the strikers and the SPD but failed. See Koch, *Die Bergarbeiterbewegung*, p. 47.

50. While the strike leaders to some extent came to be influenced by socialist ideas, the rank and file remained for a long time sceptical towards the revolutionary ideology. Indeed, the Christian social movement was so strong in the Ruhr that a separate miners' union was formed in 1894 to rival that founded in 1889 as a result of the great strike. Koch, *Die Bergarbeiterbewegung*, pp. 48–51.

51. Jürgen Kuczynski, *Die Geschichte der Lage der Arbeiter in Deutschland 1871–1932*, vol. I, part 2, 1871–1932, p. 37. Kuczynski cites here the 1872 Ruhr miners' strike.

52. Jacob Reindl, *Die deutsche Gewerkschaftsbewegung*, pp. 90–91.

53. Koch, *Die Bergarbeiterbewegung*, pp. 37–8. As a result of a miners' meeting in the Dortmund suburb of Dorstfeld. This local initiative found widespread approval.

54. *Ibid.*

55. *Ibid.*, p. 41.

56. *Ibid.*, pp. 53–4. The so-called *Alter Verband* was founded (after a series of preliminary attempts) on 27 October 1889 when an executive was elected representing 147 branches. The first congress of German miners took place in Halle, September 1890. This meeting constituted the *Verband der Deutschen Bergleute*.

57. *Ibid.*, p. 42.

58. *Ibid.*

59. Schröder, *Klassenkämpfe*, p. 46.

60. *Ibid.*, p. 63.

61. *Ibid.*

62. W. G. Hoffmann, *Das Wachstum der deutschen Wirtschaft seit der Mitte des 19. Jahrhunderts*, pp. 173, 194–95, 197.

63. Dawson, *Germany and the Germans*, vol. II, pp. 199–200.

64. Wolfgang Pack, *Das parlamentarische Ringen um das Sozialistengesetz Bismarcks 1878–1890*, p. 205. See also Lidtke, *The Outlawed Party*, p. 344. It was planned to drop sections 22–25 of the act which empowered the authorities in a given district to deny the right of domicile to suspected agitators. However, this concession would have been meaningless if the law had been given permanent force and the expatriation powers extended to the entire Reich. That is to say, the key section 28 (see footnote No. 2) would have been amended to exclude subjects not only from their own districts but from the nation as a whole.

65. Pack, *Das parlamentarische Ringen*, p. 210. The Cartel consisted of the National Liberals, the Free Conservatives and the moderate or national wing of the Conservative Party. These had been united in a coalition supporting Bismarck since 1887. It was broken up as a result of the election of 20 February 1890 when the SPD won a majority of votes and thirty-five seats. The constellation in the Reichstag now appeared as follows:

SPD	1,427,298 votes	35 seats
Radicals	1,159,915 ,,	66 ,,
Centre	1,342,113 ,,	106 ,,
Nat. Liberals	1,177,807 ,,	42 ,,
Reichs Party	482,314 ,,	20 ,,
Conservatives	895,103 ,,	73 ,,

(Source: *CHRONIK*, p. 149.) See also J. C. G. Röhl, 'The Disintegration of the *Kartell* and the Politics of Bismarck's Fall from Power, 1887–90', pp. 61, 85–6. The Kartell had lost 83 seats, its strength in the Reichstag of 397 members falling from 223 to 140. That the struggle over the Anti-Socialist Law was a contributing factor, also to Bismarck's final dismissal is quite beyond doubt.

66. Dawson, *Germany and the Germans*, vol. II, p. 200.
67. Reindl, *Die deutsche Gewerkschaftsbewegung*, p. 92.
68. For an account of the differences of opinion between the Kaiser and Bismarck over the 'social question' see Karl Erich Born, *Staat und Sozialpolitik seit Bismarcks Sturz*, pp. 20–32.

Chapter Five

1. The most notable of those aware of the need to integrate the working class into the nation would have been the famous *Kathedersozialisten* or 'socialists of the chair' meaning those professors of history, sociology and economics who made a serious study of working-class conditions. The most prominent would be men like Lujo Brentano, 1844–1931; Werner Sombart, 1863–1941; Gustav Schmoller, 1838–1917 and Ferdinand Tönnies, 1855–1936. Also noted for his efforts at reconciling the working class with the Wilhelmine state was Friedrich Naumann, 1860–1919. Among the most famous of German Social Democrats who very early saw the need for promoting social harmony in Germany was the trade union leader, Carl Legien, 1862–1920. See the present writer's articles on Legien in the bibliography.
2. Hans-Josef Steinberg, 'Sozialismus, Internationalismus und Reichsgründung', *APUZ* 6 (7 Feb 1970), 40.
3. Roger Morgan, *The German Social Democrats and the First International*.
4. Dieter Groh, 'Das Verhältnis der deutschen Arbeiterbewegung zur nationalen Bewegung von den Anfängen bis 1914', *RDA* (1969), 346.
5. Franz Mehring, *Geschichte der deutschen Sozialdemokratie*, part 2, p. 540.
6. See for example the following: Gunther Roth, *The Social Democrats in Imperial Germany*; Vernon Lidtke, *The Outlawed Party*; Hans-Josef Steinberg, *Sozialismus und deutsche Sozialdemokratie*; Erich Matthias, 'Kautsky und der Kautskyanismus', in Iring Fetscher (ed.), *Marxismus Studien 2* (Tübingen, 1957).
7. Peter Lösche, 'Arbeiterbewegung und Wilhelminismus' p. 522.
8. See the publications of the free-thinking liberal, Eugen Richter 1838–1906 (member of the *Fortschrittspartei* and later the *Deutsche Freisinnige Volkspartei* in the Reichstag), who ridiculed the ideology of the

SPD with an irony reminiscent of Jonathan Swift: *Die Irrlehren der Sozialdemokratie* (1890) and *Sozialdemokratische Zukunftsbilder* (1892).

9. Friedrich Engels, 'Der Sozialismus in Deutschland', *NZ* X, 19 (1891–2).
10. This aspect of Engels' teaching is ably analysed by Hans-Josef Steinberg, 'Friedrich Engels' revolutionäre Strategie nach dem Fall des Sozialistengesetzes' in Hans Pelger (ed.), *Friedrich Engels 1820–1970*, pp. 115–126.
11. Karl Erich Born, *Staat und Sozialpolitik seit Bismarcks Sturz*, pp. 7–20.
12. *Ibid.*, p. 31. See also Born's account in Gebhardt's *Handbuch der deutschen Geschichte*, paperback edn., vol. 16, pp. 165–173.
13. *Ibid.*, p. 98.
14. A. Schäffle, *The Theory and Policy of Labour Protection*, p. 1. This work provides a translation of the actual amendments on pp. 211–252.
15. Born, *Staat und Sozialpolitik*, pp. 99–112.
16. *Ibid.*, p. 100.
17. August Bebel, 'Die Gewerbeordnungs-Novelle', *NZ* IX, 2 (1891) 333, and Schäffle, *The Theory and Policy*, p. 222.
18. Schäffle, *The Theory and Policy*, pp. 229–230.
19. Bebel, 'Die Gewerbeordnungs-Novelle', pp. 333–35.
20. *Ibid.*, p. 365.
21. See the draft of the bill in *Sten. Ber. 8. Leg. Per.* I *Session* 1890/91 *Erster Anlageband*, Aktenstück Nr 4, p. 10.
22. *Ibid.*
23. See the debate in *Sten. Ber. Band* 117 (23 April 1891), p. 2540.
24. *Ibid.*, p. 2517 for the views of the Centre Party deputy, Stözel.
25. *Correspondenzblatt*, 25 April 1891, p. 44.
26. *Sten. Ber. 9 Leg. Per.* III *Session* 1894/95 *Erster Anlageband Aktenstück* Nr. 49, p. 224.
27. *Ibid.*, pp. 224–25.
28. Born, *Staat und Sozialpolitik*, p. 118.
29. *Ibid.*, pp. 137–38.
30. *Ibid.*, p. 139.
31. *Ibid.*, p. 145.
32. *Ibid.*, pp. 146–166.
33. *Sten. Ber. 10. Leg. Per.* I *Session* 1898/1900 *Aktenstück* Nr. 347, *Dritter, Anlageband*, p. 2238. This volume contains the draft and justification for the bill as well as a detailed memorandum (*Denkschrift*) on alleged 'excesses' (*Ausschreitungen*) during strikes of workers against employers, pp. 2238–98.
34. *Ibid.*, p. 2239.
35. *Ibid.*, p. 2241.
36. *Sten. Ber. Band* 167 (19 June 1899), p. 2644. Bebel in arguing against the government supporters in the Reichstag stated, 'Gentlemen, do not deceive yourselves! With this bill you will achieve nothing against social democracy; rather you will drive hundreds of thousands of workers who today do not belong to social democracy into its arms.'
37. *Ibid.*, p. 2920 and Born, *Staat und Sozialpolitik*, pp. 160–64.
38. This was an occasion for Bebel to declare the SPD's implacable hostility to the Wilhelmine social and political order. That this was not without its

impact on bourgeois circles is indicated by the fact that in 1904 a national association against social democracy was formed (*Reichsverband gegen die Sozialdemokratie*). See Peter Lösche, 'Arbeiterbewegung und Wilhelminismus', pp. 519–20.

39. Born, *Staat und Sozialpolitik*, p. 199.
40. *Ibid.*, p. 201.
41. *Ibid.*, pp. 202–204.
42. Saul, *Staat, Industrie, Arbeiterbewegung im Kaiserreich*, especially pp. 188–282. Saul has painstakingly shown how industry and the law combined forces with the government to stamp out the influence of social democracy among workers. Here the government is portrayed very much as the executor of the will of 'big business' and privilege against organized labour.
43. *Ibid.*, p. 188.
44. Born, *Staat und Sozialpolitik*, pp. 212–13.
45. *Ibid.*, p. 216.
46. *Sten. Ber. Band* 231, (2 April 1908), p. 4584, and *Band* 229 (11 Dec 1907), p. 2179.
47. See the text of the law in *Sten. Ber. 13. Leg. per. II Session Aktenstück* Nr. 133 *Band*, 316.
48. Born, *Staat und Sozialpolitik*, p. 233.
49. Saul, *Staat, Industrie*, pp. 393–94.

Chapter Six

1. See Wolfgang Schröder, *Partei und Gewerkschaft* . . . and John A. Moses, 'The Trade Union Issue in German Social Democracy 1890–1900', *IWK* 19/20 (December 1973), for reference to the views of East German historians regarding the alleged opportunism of the General Commission. The union leaders had always understood their role to be strictly distinct from that of the party, and hence there was never a question of acknowledging the primacy of the party.
2. See Langerhans, 'Richtungsgewerkschaft und gewerkschaftliche Autonomie 1890–1914', *IRSH* II (1957) and Gerhard Beier, 'Elemente einer Theorie der gewerkschaftlichen Entwicklung, Funktion, Struktur und Aktion'.
3. Richard Seidel, *Gewerkschaften und Politische Parteien in Deutschland*, p. 25.
4. The article series appeared between February and October 1891 in Numbers 4, 5, 11, 13, 14, 15, 16, 19, 21, 23, 24, 25 and 31 of *Correspondenzblatt*. (Hereinafter cited as *Corr.*).
5. *Corr.*, 3 (7 Feb. 1891), pp. 9–10.
6. For a fuller analysis of Kloss' argument see Moses, 'The Trade Union Issue', pp. 5–6.
7. For a discussion of the radical movement within the party ranks known as *Die Jungen* and their relationship to the localists, see Dirk H. Müller, *Idealismus und Revolution*, pp. 160–1. The tactics of the young radicals in the party envisaged using the locally organized unions for political strikes.

By keeping the unions for this purpose it was hoped to inspire them with a truly social–revolutionary spirit. Such a function for trade unions was diametrically opposed to the concepts of the centralists.

8. *Corr.*, 4 (21 Feb. 1891), p. 14.
9. *Corr.*, 5 (28 Feb, 1891), pp. 17–18.
10. *Corr.*, 11 (25 April 1891), p. 43.
11. *Ibid.*
12. *Corr.*, 13 (23 May 1891), p. 52.
13. *Ibid.*
14. Seidel, *Gewerkschaften*, p. 26.
15. *Corr.*, 22 (1 August 1891), p. 27.
16. *Ibid.*, pp. 87–8.
17. *Corr.*, 27 (19 September 1891), p. 113.
18. *Protokoll der Verhandlungen des ersten Kongresses der Gewerkschaften Deutschlands.* Abgehalten zu Halberstadt vom 14. bis 18. März 1892, p. 11 (hereinafter cited as *Gewerk. Prot.* Halberstadt).
19. The powerful metal-workers' union was in favour of the industrial union principle and was initially sceptical of Legien's plans. See Fritz Opel, *Der Deutsche Metallarbeiter-Verband* (Frankfurt am Main, 1966), pp. 14–17.
20. *Gewerk. Prot.* Halberstadt, p. 31.
21. *Ibid.*, p. 32.
22. *Corr.*, 7 (4 April 1892), pp. 25–6.
23. *Ibid.*, p. 30.
24. *Corr.*, 17 (18 July 1892), p. 69.
25. *Ibid.*
26. *SPD. Prot.* Berlin 14–21 November 1892, p. 239.
27. *Corr.*, 18 (11 Sept. 1893), p. 71.
28. The views of *Vorwärts* (No. 215) reported in *Corr.*, 19 (25 Sept. 1893), p. 73
29. See Legien's address in *SPD Prot.*, Köln 22–28 October 1892, p. 183.
30. *Ibid.*, p. 186.
31. *Ibid.*, p. 205.
32. *Ibid.*, p. 188.
33. *Ibid.*, p. 202.
34. *Ibid.*, p. 204
35. *Ibid.*, p. 208.
36. *Ibid.*, p. 221. Paul Umbreit, *25 Jahre Deutsche Gewerkschaftsbewegung 1890–1915*, p. 27.
37. See G. A. Ritter, *Die Arbeiterbewegung im wilhelminischen Deutschland*, p. 127.
38. Hans-Josef Steinberg, *Sozialismus und deutsche Sozialdemokratie*, p. 43.
39. *Corr.*, 24 (6 Nov. 1893), p. 101.
40. Statistics of membership, Paul Barthel, *Handbuch der deutschen Gewerkschaftskongresse*, p. 301:

1891—277,659	1895—259,175	1899—580,473
1892—237,094	1896—329,230	1900—680,427
1893—223,530	1897—412,359	1901—677,510
1894—246,494	1898—493,742	

SPD membership lagged significantly behind that of the unions. In 1906 when statistics were first made the SPD counted only 384,327 members rising to 633,309 by 1909. See Wilhelm Schröder (ed.) *Handbuch der sozialdemokratischen Parteitage von 1863 bis 1909* (München, 1910), p. 333.

41. *SPD Prot.* Köln, p. 205.
42. Ritter, *Die Arbeiterbewegung*, pp. 150–151.
43. *Ibid.*, p. 157. See also *Corr.*, 4 (4 Feb. 1895), p. 14.
44. The Glove Makers' Union. See also article, 'Was geht vor', *Corr.*, 1 (14 Jan. 1895).
45. *Vorwärts*, 27 Jan 1895.
46. *Der Bauhandwerker*, 19 Jan. 1895.
47. *Gewerk. Prot.* Berlin, 4–8 1896, pp. 69–72.
48. *Corr.*, 4 (17 Feb. 1896), pp. 13–14.
49. *Ibid.*
50. *Gewerk. Prot.* Berlin, pp. 88, 110–111.
51. *Ibid.*, p. 95.
52. Ritter, *Die Arbeiterbewegung*, p. 154. By 1899 the General Commission had become the focal point for most trade union social political agitation. Another feature of the 1896 Congress in Berlin was the frankness with which some pro-Legien delegates spoke of the need to become independent from the SPD. One stated: 'We trade unions must not come under the authority of the party.' Another stressed that the union ought not to become dependent upon the party, and pointed out that it would be a good thing if the *raison d'être* of the unions was recognized by the party. See *Gewerk. Prot.* Berlin 1896, pp. 81–2.
53. Ritter, *Die Arbeiterbewegung*, pp. 150, 161. *Corr.*, 29 (7 Sept. 1896), pp. 133–35. See footnote 40 for statistics.
54. Ritter, *Die Arbeiterbewegung*, pp. 160–1.
55. Parvus, *Die Gewerkschaften und die Sozialdemokratie*. See also Ritter, *Die Arbeiterbewegung*, p. 154.
56. *SPD Prot.* Gotha, 11–16 October 1896, pp. 153–54.
57. *Ibid.*, p. 157.
58. *Ibid.*, pp. 182–83.
59. *Ibid.*, p. 157.
60. Karl Erich Born, *Staat und Sozialpolitik seit Bismarcks Sturz*, pp. 162–164.
61. *Gewerk. Prot.* Frankfurt, 8–13 May 1899, p. 103. An interesting feature of the third trade union congress was that its agenda included as a central issue the question of *Koalitionsrecht*—the right of association. It was precisely this type of *Sozialpolitik* which Legien had wanted to introduce in 1894 when he was accused of forging 'dark plans'. By 1899 the vast majority of unionists had moved solidly behind Legien's aim to make the unions into a social–political pressure group. His speech which attacked the *Zuchthausvorlage* was nothing more or less than a fiery declaration of independence by the General Commission. It was received with strong enthusiasm by the delegates. The self-perception of the unions as an independent arm of the labour movement had completely formed. See pp. 103–104, 221.
62. Josef Deutz. *Adam   Stegerwald   Gewerkschafter-Politiker-Minister*.

1874–1945 (Köln, 1952), p. 23. The origins of the Christian workers' movement are, of course, much earlier and go back to the R.C. Bishop of Mainz's (Ketteler) efforts in 1869 when the Christian–social workers' associations were founded.

63. See Karl Kautsky, 'Die Neutralisierung der Gewerkschaften', *NZ*, 18 (1899/1900), vol. II, p. 391, where he stated that, 'the neutralisation of the trade unions is, therefore, the precondition for the growth of the proletarian movement in Germany'.

64. H. Ströbel, 'Zur Frage der Neutralisierung von Gewerkschaften', *NZ*, 18 (1899/1900), vol. II, pp. 270, 274.

65. Karl Kautsky, 'Partei und Gewerkschaft', *NZ*, 17 (1898/99), vol. I, p. 423.

66. Eduard Bernstein, 'Geschichtliches zur Gewerkschaftsfrage', *Sozialistische Monatshefte*, 4 (1900), No. 7, p. 378.

67. H. Fischer, 'Neutrale oder parteiische Gewerkschaften', *NZ*, 18 (1899/1900), vol. II, p. 538.

68. *SPD Prot.* Hannover, 9–14 October 1899, p. 235.

69. Carl Legien, 'Die Neutralisierung der Gewerkschaften', *SM*, 4 (1900), No. 7, p. 375.

70. August Bebel, *Gewerkschaftsbewegung und politische Parteien* (Stuttgart, 1900), p. 15. The third union body was the Hirsch–Duncker organization.

71. *Ibid.*, p. 18.

Chapter Seven

1. Quoted in Franz Mehring, *Geschichte der deutschen Sozialdemokratie* II, p. 695.

2. Heinz Langerhans, 'Richtungsgewerkschaft und gewerkschaftliche Autonomie 1890–1914', I, 51.

3. *Ibid.*

4. Sophie Klärmann, *Die freien Gewerkschaften in Gesetzgebung und Politik*, p. 76.

5. Paul Barthel, *Handbuch der deutschen Gewerkschaftskongresse*, p. 299.

6. Klärmann, *Die freien Gewerkschaften*, p. 89.

7. *Ibid.*, p. 85. *Corr.*, 31 (5 August 1900), 481–86.

8. *Corr.*, 33 (19 August 1901), 518–23.

9. *Corr.*, 35 (2 Sept. 1901), 561–64.

10. *Corr.*, 40 (7 Oct. 1901), 643.

11. Klärmann, *Die freien Gewerkschaften*, p. 82.

12. Barthel, *Handbuch*, pp. 289–79.

13. *SPD Prot.* Essen, 1903, p. 409.

14. Barthel, *Handbuch*, p. 281.

15. Wilhelm Schröder, *Handbuch der sozialdemokratischen Parteitage 1863–1909*, p. 279.

16. Barthel, *Handbuch*, p. 282.

17. Schröder, *Handbuch*, p. 286.

18. Klärmann, *Die freien Gewerkschaften*, p. 50.

19. Schröder, *Handbuch*, p. 287.

20. Barthel, *Handbuch*, p. 284.

21. Schröder, *Handbuch*, pp. 287–88.
22. *SPD Prot.* Bremen, 1904, p. 283.
23. Schröder, *Handbuch*, pp. 288–89 (Speech by Richard Fischer).
24. *Gewerk. Prot.* Köln, 1905, p. 233.
25. *Ibid.*, p. 235.
26. *Ibid.*, p. 248.
27. *SPD Prot.* Jena, 1905, p. 232.
28. *Ibid.*, p. 243.
29. *Ibid.*, pp. 264–65.
30. Klärmann, *Die freien Gewerkschaften*, p. 56.
31. *SPD Prot.* Jena, pp. 141, 279.
32. *Ibid.*, p. 295.
33. *Ibid.* See also Barthel, *Handbuch*, pp. 292–93. This agreement was ratified by the trade union congress of 1908 in Hamburg.
34. Karl Kautsky, *Der politische Massenstreik*, p. 21.
35. *Ibid.*, pp. 23–4. N.B. The concept of general strike had an anarchistic connotation, and so a distinction was often, though not rigorously, made between mass and general strikes.
36. Klärmann, *Die freien Gewerkschaften*, p. 62.
37. *SPD Prot.* Dresden, 1903, p. 432.
38. *Ibid.*, pp. 432–33.
39. Schröder, *Handbuch*, pp. 300–301. See *SPD Prot.* Bremen, p. 307 for Bebel's attitude. For a perceptive analysis of the mass strike debate within German social democracy from the point of view of an apologist for the radical (Rosa Luxemburg) position, see Antonia Grunenberg, *Die Massenstreikdebatte*, pp. 20–44. East German accounts are given by Günter Griep, 'Über das Verhältnis zwischen der Sozialdemokratie und den freien Gewerkschaften während der Massenstreikdebatte 1905/1906 in Deutschland', *ZFG* 2 (1963), and Dieter Fricke, 'Auf dem Weg nach Mannheim', *ZFG* XXV (1977).
40. Schröder, *Handbuch.*, p. 301.
41. *Gewerk. Prot.* Köln, pp. 218–19.
42. *Ibid.*, p. 221.
43. *Ibid.*
44. *Ibid.*, p. 30.
45. *Ibid.* p. 229.
46. See *SPD Prot.* Bremen, p. 307. Bebel stated that in view of the latest events in Italy as well as the mass demonstrations in Berlin the SPD would not be able to side-step this question.
47. Klärmann, *Die freien Gewerkschaften*, pp. 63–5.
48. *SPD Prot.* Jena, 1905, p. 305.
49. *Ibid.*, pp. 306–307.
50. *Ibid.*, p. 322 (emphasis added).
51. *Ibid.*, p. 342. The text of the resolution is given on pp. 142–43.
52. *Corr.*, 39 (30 Sept. 1905), 636.
53. Klärmann, *Die freien Gewerkschaften*, p. 69.
54. *Protokoll der Konferenz der Vertreter der Vorstände der Zentralverbände Berlin 19–23 Feb. 1906.* Section '*Partei und Gewerkschaft*', p. 41. (Cited hereinafter as '*Partei und Gewerkschaft*').

55. *Ibid.*
56. *Ibid.*, p. 90.
57. Quoted after Schröder, *Handbuch*, p. 307. See also Langerhans, 'Richtungsgewerkschaft', vol. II, p. 189.
58. *SPD Prot.* Mannheim, 1906, p. 233.
59. *Ibid.*, p. 239.
60. Schröder, *Handbuch*, p. 309.
61. *SPD Prot.* Mannheim, pp. 247–49.
62. *Ibid.*, p. 250.
63. For full text see Schröder, *Handbuch*, p. 310.
64. Karl Kautsky, 'Partei und Gewerkschaft' (19–23 Feb. 1906), p. 55.
65. Langerhans, 'Richtungsgewerkschaft', II, p. 188.
66. Karl Kautsky, 'Partei und Gewerkschaft', p. 423.

Chapter Eight

1. There is an extensive literature available on aspects of this subject. It will suffice here to note the work of the East Germans, Paul Merker, Wolfgang Schröder, Walter Bartel and Günter Griep. Among the West Germans, H. J. Varain, Gerhard A. Ritter, Dieter Groh, Klaus Saul and Heinz Langerhans are highly informative. (For details of publication see Bibliography.)
2. Robert Michels, 'Die Sozialdemokratie im internationalen Verbande', 150. For a concise and accurate description of the Second International see Gerhard Schulz, 'Die deutsche Sozialdemokratie und die Entwicklung der auswärtigen Beziehungen vor 1914' (Ph.D. dissertation, Berlin, Free University, 1952), p. 49: The International of 1889 was no longer the umbrella organization of a brotherhood of the international proletariat without a fatherland, but a cartel of solidarity of nationally organized labour parties who saw their decisive task to function within the national framework under the specific prevailing conditions. Even the old Engels finally recognized this transformation in the idea of the International.
3. Julius Braunthal, *Geschichte der Internationale*, vol. I (Hannover, 1961), p. 207.
4. Cited by Wolfgang Schröder, *Partei und Gewerkschaften 1868/69 bis 1893*, p. 241.
5. Michels, 'Die Sozialdemokratie', p. 167.
6. See Hans-Josef Steinberg, *Sozialismus und deutsche Sozialdemokratie* (Hannover, 1967), pp. 13–23.
7. *Protokoll des Internationalen Arbeiter-Congresses zu Paris—abgehalten vom 14 bis 20 Juli 1889*, German translation with a foreword by Wilhelm Liebknecht (Nürnberg, 1890), p. 24.
8. *Ibid.*, p. 126.
9. *Corr.*, 3 (1893) No. 18, pp. 69–71.
10. *Protokoll des Internationalen Sozialistischen Arbeiterkongresses in der Tonhalle, Zürich vom 6 bis 12. August 1893*, p. 19.
11. *Corr.*, 3 (1893) No. 18, p. 71.
12. The refusal of the German trade union leaders to concern themselves with

the question of the mass strike was acidly attacked by Rosa Luxemburg in her treatise, *Massenstreik, Partei und Gewerkschaften*. The famous agitator accused the trade unionists of having no idea of the real content of the issue. Mass strikes occurred quite spontaneously out of a constellation of factors and were not by their nature events which could be staged by a committee decision. They were, in short, historical phenomena. However, this kind of historical–philosophical instruction made no impression on the trade union leaders whose minds functioned on an entirely more practical level. See *Protokoll der Konferenz der Vorstände der Zentralverbände—abgehalten im Berliner Gewerkschaftshaus vom 19. bis 23 Februar 1906*, p. 427.

13. *Prot. Gewerk*. Frankfurt 1899, pp. 99–104.
14. *Corr.*, 3 (1893), No. 24, p. 99.
15. *Ibid*. p. 100.
16. *Prot. SPD* Jena 1905, p. 322f.
17. *Corr.*, 3 (1893), No. 18, p. 70.
18. *Ibid.*, p. 71.
19. *Corr.*, 5 (1895), No. 6, p. 21.
20. *Ibid*.
21. *Ibid.*, p. 22.
22. *Corr.*, 11 (1901), No. 45, p. 722 (emphasis in original).
23. *Ibid*. Compare the attitude of German trade unionists in 1905 towards the recommendations of the International regarding the May Day celebration: 'Where is that supposed to lead? After all, at international congresses the English, Botokuden [sic] and Chinese vote on what we Germans have to do. We have without doubt the right to disregard the Amsterdam resolution'. See the speech of Leimpeters in *Prot. Gewerk*, Köln, 1905, p. 239.
24. *Corr.*, 12 (1902) No. 29, p. 497.
25. *Ibid*.
26. See John A. Moses, 'The Trade Union Issue in German Social Democracy 1890–1900', p. 5f.
27. *Corr.*, 12 (1902), No. 29, p. 498.
28. *Ibid*.
29. Michels, 'Die Sozialdemokratie . . .' p. 171f.
30. Varain, *Freie Gewerkschaften. Sozialdemokratie und Staat 1890–1920*, p. 71.
31. Langerhans, 'Richtungsgewerkschaft und gewerkschaftliche Autonomie 1890–1914', *IRSH* II (1957), 207. See also Moses, 'Carl Legien und das deutsche Vaterland im Weltkrieg 1914–1918', *GWU* 10 (1975), pp. 595–611.
32. See Legien's own brief account of these events in *Prot. Gewerk*. Nürnberg, 1919, p. 315f. In Brussels he had taken the view that the convening of an international conference of socialists to try and avert war would be in vain. However, he did not believe the powers would be so insane as to lead the nations of Europe on to the battlefields. That was on 29 July. On 30 July Legien travelled to Hamburg where he received news of an important meeting of the General Commission on the next day in Berlin. In the meantime mobilization was in progress, and Legien having arrived in Berlin on 31 July was convinced that war was unavoidable. He explained,

however, that the General Commission meeting of that day was concerned with what measures to adopt to preserve the unions from destruction. For this a meeting of the affiliated chairmen had to be called for 2 August. Legien insisted that this meeting was not called to discuss national defence or how to support the government, but rather what to do if the unions were threatened with dissolution. They were concerned first and foremost with the continuation of legitimate trade union activity. See also Edwyn Bevan, *German Social Democracy during the War 1914–1918* (London, 1918), p. 10 and Georges Haupt, *Socialism and the Great War* (Oxford, 1972), p. 214 where Haupt observes that reports of Legien's conversations with his foreign colleagues in Brussels on 27 July at the Belgian Trade Union Congress are 'confused, brief and contradictory. There seems to have been no more than an unofficial exchange of views over a meal'. (fn. 44).

33. For confirmation of the General Commission's 'official' analysis of the causes of the war see *Corr.*, 24 (1914), No. 51, pp. 653–655 under the title *Englands Handelskrieg* (England's Commercial War), and Wilhelm Ribhegge, *August Winnig* (Bonn-Bad Godesberg, 1973), pp. 85–90. The latter work investigates the remarkable career of a former 'vagabond without a fatherland' who became a most eloquent champion of a proletarianized form of Germanism (*Deutschtum*).

Chapter Nine

1. *Gewerk. Prot.* Munich 1914, p. 451.
2. Franz Neumann, *Koalitionsfreiheit und Reichsverfassung*, p. 3.
3. See Fritz Fischer, *Krieg der Illusionen*, pp. 46–7.
4. See the author's article, 'Bureaucrats and Patriots—The German Socialist Trade Union Leadership from Sarajevo to Versailles, 1914–1919'.
5. Wilhelm Deist. *Militär und Innenpolitik*, vol. I, pp. xxxi–xxxvi.
6. *Ibid.*, p. xxxviii.
7. *Ibid.*, p. xxxviif. The Prussian war ministry was clearly aware of the effects of a too rigorous and overtly ruthless behaviour of the military might have on the public, and it was concerned about the possible legal consequences of such action. For this reason it was agreed that the military would only be called in if civil authorities could not cope, and then only if the action was guaranteed complete success.
8. *Ibid.*, Document 77, p. 191.
9. *Ibid.*, p. xxxix.
10. See Dieter Groh, *Negative Integration und revolutionärer Attentismus*, pp. 603–610.
11. Helmut Bley, *Bebel und die Strategie der Kriegsverhütung 1904–1913*, p. 145. Here Bebel's views on the inability of the SPD to hinder the outbreak of war—even if they had a Reichstag majority—are reported.
12. Groh, *Negative Integration*, p. 601.
13. *Ibid.*, pp. 604–605.
14. St. A. Potsdam 15870 Bl 88–90. Abteilung VII Exke 3. Kommisariat, Diener, Berlin, 15 Dec 1913. I am indebted to Professor Klaus Saul for a copy of this document.

15. Groh, *Negative Integration*, p. 607.
16. *Ibid.*, pp. 607–608. Groh alludes to the 'damocles sword strategy' of the SPD leadership here. This meant that it was considered bad tactics to admit openly that there could be no general strike. Rather it was better to let the governments go on thinking that an international anti-war strike was a real possibility.
17. Susanne Miller, *Burgfrieden und Klassenkampf*, pp. 48–51.
18. Groh, *Negative Integration*, pp. 655–60.
19. *Ibid.*, p. 610 fn. 87.
20. *Corr.*, 24 (1 August 1914), 469.
21. *Ibid.*
22. See Lewis, L. Lorwin, *Labor and Internationalism*, pp. 174–178, for a discussion of the efforts of trade union leaders of the various nations to maintain contact despite the war.
23. See Paul Umbreit, *Die Gewerkschaften im Weltkrieg*, p. 21 where he gives the text of the government's response to the unions' negotiations: 'We are not planning any moves against you if you do not create difficulties; rather we are pleased to have large organizations of the working classes upon which the government can rely in the necessary emergency actions'.
24. See *Beschlüsse der Konferenzen von Vertretern der Zentralvorstände 1914–1919*, p. 4.
25. *Corr.*, 32 (8 August 1914), 485–7.
26. See Paul Lange, *Die Politik der Gewerkschaftsführer von 1914 bis 1919*, p. 3.
27. Miller, *Burgfrieden*, p. 49.
28. Klaus Böhme, *Aufrufe und Reden deutscher Professoren*.
29. *Corr.*, Nos. 36, 37, 38, 39, 41 (1914).
30. *Corr.*, 36 (5 August 1914), 522.
31. See the Kaiser's speech to the crowd assembled before the *Schloss* on 1 August 1914, the first day of mobilization when he said, 'If a war should come, all parties will cease. We are only German brothers.' Cited in Ernst Johann, *Reden des Kaisers*, pp. 125–6.
32. *Corr.*, 36 (5 August 1914), 522.
33. *Ibid.*, p. 530.
34. *Ibid.*, p. 531.
35. *Corr.*, 41 (10 Oct 1914), 569–70.
36. *Ibid.*, p. 571.
37. See Böhme, *Aufrufe*, pp. 12–15. Here is documented the expressions of satisfaction from many academic quarters with the apparently unexpected patriotism of Social Democrats and trade unionists. However, very few (e.g. Hermann Oncken and Gerhard Auschütz) were willing to allow that the forces of labour by virtue of their declarations and gestures of national solidarity should be rewarded with constitutional concessions.
38. *Corr.*, 38 (19 August 1914), 539.

Chapter Ten

1. Apart from the East and West German studies discussed in Chapter 1, attention is drawn to works by U.S. historians such as Peter Gay, Carl

Schorske, Joseph Berlau, Erich Waldman, Guenther Roth, William H. Maehl and Richard Hunt. See John A. Maxwell, 'On American Studies of the German Labour Movement, 1848–1933', for a comprehensive discussion of the scholarship in this field.

2. The newspaper, *Internationale Korrespondenz* financed by the General Commission after the war had broken out, ostensibly to keep up the international connections of the union movement, served in effect as a vehicle to justify the wartime policy of the German unions. In doing so the policies of the other belligerents (especially Great Britain) were often severely attacked. This publication replaced *Internationale Gewerkschaftliche Korrespondenz* which had been established by the international secretariat of the trade unions in 1913 as a means of contact among the member countries.

3. *Corr.*, 6 (6 Feb. 1915), 62–4.

4. See Paul Umbreit, *Die deutschen Gewerkschaften im Weltkrieg*, p. 100 and Eugen Praeger, *Geschichte der USPD*, pp. 53–4.

5. Susanne Miller, *Burgfrieden und Klassenkampf*, pp. 49–50.

6. *Corr.*, 6 (6 Feb. 1915), 62.

7. Praeger, *Geschichte*, pp. 86–96.

8. *Ibid.*, pp. 89–90.

9. Carl Legien, 'Parteizerstörer', p. 637.

10. Carl Legien, 'Warum müssen sich die Gewerkschaftsfunktionäre mehr am inneren Parteileben beteiligen', p. 38.

11. *Beschlüsse der Konferenzen von Vertretern der Zentralverbandsvorstände 1914–1919*, p. 31.

12. *Corr.*, 18 (29 April 1916), 195.

13. Gustav Schmoller, 'Der Weltkrieg und die deutsche Sozialdemokratie', *SJGVV* XXXIX (1915), 1105–7.

14. A telling illustration of the trade union view of their role in society is provided by Paul Umbreit's article series in twelve parts in the *Correspondenzblatt* from 12 February until 29 April 1916 entitled, 'Soziale Arbeiterpolitik und Gewerkschaften'. The conceptions revealed here are a complete vindication of Schmoller's observations.

15. Schmoller, 'Der Weltkrieg', pp. 1110–13.

16. For the background history to the emergence of this highly significant work, see Ursula Ratz, 'Eine proletarische-bürgerliche Arbeitsgemeinschaft im Weltkrieg'.

17. *Sten. Berichte*, 10 May 1916, *Band*. 307, pp. 1016–7.

18. *Ibid.*

19. *Beschlüsse der Konferenzen*, p. 34.

20. Ludwig Preller, *Sozialpolitik in der Weimarer Republik*, p. 38. Preller also reports that the other great obstacle to a completely free right of association, viz. paragraph 153 of the Industrial Code, was finally removed in April 1918.

21. *Corr.*, 49 (2 Dec 1916), pp. 501–2. See also *Gewerk. Prot.* Nürnberg, p. 144.

22. For a detailed account of the shaping and passage of this crucial legislation see G. D. Felman, *Army, Industry and Labour 1914–1918*, pp. 197–249. East German historians claim that the passage of this bill was the most important achievement of monopolistic capitalism in establishing its

dominance over the German nation. In consenting to it for such minor concessions, the German 'social chauvinists' had betrayed their class yet again. See Fritz Klein (ed.), *Deutschland im ersten Weltkrieg*, vol. II, pp. 470–89. A more differentiated analysis is provided by Kocka, *Klassengesellschaft im Krieg 1914–1918*, pp. 118–20. The state here was clearly not acting solely in the interests of the bourgeoisie. Indeed, it had taken up a position 'between' the classes.

23.   Heinz Josef Varain, *Freie Gewerkschaften, Sozialdemokratie und Staat*, pp. 90–91. The fact that the Auxiliary War Service Bill was passed at a time when union strength was numerically very low, raises the question why General Groener believed that without the unions and their parliamentary representatives the legislation could not have been implemented. A clue is provided in Groener's statement that the war could not be won by fighting against the workers, too. In other words, a working class hostile to the state would have rendered the war effort even more problematic than it had become. It was therefore necessary to make a conciliatory gesture towards the working class to head off their increasing radicalization and overt opposition to the war and monarchy. It had become clear to Groener that the initial general enthusiasm for the war was no longer shared by all classes in 1916, and he for one began early to envisage the possibility of a defeat and the social upheaval that must accompany it. See Gerald D. Feldman, *Army Industry and Labour*, pp. 209–210, also Kocka, *Klassengesellschaft* for the question of social fragmentation and polarization under the stresses of war.

24.   *Corr.*, 51 (16 Dec. 1916), 521–28. Among the concessions resulting from the implementation of the new bill was the appointment of the chief of the metal workers' union, Alexander Schlicke, to a post in the War Office. See Feldman, *Army*, pp. 235–6 and Kocka, *Klassengesellschaft*, p. 113.

25.   On Helfferich see John G. Williamson, *Karl Helfferich 1872–1924*.

26.   An early reference to socialization being accelerated by the war through the state assuming control over production is given by the prominent trade union writer, Wilhelm Jansson, 'Gewerkschaftliche Randbemerkungen zum kommenden Frieden' in Wilhelm Jansson (ed.), *Arbeiterinteressen und Kriegsergebnis—Ein gewerkschaftliches Kriegsbuch*, Berlin 1915, p. 163.

27.   *Corr.*, 14 (1 April 1916), 148.

28.   See Moses, 'The trade union issue.' *Sozialpolitik* is defined by Ludwig Preller, *Sozialpolitik*, p. xviii as that aspect of politics which includes all the efforts and measures which are aimed at producing the best possible order in the social structure in respect of the working life (*Arbeitsleben*) of human society.

29.   *Corr.*, 1 (5 Jan. 1918), 3. Further evidence of union expectations on the resumption of peace is documented in the article series, 'Der gewerkschaftliche Wiederaufbau nach dem Kriege' in *Corr.*, 6 April–6 June 1918 in thirteen parts. It was hoped that the coming demobilization of the army would see the beginning of the 'mobilization of the trade union movement' (6 April 1918, p. 125).

30.   See 'Gewerkschaftliche Forderungen zum Friedensvertrag' in *Corr.* (26 May 1917), 201–204.

31.   *Corr.*, 1 (5 Jan. 1918), 3.

32. *Corr.*, 49 (8 Dec. 1917), 454–55. See also Protokoll der 15. (ausserordent-lichen) Konferenz von Vertretern der Zentralverbandsvorstände, 1 Feb. 1918, Hiko-ABI-Archiv ADGB-Restakten NB 528/007, for a detailed assessment of these strikes and the warning to the government. Around the same time, the Association of German Employers submitted a lengthy memorandum (March 1918) to the government with their demands for effecting the transition from a war to a peace-time economy. In complete contrast to the wishes of the unions, the employers demanded the dismantling of the Auxiliary War Service Bill. In peacetime, it was argued, there was no more justification for such government interference in the economy which flourished best under private enterprise. Nothing could illustrate better the polarization of views between unions and management as to how the national economy should be organized. See *Denkschrift der Vereinigung der Deutschen Arbeitgeberverbände* in Otto Leibrock, *Geschichte, Organisation und Aufgaben der Arbeitgeberverbände* (Appendix).
33. See above footnote 32. See also Kocka, *Klassengesellschaft*, p. 54.
34. Kocka, *Klassengessellschaft*, p. 55.
35. *Ibid.*, p. 56.
36. *Ibid.*, p. 57.
37. As examples of contemporary criticism of the General Commission's identification with the state during the war see Hermann Leibmann, *Die Politik der General Kommission*, as well as Paul Lange, *Die Politik der Gewerkschaftsführer von 1914 bis 1919*.

Chapter Eleven

1. *Corr.*, 1 (4 Jan. 1919), p. 3.
2. Karl Dietrich Bracher, *Die Auflösung der Weimarer Republik*, p. 23.
3. See Legien's observations at *Vorständekonferenz 4 Oct. 1918*
4. Gerald D. Feldman, *Army, Industry and Labour*, p. 525ff. See also *Corr.*, 18 (3 May 1919), p. 178.
5. *Ibid.*, p. 526.
6. *Eine Kriegsgemeinschaft gegen Arbeitslosigkeit*, Hiko NB603/009.
7. Gerald D. Feldman, 'German Business between War and Revolution: The Origins of the Stinnes–Legien Agreement' in Gerhard A. Ritter (ed.), Enstehung und Wandel der modernen Gesellschaft (Berlin, 1970) 322.
8. *Ibid.*, p. 322.
9. On the annexationist plans of German industrialists generally, see Fritz Fischer, *Griff nach der Weltmacht*, pp. 316–321.
10. Feldman, 'German Business', p. 333.
11. *Ibid.*, p. 324.
12. *Vorständekonferenz*, 4 Oct 1918, Hiko NB528/004. At this conference the chairman of the affiliated unions voiced their reactions to the constitutional changes and the nomination of Gustav Bauer instead of Legien to the newly created office of Secretary of State for Labour. The general feeling was that Legien, although deserving of the honour, was really needed in his existing post.

13. Feldman, 'German Business', p. 324. See also Feldman's publication of documents gleaned from the archives of German firms which illuminate the background to the November Pact from the employers' side, entitled 'The Origins of the Stinnes–Legien Agreement: A Documentation' (cited hereinafter as 'Documentation'), p. 49.
14. Legien at the *Vorständekonferenz*, 4 Oct 1918.
15. *Corr.*, 28 (19 Oct 1918), p. 383.
16. *Ibid.*, p. 384.
17. There was a vast body of pamphlet material emanating from trade union presses during the 1920s polemicizing against Versailles. For a summary of views see the ADGB pamphlet, *Gewerkschaften, Friedensvertrag Reparationen* (Berlin 1932).
18. Feldman, 'Documentation'. Here Feldman draws attention to the phenomenon of trade union patriotism with the example of the miners' leader Otto Hué who was prepared in October 1918 to make propaganda for a *levee en masse* which would result from a fusion of industrialist and labour forces in a final struggle for the fatherland.
19. *Ibid.*, p. 46.
20. *Ibid.*, p. 49.
21. *Ibid.* p. 51f.
22. *Ibid.*, p. 54.
23. *Ibid.*, p. 62f.
24. Feldman, *Army, Industry and Labour*, p. 524.
25. Feldman, 'Documentation', p. 77.
26. *Ibid.*, pp. 77, 79, 81, 89.
27. *Protokoll der Konferenz der Vertreter der Verbandsvorstände* 3 Dec. 1918 Hiko NB1/0011 (cited *Protokoll Verbandsvorstände*).
28. Feldman, 'Documentation', p. 81.
29. Schuchmann, *Codetermination. Labour's Middle Way in Germany*, p. 52.
30. Feldman, 'Documentation', p. 47.
31. Hartwich, *Arbeitsmarkt, Verbände und Staat 1918–1933* (Berlin, 1967), pp. 4, 402.
32. *Ibid.*, p. 403f.
33. Feldman, 'Documentation', p. 46f.
34. *Protokoll Verbandsvorstände*, 3 Dec. 1918.
35. Feldman, 'Freie Gewerkschaften und Zentralarbeitsgemeinschaft', p. 241. 241.
36. Friedrich Zunkel, *Industrie und Staatssozialismus*, pp. 172–200.
37. *Ibid.*, p. 196.
38. Feldman, 'Freie Gewerkschaften', p. 232f. In chiding both the Marxist–Leninist and censorious left wing schools of historians in Germany for their hyper-critical approach to the policies of the free trade union leadership, Feldman makes a point no less telling for its being obvious, namely that while both the revolution and the ZAG failed to achieve their objectives, the trade union movement is still with us pursuing its traditional goals. In 1918/19, the Bolshevist inspired left tried to eliminate the unions while capital had tried to neutralize them in the ZAG. They have, however, survived in West Germany whereas the other forces have been radically transformed.

39. *Gewerk. Prot.* Nbg., p. 467.
40. *Ibid.*, p. 463f. Legien adumbrated these views in his chairman's report (*Rechenschaftsbericht*) at the same congress when he said that the ZAG was the hope for a future peacetime economy. It would serve to eliminate industrial dispute, a factor which could only advantage the victor powers (p. 201).
41. Schuchman, *Codetermination*, p. 62, and Zunkel, *Industrie*, pp. 56–68. The idea of *Gemeinwirtschaft* is best summed up as a socio–economic order in which the social partners (capital and labour) rejecting all thought of egoistic group interest (profiteering or ruthless strikes) combined forces for the general welfare and national survival. This presumed a willingness on the part of the social groups and individuals to submerge former rivalries for the sake of national solidarity in economic life by submitting the economy to state direction.
42. Zunkel, *Industrie*, p. 172.
43. Cited in Werner Richter, *Gewerkschaften, Monopolkapitalimus und Staat im ersten Welkrieg und in der Novemberrevolution (1914–1918)*, p. 203.
44. Feldman, 'Freie Gewerkschaften', p. 237.
45. Zunkel, *Industrie*, p. 198f.
46. Feldman, 'Freie Gewerkschaften', p. 243. The ZAG as a long term enterprise had certainly become a dead letter by 1924. However, its immediate function in the demobilization has been highly evaluated by Wolfgang Elben, *Das Problem der Kontinuität der deutschen Revolution*, pp. 70–81 and also by B. J. Wendt 'Mitbestimmung und Sozial-partnerschaft in der Weimarer Republik', *APUZ* 26 (28 June 1969), p. 31, where Wendt pays tribute to the ZAG for keeping supplies flowing sufficiently during the winter 1918/19 in the face of the continued Allied blockade to keep the population basically fed etc. See also Gerald D. Feldman, 'Economic and Social Problems of the German Demobilization 1918–19' in which the author seeks to examine the German demobilization as a segment of the general process of demobilization throughout Western industrial society in both its character and intent. The role of Colonel Koeth as head of the demobilization office was most significant. He seems to have enjoyed the confidence of both the labour as well as the industrial leadership since he approached his task in a purely pragmatic way. Feldman characterizes Koeth thus: 'Koeth and his office served precisely those groups which had emerged strongest from the war, big business and organized labour, and sought to pacify them both (p. 20). But the point is that Koeth was not concerned with laying permanent foundations for the ZAG; he simply wished to effect the *ad hoc* measures necessary to get the economy functioning again by refereeing the 'social partners'. He was not interested in planned economy schemes. Hence the ZAG which had virtually established the demobilization office was ignored. Koeth's independent economic decisions did not serve to strengthen the concept. For example, 'the basic pattern of uncontrolled price and wage increases which characterized the inflation was also a direct outcome of Koeth's "revolutionary economics"' (p. 20). So while Koeth satisfied both labour and industry for a short time he allowed trends to develop which ultimately sabotaged the ZAG.
47. Hans Schieck, 'Die Behandlung der Sozialisierungsfrage in den Monaten

nach dem Staatsumsturz' in Eberhard Kolb (ed.) *Vom Kaiserreich zur Weimar Republik*, p. 153.

48. Cited by Schieck 'Die Behandlung. . .', p. 163 fn. 102.
49. *Corr.*, 28 (16 Nov. 1918), p. 417.
50. Ulrich Kluge, *Soldatenräte und Revolution*, p. 124.
51. *Ibid.*, p. 122.
52. von Oertzen, *Die Arbeiterräte*, p. 187.
53. *Ibid.*
54. *Corr.*, 28 (6 Nov. 1918), p. 416.
55. See decree of 12 Nov. 1918 from the People's Commissars in which the government pledges the maintenance of orderly production and guarantees the security of private property as well as of individual freedom. Published in *Corr.*, 28 (16 Nov. 1918), p. 416.
56. *Corr.*, 28 (30 Nov. 1918), p. 439.
57. *Ibid.*
58. At the First Congress of Workers' and Soldiers' Councils 16–20 December 1918, the Majority Social Democrats, with whom the General Commission was in full accord, had 292 members out of a total of 489 delegates. The USPD controlled 94 members with whom ten so-called 'united revolutionaries' being left-wing soldiers' and workers' delegates from Hamburg and Bremen were aligned. The Democratic Party was represented by 31 men while there were 27 apparently independent delegates who formed a separate soldiers' 'fraction'. Public interest focused naturally on the question, 'National Assembly or Councils' System?' However, with such an overwhelming Social Democratic majority—a fact which was in the circumstances quite predictable—the outcome was something of a foregone conclusion. The attempt by the USPD leader, Däumig, to make Germany a councils' republic was rejected 344 to 98 votes. See *Der Zentralrat der deutschen sozialistischen Republik*, pp. xxviii–xxix and Charles B. Burdick and Ralph H. Lutz, *The Political Institutions of the German Revolution 1918–1919*, pp. 12–13, 222–26. 222–26.
59. *Der deutsche Kommunismus-Dokumente*, ed. Hermann Weber (cited, Weber, *Dokumente*), pp. 162–63. The line to be taken by the Communists against the trade union leadership had already been outlined by Rosa Luxemburg in her 1916 pamphlet *Hundepolitik* in which she attacked those Social Democrats who supported the war effort.
60. Quoted by Werner T. Angress, *Stillborn Revolution*, p. 13.
61. *Ibid.*, p. 16.
62. *Ibid.*, p. 17f.
63. *Der Grundungsparteitag der KPD–Protokoll und Materialien*, ed. Hermann Weber (cited, Weber, *Gründungsparteitag*), pp. 138–67. In the debate on the 'economic struggles' the Communist or Spartacist views on the trade unions were ventilated.
64. See Ossip Flechtheim, *Die KPD in der Weimarer Republik*, pp. 129–37 for an analysis of these particular events. The *Correspondenzblatt* as official organ of the General Commission evaluated the Spartacist Putsch in an article 'Die Niederlage des Spartakismus und die Gewerkschaften' on 18 Jan. 1919, pp. 9–11, from which the following account is taken.

65. See both Weber, *Gründungsparteitag*, pp. 159–60 and *Corr.*, 29 (18 Jan 1919), p. 10.
66. Weber, *Gründungsparteitag*, p. 162.
67. *Ibid.*, p. 163.
68. *Corr.*, 29 (18 Jan 1919), p. 10.
69. Legien, for example, made no distinction between anarcho–syndicalist tactics and those of the Communists. See Hans-Manfred Bock, *Syndikalismus und Linkskomunismus von 1918–1923*, p. 85.
70. *Vorständekonferenz am 1. und 2. Februar 1918*. Hiko NB529/126.
71. *Auszug aus dem Protokoll der Verhandlungen der Konferenz der Vertreter de Gewerkschaftlichen Zentralvorstände vom 25 April 1919*, p. 8, Inv. nr. Nr. W1235.
72. *Ibid.*, pp. 8–9.